Jean Sasson is the sharp-eyed and compassionate chronicler of women's lives in the Muslim world. Author of the worldwide bestsellers *Princess*, *Daughters of Arabia*, *Desert Royal*, *Mayada: Daughter of Iraq*, *Love in a Torn Land* and *Growing up Bin Laden*, she lived in Saudi Arabia for twelve years, and has travelled throughout the Middle East for thirty years. She currently makes her home in the southern United States.

For more information on Jean Sasson and her books, see her website at www.jeansasson.com

Maryam with her father and sister Nadia in Kabul Park

For the Love of a Son

Jean Sasson

BANTAM BOOKS

LONDON • TORONTO • SYDNEY • AUCKLAND • JOHANNESBURG

TRANSWORLD PUBLISHERS
61–63 Uxbridge Road, London W5 5SA
A Random House Group Company
www.rbooks.co.uk

FOR THE LOVE OF A SON
A BANTAM BOOK: 9780553820201

First published in Great Britain
in 2010 by Doubleday
an imprint of Transworld Publishers
Bantam edition published 2011

Copyright © The Sasson Corporation 2010

Map of Afghanistan by Evan T. White

Jean Sasson has asserted her right under the Copyright, Designs and
Patents Act 1988 to be identified as the author of this work.

Addresses for Random House Group Ltd companies outside the UK
can be found at: www.randomhouse.co.uk
The Random House Group Ltd Reg. No. 954009

The Random House Group Ltd supports The Forest Stewardship Council
(FSC), the leading international forest certification organization. All our
titles that are printed on Greenpeace-approved FSC-certified paper carry
the FSC logo. Our paper procurement policy can be found at
www.rbooks.co.uk/environment

Typeset in 11/14pt Sabon by Falcon Oast Graphic Art Ltd
Printed in the UK by CPI Cox & Wyman, Reading RG1 8EX

2 4 6 8 10 9 7 5 3 1

From our heroine Maryam Khail
These memories of Afghanistan are dedicated to three
people who loved Afghanistan with all their hearts:
to my beloved parents, and to Farid, my 'big brother',
I miss you every day of my life.

From author Jean Sasson
For every woman in Afghanistan who silently suffers
unimaginable abuse at the hands of the men who
should love and respect her. I'm sure these women
wonder if anyone in the world cares.
I care.

A special thank you

to Paul Hams and Alison-MacColl

There's a little story attached to all important events in our lives. A few years ago while on book tour in London, I was fortunate to meet a unique man named Paul Hams. Paul is a loving husband to Claire and a devoted father to sons Robert and Richard and a talented chef who also owns a London black cab. Paul is a very skilled driver who escorts favoured customers around London and other areas in the UK.

Paul and I hit it off immediately. He's a skilled driver who makes life in London much easier for an out-of-towner like myself. Paul and I had some fun days as he was delivering me to various business meetings. He's an interesting man with a wonderful family and I adored hearing about Claire and the boys. When I had a little free time, Paul transported me to Harrods and other fun shopping spots, accompanying me inside the stores to keep me company and kindly volunteering to help me carry bags. Paul and I had a great time and I came to appreciate what a fine young man he is. Later he took me to his warm and inviting home to meet the very lovely Claire who, like her husband, made me feel a member of the family.

A solid friendship was born and from that time on I knew I'd never call on anyone but Paul when I was lucky enough to be in London, one of my favourite cities in the world.

Paul and I kept in email touch, exchanging news about our families. A year or so later, Paul sent an email saying he had met a woman named Alison MacColl while holidaying in Spain. This woman was talking about the books I had written, telling Paul that she had a wonderful friend, Maryam Totakhail, who grew up in Afghanistan. According to Alison, Maryam's story was very compelling. She had previously written her story and had even hired an editor to clean it up; yet the book failed to interest publishers. Alison said that it was a great disappointment to all that the book remained unsold. Alison had the idea that I would be the perfect writer to make Maryam's dream come true. That's when Paul told an astonished Alison that he and I were friends, and then Alison asked how she might contact me, to tell me about Maryam's compelling story and to ask if I might consider writing it. Paul, always protective of my privacy, said that he would give me a call to see what I thought of the idea.

I'm lucky enough to receive five to ten requests each month from women who have lived through dramatic times, stories that I believe the world should know. Sadly, I can only write one book every year or so and therefore, I must turn down most requests. Also, once I have written a story that takes place in a specific country, I rarely write another story set in that same land. At the time Paul contacted me, I had written about Princess Sultana of Saudi Arabia, Mayada of Iraq and Joanna of Iraqi Kurdistan. For years I have wanted to write stories set in Lebanon, Afghanistan, Yemen, Pakistan, India and Thailand, but thus far the moon and stars had not come together for me to write a book with those countries as a backdrop.

Trusting Paul's judgement completely, after he told me about Alison's enthusiasm for her friend's dramatic story, I said that he should feel free to pass along my private email address.

Soon I heard from Alison, who wrote a heartfelt letter about Maryam. Alison was a sincere friend of Maryam's, wanting nothing more than to jump-start the project that at that time remained unsuccessful. After speaking to Alison, I agreed to speak with Maryam. It's important for me to get to know the subjects I write about, to deeply feel their intense emotions. Unfortunately, there are times when there is no heart-to-heart connection and I must turn away from a promising book project. Therefore, until I met Maryam I had no way of knowing if her story would be my next project. Maryam and I spoke several times and I heard her story from her own lips, as I did not want to read the story previously written about her. Soon I felt connected to Maryam and her family life, and so I asked her to fly to London to meet with my publisher there, and to travel on to the USA to meet with my literary agent in New York. For those who question whether my heroines/heroes live, I'd like to add the fact that I've never written about any heroine or hero who did not first meet, or at least speak with my publisher(s) and literary agent(s), and this goes for Princess Sultana, Mayada, Joanna, Omar and Najwa Bin Laden and Maryam. Publishers routinely speak with, or meet, all the subjects of my books.

My publisher fell in love with the very beautiful and dramatic Maryam, agreeing that her story was one that should be told.

Given the green light, I notified Maryam and Alison, who were both estatic. I saw that Alison's joy matched Maryam's excitement. I knew that Maryam was lucky to have such a staunch friend.

This is a book that I would have never written had Paul Hams not met Alison MacColl. I am very pleased and happy to thank Paul and Alison for their role in bringing this very important story to my attention.

Maryam feels exactly the same.

Thank you Paul! Thank you Alison!

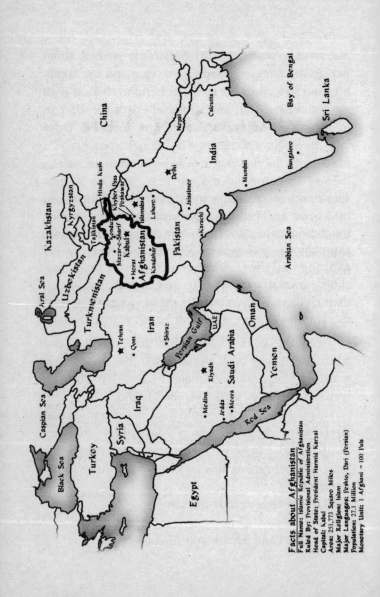

Facts about Afghanistan

Full Name: Islamic Republic of Afghanistan
Ruled By: Provisional Administration
Head of State: President Hamid Karzai
Capital: Kabul
Area: 251,773 Square Miles
Major Religion: Islam
Major Languages: Pashto, Dari (Persian)
Population: 27.1 Million
Monetary Unit: 1 Afghani = 100 Puls

Author's Note

The heart of evil beats in Afghanistan. When men hold every advantage, neither wealth, nor beauty, nor intelligence, nor education, nor strength, nor family can compete with gender. Women have only prayer and hope as allies. Whether the men in their lives choose to marry them off to an old man, take away their children or even murder them, women live with the knowledge that there will be no rescue. Female liberation is not in the Afghan culture.

This is the story of Maryam Khail, a beautiful Afghan woman born into one of the most influential families in Afghanistan, a family of wealth and power. Despite her beauty, her education and her strength, the evil that lurks in every home in Afghanistan finally caught up with Maryam.

This is Maryam's story. Pray that her story does not become yours.

Jean Sasson

On holiday with family in Afghanistan. Maryam is
sitting on the truck, in her customary garb.

Prologue

In Afghanistan girls can dream, but only the dreams of boys come true. Boys own the world they live in, while girls are basically servants, compelled to please the men in their families. Although Afghan boys are supposed to be tough towards females, my heart plunged in pity as I observed little girls shyly making their way into the Kabul Share-i-Now school to begin their first day of kindergarten.

But I straightened my shoulders, puffed out my chest and tugged at my mother's hand, pulling her along as I walked smugly past the timid creatures fearfully huddled near their older sisters or mothers.

I felt the importance of the moment, for everything I was wearing was crisp and new, from my collared white shirt to my grey shorts and even my black loafers. I glanced down to double-check that the dust of Kabul had not ruined their shine, so glossy I could nearly see my reflection. I was expensively dressed, for families in Afghanistan will spend their last pul to provide their sons with the best, although such sacrifices were not necessary in our home, for we were financially comfortable.

The year was 1966 and I was five years old. Afghan boys and girls were segregated at puberty but when they were younger they were permitted to associate. Thus I would be in the same classroom as girls my age although, as a boy, I would be considered more important.

We filed into the classroom and my mother and I selected a small desk and chair in the area where all the boys were congregating. My mother leaned forward to brush my cheek with her lips, but I pulled away, feeling all grown up, scorning public displays. My mother caressed my head, her hands fingering my newly shaved head, a good fashion for a young boy. She gave me one last poignant look before she reluctantly turned and left her only son, Yousef Agha Khail. That was the happiest moment of my young life, for I knew that I was on my way to becoming a man, something I had always yearned to be.

I glanced around the room. Girls were gathering on one side and boys on the other. Unaccustomed to being without their mothers, the little girls looked paralysed by anxiety, their small heads bowed, while the boys were sitting up straight with self-belief. I glanced back at my mother lingering in the doorway and gave her a quick, self-possessed nod.

During those first months of kindergarten I remember playing, assuming my position as the boldest of the boys and working hard on my lessons, for much was expected of male children. Daily school life was basically repetitive, until one dreadful day when my old nanny, whom we all called Muma, thoughtlessly dressed me in a pair of shorts that were difficult to unfasten.

I can forgive her now for that critical mistake, because Nanny Muma was so old that her hair had turned as white as the mountain snow, although she sometimes coloured it with henna. She was from Pansher, an area of Afghanistan where women are rumoured to produce more milk than they need for their babies. For that reason, many educated families hired Pansheri women as wet nurses. Muma had been a wet nurse for my mother's family for many years. When my mother was pregnant for the first time, my grandmother Hassen sent Muma to my mother to care for her. Once my sister Nadia was born it quickly became apparent that Muma's milk had long since run dry, but my mother kept the faithful nurse by her side all the same.

Later that morning when I felt the urge to answer nature's call, I found my small fingers could not release the buckles. The attendant assigned to the boys' toilets offered to assist me, but I had a secret I did not wish to reveal so I brushed him away. But soon I became desperate, for I was in danger of urinating in my clothes. My customary confidence melted away, replaced by sobs of alarm. Just then the attendant grabbed my hand and returned me to my teacher in the classroom. When my teacher leaned down to help, I whipped away, trying to escape her prying hands.

My extreme distress increased the volume of my cries, so my bewildered teacher sent the attendant to locate my older sister, Nadia. Nadia rushed into the room and unbuckled the waistband of my shorts. My sister was not thinking clearly, because instead of leaving it there, she pulled down my shorts in front of the whole class.

Everyone gasped.

I looked down, struggling for breath. My secret was exposed. Yousef Khail was not a boy! Yousef Khail was a girl!

In horror, I yanked up my shorts and ran from the room and into the boys' toilets, where I finally relieved myself. Afterwards I lurked in the hallway of the school, too embarrassed to face my teacher or my classmates, but I was soon told to return to my classroom. When I entered, my classmates stared openly, their faces twisted in puzzlement. I overheard some of them sniggering so I hurried to my seat and sat with my head bowed, suddenly resembling the little girls I had so scorned. In a matter of moments, I had gone from being a popular boy to a lowly girl.

My teacher was kind and didn't say a word about the fact that our class had suddenly gained an extra female pupil. The mortifying day finally ended and I fled to the front of the building to wait impatiently for my nanny to arrive. I ached to take my shame home.

Our family home in the city suburb of Share-i-Now was so near the kindergarten that Muma walked me to school in the mornings and collected me each afternoon. I breathed a sigh of relief when I saw her familiar figure walk up, but then my teacher stepped out to greet her and led her into the office of the school principal. I watched in dismay, my face flushed and my heart beating rapidly.

I longed for my mother, who was out of the country with a medical condition. At the time, most educated and well-connected Afghans travelled out of Afghanistan for medical treatment, and my father had recently taken my mother to Moscow with her overactive thyroid. My mother was so clever and bold she would have succeeded in convincing the principal that a bizarre misunderstanding had occurred, that her youngest child was indeed male, but I knew my poor nanny would never find the courage to stand up to authority. My shoulders slumped. Nanny would tell my teachers everything, explaining why the daughter of a prominent Afghan

Pashtun, Ajab Khail, had passed herself off as a male child.

The meeting unfolded just as I feared. The principal quickly learned my life story: that I so longed to be a boy I had acted out the role for my entire life, that I refused to play with those of my sex and reacted angrily if anyone refused to accept I was male.

The principal sent a teacher to find me. My heart fluttered when I was told that all the teachers of the school were waiting to see me. I was shaking. I assumed I would be punished for living such a lie and then my humiliation would be complete. Surprisingly, when the door opened and I saw the many faces looking at me, everyone was smiling. I exhaled in relief. Had Muma convinced them of the impossible, that I truly was a boy and the day's events had been nothing more than a terrible misunderstanding?

The kindly lady principal lightly touched my shoulders and led me to the front of the room, announcing, 'This is a very special day for all of us. This is the official day that our young pupil Yousef becomes Maryam.' She smiled winningly at her audience. 'Please, let me introduce you to Maryam Khail.'

I was so shocked I couldn't speak. I scratched my shaved head in puzzlement. All the teachers appeared

extremely amused, and one by one began con-
gratulating me. The principal then presented me with
the school uniform for girls, telling me, 'Maryam,
you are the most precious little girl, a beautiful girl
who is special in every way.' I was startled when
another teacher walked briskly into the room to
present me with a large bouquet of colourful flowers.
The principal even called in the school photographer,
who made a big fuss of taking an official picture.
Despite the heartfelt celebration, and the kindness of
those teachers, I was numb with misery. I glanced
at the clothes in my hand. Now I would have to wear
the uniform I so hated, a drab black dress that dipped
below the knee, with black stockings and a white
scarf. Boys could wear any combination of shorts or
long trousers with any clean shirt, but all the girls in
the school were required to wear the uniform dress.
It made it impossible for us to play with abandon, to
pedal a bike or rollerskate, for it would be a scandal
if a girl fell and exposed her limbs or her panties.

Once again my future as an Afghan girl loomed
before me. I would now be expected to remain sub-
servient to boys while they claimed centre stage.
Interesting courses of study would be offered to male
classmates, while I would be shuttled off with the
girls, taught to stitch in a straight line or to prepare
large meals for the men of the family. Before long
the blood would come and I would be staring into

the mirror at a mature face. Then I would leave my family to marry into a strange household, becoming a house servant to the mother of my new husband.

I had still not spoken a word when a very quiet Muma led me away, my feet and legs dragging from the weight of my despair. I truly felt I had lived the last happy day of my life. I had relished every moment of my life as Yousef. I had no desire to be Maryam, for over the years I had heard too many family members express disappointment over my gender.

I was the second daughter and last child born to my parents, Ajab Khail and Sharifa Hassen. After my sister Nadia was born, family and friends were desperate for the second child to be a son because in Afghanistan there is no respect shown to a mother, or a father, who produces only daughters. So I was a disappointment for many from the moment of my first noisy appearance. Although I was not the boy they were longing for, I did bring a lot of excitement, for I made a spectacular entrance into their world.

I was born late on a Friday night, on 16 December 1960. Earlier in the day my mother had had her final pregnancy examination. Mother told the doctor that she felt so uncomfortable she was certain her second child would be born soon, but the doctor disagreed, telling her that she might as well relax because in his expert opinion her second child would not be coming for at least another ten days. I proved the doctor wrong only a few hours later when I awoke my mother during the early part of the night. I was ready to get out, already prepared to create a bit of mischief in the world.

Afghanistan suffers through long and brutal winters, and on that December night snow was piled over a foot deep, with more on the way. My mother was scheduled to deliver in hospital, so transport was needed. At the time of my birth few homes in Afghanistan had their own telephone so my father had to dash to the main road to use the public one. He phoned the ambulance service, telling them, 'Come quickly! You must take my wife to the hospital!'

But nothing moves fast in Afghanistan, so my poor father waited in the snow for at least two hours, remaining at the agreed-upon spot so he could escort the ambulance driver directly to our front door. He was delayed for so long that Mother's labour pains grew more and more intense. To calm her, Nanny Muma and Grandmother Mayana Khail, my father's mother who lived with us, took turns rubbing her back. Finally the three women heard the ambulance siren, and Grandmother carefully bundled Mother in a heavy winter coat. They hurried outside the house to wait on the front porch.

After a particularly powerful contraction, Mother

slumped down on the top porch step. As she sat down, I came out. Thankfully, Muma was a capable baby-catcher. She pounced to grab me as I popped out, for I had become airborne on that high step. Perhaps the icy cold air made me more alert than most newborns because Muma later told me that I was bright-eyed and eager from the first moment.

I've been told that from the beginning I was a wilful, difficult daughter, never sweetly obedient as Muslim daughters are expected to be. Perhaps my attitude came from the fact that any time our family would gather for a celebratory occasion, I would be greeted by aunties and uncles and cousins with hurtful comments such as, 'What a pity she wasn't a boy!' Although my parents were more modern and wise than most, brushing off such stinging remarks by retorting, 'But Maryam is our boy,' my feelings about being a girl were forever tainted.

I started feeling apologetic about my sex, but later I became angry at myself for not being the boy I wanted to be. I hated being a girl so much that I foolishly thought I could will myself into becoming a boy. I rebuffed girls my own age and instead played with male cousins or the boys in the neighbourhood. My parents went along with me, allowing me not only to dress in boys' clothes, but also letting me keep my thick hair cut short. They made no objection when I later insisted on shaving my head. I collected toy cars, and over the years I became quite skilled at flying kites, a favourite hobby for Afghan boys, and I rollerskated and pedalled boys' bikes. I felt I was as good as any boy.

I was so good at hiding my sex that soon almost everyone in the neighbourhood and in my family appeared to forget I was not what I pretended to be. I foolishly thought I could carry on the charade but reality was quick and painful when my sister unthinkingly exposed my secret. School had become the biggest part of my small world, and never again would I be accepted as a boy in that very important arena outside my home and neighbourhood.

A short while before, my parents had left Afghanistan to seek medical treatment for my mother. I could not stop worrying about my mother and now the day's events made me miss my parents more. My parents were wonderfully advanced, so different from most other Afghan adults, and I longed for a miraculous intervention from them. Both were highly educated and adept at accepting new ideas, and they doted on me, rarely failing to support their youngest child's eccentric behaviour. I believed my parents could protect me from my fate, but of course I was too young to realize the full impli-cations of being a woman in Afghanistan. What I was to learn was that even the queen could be murdered on a whim by her king husband or even by her father, brother or a cousin. Should such a thing happen, no one would stand up to defend her. They would accept any flimsy explanation given out by her family, because if a man feels he must murder a female member of his family, everyone will assume the woman was to blame. The only question they would ask is: 'What sin did she commit to cause her poor male relatives to have to kill her?'

My pace picked up when I spotted the outlines of our home. I wanted nothing more than to seek refuge in a small corner.

I didn't know it at the time but we lived in the most plush area of Kabul, the capital of Afghanistan. It is an ancient city, over three thousand years old, situated in the dramatic Hindu Kush mountains, straddling the Kabul River. In my youth it was the economic and cultural heart of north-eastern Afghanistan. Kabul was a beautiful city in those days, and every schoolchild learned by heart poems praising its beauty, the most popular being 'Kabul', by the Persian poet Saibi Tabrizi.

Kabul

The beautiful city of Kabul wears a rugged mountain
  skirt,
Even the rose is jealous of its lash-like thorns.
The dust of Kabul's blowing soil smarts lightly in my
  eyes.

But I love Kabul, for knowledge and love come from
   her dust.
I sing bright praises to her sparkling water,
colourful flowers and the beauty of her trees.
Men choose Kabul over Paradise, for her mountains
bring them near to heaven's delights.
Every street in Kabul fascinates the eye.
In the bazaars, Egypt's caravans pass through the
winding streets.
Hundreds of lovely suns hide behind her walls.
No one can count the moons on her rooftops.
Kabul's morning's laugh is as gay as flowers,
while her dark nights shine like beautiful hair.
Kabul's tuneful nightingales sing with flame in their
   notes.
Fiery songs like burning leaves fall from their throats.
Even Paradise is jealous of Kabul.

Everyone found Kabul splendid in those days,
never imagining the horrific ruinous wars lurking in
my country's dark future that would take nearly
every building in the city down to dust.

Although we lived in a wealthy neighbourhood,
our family home was not elaborate – it was a modest,
one-storey building. There was a small living room, a
second family room and a tiny but adequate kitchen.
The largest room in the house was my parents' bedroom, so spacious that four beds were positioned

there. Nadia and I slept in two American standard-sized beds located in one corner while our parents' larger beds were in the back of the room. My father's bed was the nicest of the four, distinctive with solid expensive wood, a gift from a British general who once lived in Afghanistan. There was also an ancient wooden side table beside my father's bed, ornately carved, a present from a maharaja of India. Wood has always been prized in my country because trees are quite scarce in most of Afghanistan.

I remember how I enjoyed the pleasure of slipping into my mother's bed to sleep for a few hours and then, after becoming restless, leaving her bed to climb into my father's bed for a few extra hours of sleep. Those were such innocent, sweet times. There was a second tiny bedroom and that is where Grandmother Mayana slept, but she was a sad loner and we saw less of her than we should have.

Just as Muma and I were about to enter the front garden, I caught a glimpse of my grandmother walking around, her head bowed, an old woman deep in thought. I slowed down and seized Muma's hand and pulled back. Grandmother Mayana was as sweet as sugar, yet she was the last person I wanted to see on that day because she had the most depressing aura of anyone I had ever known. Father once said that all the grief she had suffered over her lifetime had moulded her face into a mask of eternal sadness.

I kept a tortoise's pace, hoping she would disappear into her small room, her little haven, a place she rarely left. At that moment she glanced up and saw me, but her eyes remained without expression and her lips failed to spread in a smile. But then I didn't smile at her either. After my awful day I was in no mood to be reminded that her past might be my future.

Family legend claimed that Grandmother Mayana had been one of the most beautiful girls in the country. But as with any Afghan woman, even celebrated beauty could not save her from the evil lurking in Afghanistan.

Chapter 1

There was a time when Grandmother's girlish dreams held great promise. Although her family was deprived when it came to worldly goods, even the poor of Afghanistan dream of neat huts, a shoulder of lamb to serve at occasional feasts and a satisfactory marriage followed by many sons.

Mayana's father was a poor farmer from Sayid Karam, a district in the Paktia province, an area sixty miles south of Kabul inhabited by members of the Khail tribe. Largely mountainous and lacking trees and most other greenery, it suffers from a particularly dry climate and it is difficult for any farmer to grow enough produce to support his family.

Despite the harsh climate, which multiplied demand on a farmer's labours, Mayana's father was not dissatisfied, for he had a wife who worked hard and children he held dear. The family was known to breed handsome sons and attractive daughters, but none was more alluring than the farmer's daughter

Mayana. She was so beautiful that even other women noticed her appeal, whispering that Mayana Khail was exquisite, with a dimpled mouth, lips sensually full and large dark eyes that danced.

Although birth records were not kept on female children, the family believes that Grandmother Mayana was born around 1897, at a time when Afghanistan's affairs were relatively quiet. The Afghanistan of Grandmother's youth was one of nearly total isolation, created both by rulers who distrusted their neighbours and the inaccessibility of the country due to the lofty mountains encircling the entire land. Afghanistan was then a country of approximately six million citizens composed mainly of fanatic tribes, warring with each other or with any foreigner foolish enough to cross its borders. The British had tried to occupy Afghanistan, as it was the shock absorber between their interests in the area and Russia, but defeat and retreat had left scattered British bones bleaching white in the hot Afghan sun.

'Keep Out' was the signal at every border crossing, guarded by soldiers. Stone watchtowers were scattered along the ancient caravan trails, the same trails that had been used by Alexander the Great and Genghis Khan. There were no railways or telegraph lines. Any products coming in or going out were loaded on to pack animals, caravans consisting of donkeys, horses, camels and even elephants.

Cruelty was part of the culture, with state-sanctioned punishments ranging from prisoners being fired from cannons, beheadings by sabre, live burials, intentional blinding or stoning. Perhaps the most merciless punishment came in the form of starvation, when thieves were locked into metal cages and raised high above the city centres on metal poles so their friends couldn't pass them poison or food. An agonizing death came from lack of water and food, with the lucky ones dying more quickly from either heatstroke or hypothermia, depending on the time of year.

A monarch ruled with undisputed authority, but the royals were just as brutal to each other as they were to their subjects. Many royal heirs were deliberately blinded, because no man with a physical disability may hold a place of honour in Afghanistan.

Grandmother would have been around fifteen or sixteen years old in 1913. The Amir of Afghanistan was having a lot of trouble with outlaws, warrior bands carrying out raids across the north, escaping into the Khost valley. That was also the year a conspiracy against the Amir was discovered in Kabul. The conspirators were exposed and stoned or stabbed to death, so nothing came of the uprising. The land was abuzz with that news but Grandmother probably wouldn't have noticed the upheaval because political matters were a subject solely limited to men. Her teenage sights would have been firmly on her upcoming marriage.

Grandmother's beauty, rosy cheeks and bright eyes would have brought many suitors to the family door but her marriage had already been arranged at the time of her birth. She was destined to become the bride of her very gentle first cousin, the son of her father's brother. Everyone was pleased with the arrangement – Afghan culture encourages marriages between cousins – but fate would intervene when Mayana's exceptional beauty created a diverging path.

Government law backed by Afghan tribal culture ruled that women were forced to veil, although Grandmother's family allowed the women to dart from one family home to the other without a face covering since the houses were nestled so close to each other. Nevertheless the women did dress with great modesty, covering their bodies with cloaks and draping their heads with scarves.

And so it came to pass that one day in 1913, when my grandmother stepped out of her father's humble family home to walk to her auntie's house, at the same moment Ahmed Khail Khan, the head of the Khail tribe, happened to pass by on his horse.

Mayana's classic beauty struck Ahmed Khail with a passion so powerful he later claimed to have been rendered speechless. A man accustomed to having all his wishes granted, he decided instantly that he would make the village beauty his fourth wife. Ahmed Khail Khan had already been married six times, but on that particular day he had only three wives so there would be no need to divorce any of them in order to take a fourth. Not only was he the most powerful man in the Khail clan, he was a Pashtun Sunni Muslim, and four wives are allowed by our Muslim religion.

Although struck by great desire, Ahmed Khail kept his composure, saying nothing at the time but noting his surroundings so that he might send his emissary to arrange the marriage. The following day the Khan's representative appeared at Mayana's home, bearing many expensive gifts. The man presented the treasures to Mayana's astonished father, and at the same time asked for his most beautiful daughter for Ahmed Khail, the leader of the Khail tribe.

Mayana's father was an honourable man, and although he was surely tempted by the great wealth and prestige that would come to him and his family at such a connection, he refused the Khan's offer. He softly replied, 'Our home is most honoured, but I cannot accept these fine gifts or the proposal of marriage. My daughter is soon to be married to my brother's son. She was pledged to him at her birth.'

The emissary was struck dumb. Never had the powerful Ahmed Khail Khan been refused. The poor man squirmed, fearing he might forfeit his own life when he returned with rejected gifts rather than with the promise of a beautiful bride. He reluctantly departed and braced himself for what was to come. The bride Ahmed Khan so desired was promised to another.

As expected, the Khan flew into an uncontrollable rage. Everyone around him remained motionless, fearful to call attention to their presence. 'Who is this poor farmer who dares refuse the head of his tribe?' he demanded, flinging his arms about, shouting louder and louder. 'Where can I find this sorry groom who plans to claim such a beauty?'

While Mayana's family carried on with their wedding plans, a grisly plan was already in motion. Mayana would never marry her betrothed, the only man she had ever considered as a possible husband and the father of her children.

Two days after the Khan's emissary left their home a disappointed man, an expert horseman thundered by, tossing a large dilapidated burlap bag at the farmer's door. Mayana's father slashed the bag open before recoiling in horror. The mangled body of his dead nephew had been stuffed into the bag. Everyone understood that the ominous message must have come straight from the ruler of the Khail tribe: no one could refuse the Khan. The murder was a harsh reminder that the Khan held undisputed power over his tribe. In order to avoid any further bloodshed, the petrified family sent word to the Khan that their young daughter Mayana would arrive in a few days.

As usual, Ahmed Khail had his way.

And so it came to pass that my grandmother Mayana became a 'prize bride' like so many other beautiful Afghan women who are given to the man with the most influence and wealth.

My grandmother rarely discussed her youth or early married life with me. Although she showed me and my sister great affection, she was dolefully silent about her own life story, her stoic nature discouraging her inquisitive granddaughters' curiosity. I longed to ask about her early life but I could never muster the courage to ask if she had felt affection for her ill-fated cousin, the man she had believed would be her husband, or if she mourned his violent death.

Silence reigned around those who knew my grandmother. I was ten or eleven years old before I knew anything substantial about her history. No one in my family dared to discuss her marriage openly, for who knew if word might hit the ear of the Khan, thus condemning them all. But as I grew older, my parents and others in the family would sometimes let slip small stories about the life Mayana had lived as the wife of Ahmed Khail. I remember weeping from stories so sad. At the sight of my tears, Grandmother would caution, 'Do not speak of such depressing things in front of this child.'

But the family gossip continued.

I knew that any girl's wedding should be a cause for celebration, but instead my grandmother was given to someone she did not know. The women of the family dressed a frightened Mayana in her wedding dress, then she was placed on the back of a gaily decorated horse, with ribbons of vivid colours woven into its mane and tail, and escorted to the grand home of the Khan, approximately six miles away.

While an impatient Ahmed Khan waited to claim his bride, his three existing wives were riddled with jealousy. Through household gossip they had dis-covered that their husband was overly excited about the exceptionally beautiful daughter of an ignorant peasant. They felt themselves superior to such a simple girl, but they weren't the only ones who were infuriated. Ahmed Khan's grown-up son Shair, the proclaimed heir of the Khail Khan title and fortune, was also tormented by the realization that a youthful bride brought with her the possibility of siblings, who would be rivals for his father's wealth. Should the new bride present his father with a son, Shair would be expected to share his inheritance. And so it was that many aggrieved people were looking out, waiting to catch their first glimpse of the simple farmer's uneducated daughter.

Six miles on a horse was a long journey on Afghanistan's pitted dirt roads, but Mayana's entire family made the excursion to the Khan's home. Some family members were mourning, but others were determined to make the best of the situation. After all, one of their own would now belong to the most influential family in the district. Perhaps there would be some financial benefits for them all.

The tribal ruler's home was in reality a self-contained fortified village. The fort, or galah, was deliberately isolated, located on high ground for safety from surprise military attacks. Rival tribesmen from adjacent provinces could pose a threat at any time. The galah was self-sufficient, encircled by nearly a thousand acres of grazing land, for a rich man like the Khan owned many horses, sheep and goats. There was also land reserved for his fields of corn, wheat and other produce.

On top of its hill, the galah had been built on a foundation of Afghanistan's grey-shaded native stone. Above the stone, thick mortared bricks reached a height of more than fifty feet. Tall battle-ready parapets were constructed at each of the four corners. The fort's windows were specifically built for observation and defence, with slits through which the warriors could fire their arrows or guns.

Coming from the home of a simple peasant, all the women in the bride's party would have been intimidated at such a sight. They rarely travelled far from their homes and seldom if ever saw such displays of wealth and power as the massive fort the beautiful Mayana would now call her home.

A group of strong men were waiting to open the huge wooden gate to the galah. Once inside the gate, the wedding party arrived at the large central courtyard, which was enclosed by yet another protective wall. Tall apartments rose above the outer walls, specifically designed for the male guests who would never be allowed entrance into Ahmed Khail's main inner dwelling, where his wives lived.

My grandmother and her female relatives were then escorted to the Khan's private quarters. The Khan's personal wing was built behind large windows, so he could watch the daily activities of those who worked for him. His wives and children lived in a separate, restricted wing, their quarters isolated and their windows covered with the traditional Islamic dressing of latticed wood. Fresh breezes would flow through the open trellis, allowing the wives and children to gaze out on the life they are not allowed to take part in, while thwarting curious strangers who wanted to peek into the interior.

House servants and some of the livestock were accommodated near the family section, as well as the galah's main water supply, a deep well that provided clean water, something rare in

Afghanistan unless one lived by a fast-flowing stream.

No one remembers exactly what happened next, but it is thought that the wedding was held almost as soon as Mayana entered the home of the Khan. The Khan was very traditional, so men and women were separated for the actual ceremony.

Grandmother Mayana would have met the Khan's three senior wives at her wedding, women who felt their pride had been pricked by the inclusion of such an unsophisticated girl in their restricted circle. Although Mayana was reviled prior to her arrival, the hatred increased when her beauty was exposed. One look at Mayana's lovely face told the older wives why their husband sought to add the young girl to his harem. Little could Mayana know that she had landed in the middle of such venomous resentment. She was accustomed to a degree of camaraderie between the women in her family. Only Ahmed Khail Khan looked forward to Mayana's appearance, a man energized by lusts, dreaming of enjoying sexual pleasures with a young, beautiful and obedient bride.

Hopelessly smitten by Mayana's combination of beauty and sweetness, the Khan soon publicly acknowledged Mayana as his most favoured wife. Although the Khan had never been the sort of man to concern himself with the feelings of his wives, he nurtured his young bride. And so their union was happy.

The Khan was so pleased with his young bride that when he heard that the jealousy of his three older wives was causing Mayana such misery, he paid his harem an angry visit. He warned them all that he would not tolerate their behaviour. 'If you are seeking punishment, then you will soon receive your reward,' he threatened. 'All living in my household are commanded to regard my wife Mayana as the lady of the galah. Grant her every wish.' He stomped off, his fury expressed in every movement.

Knowing the Khan was not a man to make empty threats, the three wives attempted to suppress their jealousy and anger. But with each passing day, Ahmed Khail's favouritism grew more pronounced, creating further bitterness, which only resulted in an even bigger volcano of hate against the new lady of the galah.

Obviously Ahmed Khail remained sexually drawn to his young wife, for she bore him three children, one after the other, within three years. These three children were daughters, named Peekai, Zerlasht and Noor. The fact Mayana had given birth to three daughters delighted the Khan's jealous wives and older sons. In those days no one knew what science tells us now, namely that fathers are responsible for the sex of a child, so mothers bore the burden of blame. Those wives who did not bear sons were scorned and ridiculed. During this time, one of the older wives gave birth to a son, named Shahmast, adding to the older wives' glee that Mayana alone was known as the 'mother of daughters', a terrible slur in a culture that only values male children.

In 1917, German agents began to foment unrest in Afghanistan in an attempt to entice Afghanistan's ruler to join Germany's cause against Russia during World War I. But the wise Amir remained stubbornly neutral in that conflict. In that same year my grand-mother's status was escalated when she, his most favoured wife, bore the Khan his long-awaited son. The child was my father, Ajab Khail. The servants and soldiers of the galah erupted in festive celebration. But congratulations from the Khan's three older wives and heir Shair were muted.

For the first two years of my father's life he flourished, for love was enthusiastically bestowed on him by his mother and father, three older sisters and the many servants. But my father's joy would not last much longer.

For more years than Afghan people could remem-ber, they had been harassed and buffeted by rebellions and wars. Rival factions often stirred internal strife that was fierce but generally brief. Other wars brought about by external forces created more chaos. That's what happened in 1919 when new tensions led to a conflict with the British Empire. My father was two years old. The problems began when Afghanistan's king Amir Habibullah, an astute reformer who had kept Afghanistan at peace for many years, was assassinated. Upon his death, his son Amir Amanullah succeeded to the throne. Less experienced than his father at forging good relations with powerful nations, the successor was soon embroiled in a petty quarrel with the British. The young king quickly turned to a military solution. With the end of the devastating Great War in Europe, he believed the British were so weakened that his forces would be strong enough to defeat British India.

An eager call to arms went through Afghanistan, and the Khan of the Khail tribe, Ahmed Khail, husband to Mayana and father to my father, gathered hundreds of his warriors around him. His heir, Shair, was a general in the Afghan military and headed his own fighting force. And so the leader and the heir of the Khail tribe both marched to war, leaving nervous women and servants behind.

Although the Afghan fighting force were ill equipped, they were tenacious warriors. On 3 May 1919, Afghan troops battled their way across the Indian border and occupied the village of Bagh.

The British responded with a greater force and

fierce battles ensued. The well-equipped and well-trained British soldiers quickly gained the upper hand and drove the Afghan invasion from Indian territory. Airpower was a new and excellent asset, allowing the British to extend their reach beyond the border, even threatening the Amir's own castle when they bombed near the capital, Kabul.

During a battle mêlée, my grandfather Ahmed Khail received a fatal wound when he was shot in his left eye. Tragically, his death did not come at the moment of the bullet's entry into his brain. His passing was to be painfully slow. Shair sent his wounded father across the famous Khyber Pass for treatment by a British physician, who was living in what is today's Pakistan, but the strenuous journey on the back of a horse only added to Grandfather's anguish. He died on the way.

After Grandfather Khail drew his last breath, his men turned their horses to make a cheerless trek back to Paktia province, to the galah where his wives and children were devastated to learn of his death. Although the war was a tactical victory for the British, King Amanullah managed to negotiate the peace treaty so that at least the Afghans kept the right to conduct their own foreign affairs as a fully independent state.

This upheaval did not bode well for my family. Grandmother Mayana had enjoyed unexpected happiness with Ahmed Khail. His genuine affection for his youngest wife and their four children had been so conspicuous that it was offensive to his earlier families. Now that Shair was the head of the Khail tribe, my grandmother would be ruled by a stepson who had detested her from the first moment she had arrived at the galah. Her beauty could not save her now and neither could her former powerful position as the most favoured wife of the Khan. She was helpless without her protector husband and all she could do now was pray, hoping for the best, for that is all a woman can do in Afghanistan.

Chapter 2

My grandfather was an extremely wealthy man. Islamic law demands that when a father dies, his property is divided between his wives and children, with his sons receiving a double share. But only Shair had reached adulthood when his father died, and as such he was in charge of the birthrights of his younger siblings. Although by Sharia law wives should receive their portion at the time of their husband's death, in Afghanistan men often ignore Islamic law when it comes to females, rarely allowing surviving widows and daughters to handle their own wealth. And so Shair seized control of his father's wealth the moment he knew he was the head of the family. His wishes, decisions and commands became law for every person belonging to the Khail tribe.

My grandmother's life and that of her four children changed immediately. Shair Khan elevated his own wives to the position his father's wives had once held, and in their new positions, these women became insatiably greedy. Grandmother Mayana and her daughters were called before Shair Khan. He brusquely ordered them to deliver all their jewels and gold to him so he could drape them on the necks and arms of his own wives. But most unexpectedly and shockingly, he informed Grandmother, 'You are now a servant. You will join the servants in their duties.'

In just a day my grandmother went from the lady of the galah to a lowly servant, washing and cooking vegetables, scrubbing floors, milking cows or whatever else her stepson and his wives ordered her, to do. Menial tasks were maliciously piled upon her, and Shair's wives and children enjoyed the greatest amusement thinking up new humiliations for the woman formerly elevated above them all.

Although he was only a small child, even my father was not spared. He was ordered to forget play and told that he must earn his keep. Any time Shair left the galah, my father Ajab was to climb to the highest point of the stone tower to keep watch for his older brother's return. He must stare at the road, watching for the dust from the horses' hooves, and as soon as he saw it he was to run as fast as his little legs would take him down the stone stairway to the main gate. He was also in charge of collecting the Khan's gun and hat.

The Khan was often away until very late in the

day. My father was too young to stay awake until the early hours, so on that first night he fell into a deep sleep while on watch. He was startled awake when his brother Shair pulled him up by his arms and slapped his face. He warned him, 'If you ever fall asleep again, Ajab, your punishment will be severe.'

After that, my father was terrified of drifting off to sleep again. As well as the threat posed by his older brother, there were other dangers for the young child. Afghanistan has a huge number of venomous snakes, scorpions and tarantulas, so he spent much of his young life looking out for those deadly creatures while trying not to fall asleep. Years later he told me how his great fear would cause him to talk to himself, or jump up and down, or even pinch his flesh between his little fingers, anything to keep him awake.

Shair's next order was that the family had to move. The King of Afghanistan had recently presented Shair with a few hundred acres on the outskirts of Kabul. Shair built a much larger galah on this land. The basic design followed the model of his father's old one, but the interior was much more modern and built to the standards of an extravagant palace, including every feature needed for daily life independent of any city or village. Although the new galah was undeniably luxurious, my grandmother and her children had lost the familiarity of the only home they knew. Sadness engulfed the entire family, yet there was worse to come when further restrictions were placed on Grandmother and her daughters.

Although the poor of Afghanistan learned to satisfy themselves with simple foods like coarse bread and a little fruit and vegetables, the wealthy were accustomed to delicious dishes of fowl, mutton, rice and special sweets. The Khail ruling family ate only the finest foods but Shair ordered that from now on my grandmother and her children were only allowed enough to keep them alive. They were permitted tea, but no sugar to put in their tea. They were allowed bread, but no butter or jam to spread on the bread. Grandmother's hungry daughters pleaded for small chunks of cheese, anything to relieve the monotony of their bland diet, but their pleas were ignored. When Shair Khan heard of their hunger and cry for food, he told them, 'Lick your fingers.'

My grandmother's heart shattered when her hungry young daughters wept, pleading for something sweet. She dreaded that Shair would do something to separate her from her children and she knew she wouldn't be able to bear being far away from them, unable to offer her love as comfort.

My grandmother was still in her twenties, a young woman who remained physically lovely, despite having given birth to four children and the recent traumas she had had to endure. Shair called her to appear before him and she shivered in fear at the anticipation of this meeting, for his loathing for her seemed to expand with each passing day. When she faced her stepson, his face was contorted with hatred. His voice full of spite, he announced, 'Mayana, an old man far from our galah has offered a large sum for your dowry. You will be married soon.'

Grandmother Mayana felt faint. She understood what such a marriage would mean for her family. Cultural law demanded that her children remain under the control of Shair Khan if she remarried so she would disappear from the galah and never be allowed to see her daughters and son again. She would become the property of a man she did not know, forced to bear his children. Knowing that any protest would only serve to harden her stepson's decision, she remained silent, staring at her feet as an obedient woman should. Finally she was dismissed.

After that summons, Mayana made a hard decision. She would choose a young death rather than endure the pain of having her children torn from her arms as she was given to another man, a man who by law was free to sexually abuse every part of her body, a man who could beat her daily, a man who would surely keep her away from her children. She decided that if she was going to be wrenched from her children's lives, she preferred a quiet grave to a living hell. A favourite servant arranged for

Grandmother to acquire arsenic, putting just enough in a small snuffbox so that, if needed, she could commit a quick suicide.

But a few years passed and there was no further mention of marriage. It was 1922 and the Amir was calling out for Afghan men to devote themselves to civic duty, telling educated families that their college-age sons would be sent abroad for education. Young Afghan men would have the chance to look upon the world outside our little corner and create a future movement for change. Although our country was beginning to stir, inching forward into modernity, everything remained archaic at the galah, a fact Grandmother was reminded of when Shair tried to kill her only son, my father.

Shair had an iron-clad rule that to show respect my father must remove his hat any time he greeted him. One day my young father forgot he was wearing his hat and ran outside to greet his brother. The sight of that forbidden hat drove Shair into one of his famous rages and he ordered his horse to charge and trample on my father. My tiny father covered his head with his hands and waited for the inevitable blows from the horse's hooves.

But that horse had a special affection for my father. It danced on its hind legs, prancing with front legs in the air, refusing to trample the young boy. As soon as he recovered his wits, my father saw his escape and ran as fast as he could, finding a corner to hide away until Shair forgot his anger.

In 1923, a few months after this incident, Shair ruled that my father would be sent away to a military boarding school. My grandmother was devastated – her small son was only six years old, much too young for military training. Shair brushed her off, saying, 'Your son needs to be made into a man.' The parting was quick, for Mayana was informed only at the last moment. And so she watched helplessly as her young son's tiny figure was set upon a horse and taken from the galah.

Although the military school was only ten or so miles away from the galah, it was a long journey on horseback on Afghanistan's bumpy roads. While Ajab was allowed to visit home on occasion, he was kept busy by his older brother and only rarely saw his mother. My father's only joy at being away from the galah was the relief from his brother's cruelty. However, this too soon came to an end when Shair was appointed the dean of the military school. There would be no escape from his cruel brother.

In 1929, the year my father was twelve years old, Afghanistan was experiencing great upheaval. Amir Amanullah had grown into a progressive leader and passed reforms calling for the education of women, the introduction of European dress and the establishment of business ventures with outside firms. This created turmoil amongst the tribes who loathed any suggestion of change. Afghan clerics and tribal leaders were particularly incensed to discover that Amanullah's only wife and queen had appeared unveiled during a recent trip to Europe. Before the year ended the Amir was forced to issue proclamations cancelling his reforms, but he had lost the support of the clerics and tribal leaders. When he was forced to abdicate, Afghanistan lost an intelligent reformer who would have brought much needed change to my country.

During this year of national turmoil, my father learned that his mother was dangerously ill with influenza and so he did something he had never done before. He requested a private meeting with his brother, the dean. When admitted into Shair's office, my father asked, 'My brother, may I have permission to visit my mother? I have heard that she is gravely ill.'

Shair didn't say yes, but he didn't say no either. Instead, he brusquely told my father, 'Return to my office at the end of the day.'

My father's hopes lifted. Perhaps his brother had changed and would let him go home. However, when he returned to his brother's office later that day, Shair was waiting for him and slapped his face numerous times. He pushed my father to the floor, shouting,

'Here is your answer. *NO! Did you think you would receive special treatment because you are my brother?* Know this, Ajab, you are no more important than any other student at this school. You may not visit your mother until classes are out.'

Shair should have been his brother's protector, but instead he seemed determined to harm him. My father was constantly on guard against the next attack, never knowing when or where his brother might strike. Another more serious incident occurred a few years later. My father was innocently walking past his brother's office one day and, for no reason, Shair rushed from his office and gave him a violent shove. My father had been at the top of a long flight of stairs at this point. Caught completely unawares, he went into freefall, tumbling down head first.

At that very moment Prince Daoud, a young member of the royal family, happened to be walking past. A very surprised Prince Daoud reached out and caught my father, saving him from injury. Shair pretended he had nothing to do with my father's fall, but the prince was aware that something was seriously wrong. But he was only a young boy himself at the time and without the power that would come to him later he could do nothing against the powerful Shair Khan.

While my father was trying to stay out of his brother's way, Mayana retreated even further into herself, living only for her children. Her daughters were growing more beautiful by the day, and she became anxious about what the future might hold. In Afghanistan, beautiful girls were married young, and to the highest dowry bidder.

Peekai, the eldest, had sky-blue eyes and dark black hair. Her face was so exquisite and her eyelashes so long that some of the female servants would gather to watch her sleep and admire her beauty. Zerlasht, the middle daughter, had vivid green eyes, with blonde hair. Noor, the youngest daughter, had blue eyes and light brown hair. All the girls were exotically beautiful, although Peekai was the most lovely of the three. Word of her beauty spread throughout the land, stirring the Afghan king to inquire about her age and a possible engagement, but Shair lied, telling the king, 'She is not yet of a marriageable age.' Shair did not want one of his hated half-sisters to marry into an influential family where she might be in a position to help her mother and siblings against his brutality.

Years had passed since Shair had threatened to marry Mayana off. She had almost convinced herself that he had forgotten all about it when he summoned her once again.

Shair said, 'The day has come. Your marriage has been arranged. Your husband is old, but he is rich enough, and that is what matters.'

Burning with determination, Mayana reached for the poison she still carried in her snuffbox. The moment the guards and servants realized her intent, they all jumped on her, attempting to knock the arsenic from her hands. But Mayana was resolute and she clung to the poison, twisting, shouting, fighting with all her strength. However, she was finally overpowered by the men and they snatched the poison out of her small hands.

A red-faced Shair screeched, 'Confine her to her room!'

My frightened grandmother was dragged away and locked in her room, with guards positioned outside her door and window.

Grandmother's attempt to kill herself to avoid marrying an old man was considered a serious rebellion. Shair swore, 'I will not accept revolt from within my own household.' In a heated rage he declared that Mayana would be stoned for disobedience.

Servants slowly gathered to do Shair's bidding. Stones were gathered into tall piles in the courtyard.

There was one elderly servant who still mourned his former master, Ahmed Khan, and disapproved of the cruelty of his son. He had faithfully served Mayana during the days when she was the lady of the galah and he felt compelled to do something to save the life of a good and guiltless woman whom his master had loved. The servant believed that only Ajab, who was by then a teenager, could save his mother. He rushed from the galah, travelling many hours over jagged footpaths and irregular dirt roads. He arrived at the military school late at night, calling for Ajab to come quickly, that he must save his mother from an agonizing death by stoning. Stunned by the servant's terrifying words, my father mounted a horse and raced off to the galah. If my father did not arrive in time, he knew exactly how his mother would die. During that long ride his imagination took him to the macabre scene he feared was taking place at that very moment.

No one denies that stoning is one of the most grisly of the various death penalties. In Afghanistan, and under Islamic Sharia law, it is a legally sanctioned form of punishment for the sin of adultery. It is the only capital punishment requiring four accusers, who each must testify that they witnessed the defendants in the act of sex. But Shair made his own law. And was determined to punish Mayana for her defiance.

Accepted stoning procedures are for a narrow, deep hole to be dug into the ground. The hands of the 'guilty' female are bound. Then she is lifted and placed into the constricted hole. Dirt is packed around her so she cannot struggle. Only her head and body from the waist up are left visible.

A man of authority will become the stoning

cheerleader, encouraging a group of executioners, which in most cases will only be men, to gather around a pile of stones. It is not illegal to stone a woman to death. It is, however, prohibited to kill her quickly. Stones are selected to inflict injury rather than a quick and merciful death. The executioners are discouraged from making any lethal hits on the head at all, at least not until the victim has undergone sufficient pain and suffering. The ideal death struggle for someone so sinful should last at least an hour, if not longer.

Human flesh cannot resist unyielding stone. Two hours of being peppered by small stones will lacerate human flesh into mush. With small stones opening small wounds, the victim's vision will quickly be blinded by blood. The soft flesh on a woman's face will soon begin to shred. The victim's screams of anguish as she pleads for mercy, combined with the stoning cheerleader's shouts, will drive the stoners into a frenzy, disregarding all personal knowledge of the victim and reducing her to an object of sin and hate. By the time death draws near, the soft tissue of her face will have been replaced by blood and gore. Yet the victim will often still be conscious. After the cheerleader's voice begins to tire, and the arms of the executioners become weary, the stoners will begin to select larger stones and finally deliver the death blow.

The sun was about to rise just as my father caught sight of the galah.

He could hear the wails of his sisters and, believing his mother must have already died under a barrage of stones, he jumped from his still-moving horse. When he caught a glimpse of the stones, piled high for the stoning, he exhaled in relief, but then he saw his mother being led to the centre of the courtyard. She was staring trancelike at the hole in the ground that was awaiting her body and she did not notice her son.

Knowing he didn't have much time, my father rushed past the gathering crowd, ran inside the galah and shouted for his brother.

When he saw his brother, he fell to his knees, pleading, 'Brother! Do not kill my mother. I will take her and my sisters away from the galah. You will never see us again. I will never return here or to school. I give you all my inheritance, my brother. Only let my mother live. You cannot kill her. You have no right under Allah to kill her for such a thing.'

Without waiting for his brother's response, my father sprinted to the courtyard and wrapped his arms round his mother, shouting for his sisters. 'Come to me, sisters! We are taking our mother and leaving the galah for ever.'

The servants and guards paused, stones in their hands. They had no desire to execute Mayana. All the hatred for Mayana and her children came from within the ruling family, not from the servants' quarters. With his sisters gathered round his mother, Ajab moved quickly towards the gate. Suddenly his brother's head servant came rushing from Shair's quarters, shouting, 'Khan sahib! Wait! The Khan has said that you must stay. He will honour your demands for your mother's life. And he gives you his word that your mother will not be forced to marry another man.'

Ajab paused, knowing that his brother's order could not now be ignored. To stalk from the galah now would ensure all members of his family would surely be put to death. His brother would not tolerate such insubordination, for he would lose face and this was something he would never allow. The only advantage Ajab had now was that Shair had given his word through the mouth of his trusted servant, who had loudly announced it for all to hear. Shair would be greatly shamed if he did not keep his word.

Ajab waited for Shair and kissed his mother's cheek, comforting her, telling her, 'Do not worry.' When Shair Khan finally stepped outside to glare at his brother, Ajab moved towards him, kissing his hands. 'Thank you for your mercy, my brother.'

To save face, for the sake of the witnesses, all was forgiven, and Shair invited his brother to enter his quarters. Later that day Shair Khan ordered his driver to deliver his brother back to school in his motor vehicle.

My father had no choice but to leave his mother and sisters and return to school, knowing that he must be educated in order to find a good job and care for them all. His three beautiful sisters were of an age to be married, yet, strangely enough, Shair still had made no attempt to find them husbands. My father could only assume that Shair didn't want his sisters to slip from his control.

My father often said that despite his fear and his youth, he became a man that day, the day he saved his mother from a gruesome death by stoning.

Chapter 3

The years passed by with few changes. Grandmother Mayana and her three daughters continued to live under the cruel hand of Shair Khan, while my father pursued his education. He was an unusually solemn young man, his head filled with the responsibilities that faced him. His only goal in life was to finish his education, settle into a steady job and return to the galah to protect his mother and sisters.

After graduating with honours from the military school, Ajab was enrolled in a British military college in northern India, which is today's Pakistan. At the time, India was still a British colony and most of the students there were British. Only a few Indian students were allowed and they came from the most influential families.

The British method of schooling was very different from what my father was accustomed to in Afghanistan. The courses were more difficult and the discipline more rigorous. Yet he liked his new school, for he knew he was receiving a superlative education that would open many doors for him.

There were a few revelations. Despite the many years the British had occupied India, the British soldiers were casually racist towards the Indian boys. Although the British were cordial with the Indian boys during school events, they didn't socialize with them. My father realized that it was not the dark colour of the Indian boys' skin that caused the rift, for those same British students held no prejudice against him even though he was a dark-skinned Afghan boy. In fact, my father was often invited to accompany the British students on weekend jaunts to a popular British park. The British discouraged any Indian citizens from joining them in the park but they welcomed my father into the group. They even encouraged him to flirt with English ladies who might be taking a stroll in the park.

Despite his seriousness as a student, my father took to their social activities, and was so busy that for the first time in his life he neglected his family back in Afghanistan, forgetting to write to his mother or his brother. This lack of communication caused Shair Khan to travel out of Afghanistan to the school in order to check up on my father in person. Upon Shair's arrival, the school head informed him his brother had gone to Kashmir for a short holiday. Shair was furious and left the school determined to find his errant brother. After a few days of searching he found my father, who at the time was courting a lady while rowing her across a small lake.

Shair was a forceful man with a big voice, and he shouted loudly enough that my father could hear him right across the lake. 'Ajab, row to the shore! Now!'

My alarmed father quickly changed course towards his brother, who was waiting impatiently on the shoreline. Father's heart was beating rapidly for he not only feared a serious beating for himself, but he was also concerned that some harm might have come to his mother or to one of his sisters. When he reached him, a glowering Shair said sarcastically, 'You are all right, I see.'

My father's mouth went dry, his tongue unable to move.

Shair turned abruptly and briskly walked away. He left the resort without saying another word to my father.

Never again did my father fail to keep his brother informed of his whereabouts, yet he wondered why Shair had undertaken such a long trip just to locate him. He pondered the far-fetched idea that perhaps over the years some small affection for him had taken root in his brother's stone-cold heart.

While the world outside our borders saw enormous turmoil and change during the Second World War,

Afghanistan remained neutral, but when the war ended, many changes came to our little corner of the planet. First of all, Afghanistan was formally admitted as a member of the United Nations in 1946. In 1947 came the end of British rule over India. The Indian Independence Act passed by the British Parliament on 18 July created two dominions, Pakistan and the Indian Union. In Pakistan, Muslims of the subcontinent had finally achieved their dream of having an independent state for Muslims. However, Muslim Afghanistan voted against the new Muslim nation – the only country to do so – because of their concerns over the question of the right to self-determination for the Afghans in the North-West Frontier province.

Meanwhile, my father had graduated from the military school in India with grades so impressive that he was set to win a scholarship to the United States, but, much to his dismay, when a playboy prince at the school claimed the scholarship, my father's credentials were overlooked. However, a second scholarship for a British military school in London soon became available, and my father was presented with that award instead.

Shair expressed rare pride in his younger brother and agreed that my father could travel to London and continue his education there. My father had heard exciting tales about England from his

British classmates so he was looking forward to settling into the huge metropolis of London.

And so in 1947 my father bade an emotional farewell to his mother and three sisters. Even after all those years, the three women continued to be harassed by Shair's wives, forbidden to participate in normal family life. My father pledged that once he returned to Afghanistan he would improve all their lives. He would be better educated and better travelled than most men in the country, including even his big brother Shair, the leader of the Khail tribe.

Although the Second World War had recently ended, London had not yet recovered from the German Blitz, and the air was polluted with dust from the enormous ongoing reconstruction projects. My father's lungs couldn't cope with the damp climate, coupled with the floating debris. Before long he could barely breathe.

The last thing he desired was a disruption of his schooling. He loved London and the academy. His contemporaries were likable young men from some of the world's best-known royal families. My father knew the classmates he was meeting were the future leaders in their own countries.

But his health continued to decline, and the doctors in England warned him that his lungs were weakened and he must seek a better climate in order to recover. They recommended he travel to Switzerland and seek treatment there, so he took temporary leave from his military school. Once in Switzerland he was told that his health had been seriously compromised. Thinking he would be in the hospital for only a few weeks, he was shocked to learn his health would require fifteen months of medical treatment. Despite his illness, he was encouraged to take walks in the crisp mountain air and he soon grew to love the country and the people. He later said that those fifteen months were the best of his life. Once he was better he returned to his studies in London, where he graduated with honours. Communications were so difficult in those years, however, that contact with his family in Afghanistan was sporadic, with brief letters exchanged only a few times a year.

In 1953 Afghanistan was still squabbling with Pakistan. In September of that year, Mohammed Daoud Khan, the royal cousin who had saved my father's life so long ago when Shair threw him down the school stairs, was elevated to the position of Prime Minister. This was also the year that my father completed his schooling and was ordered by Shair Khan to return to Afghanistan.

Father's years in Europe had been so idyllic that the idea of returning to the difficult life he had known in Afghanistan filled his heart with dread. He felt a strong urge to remain in England, yet knew he must return to his family.

Even as my father embarked on his journey, he had no clue that the evil lurking in Afghanistan had been busily taking away those he loved. No joyful reunions awaited his arrival. Instead, death was everywhere. As soon as his feet touched Afghan soil, my father was told that of his five siblings, only one was still living, and that was Shair, his older brother.

His half-brother Shahmast, who was a young man of gentle temperament, had recently graduated from medical school in Turkey, only to perish of a fever in an epidemic a few days later. My father's three beautiful sisters had all recently died as well. All three sisters had been of good health shortly before they died and the Afghan mountains buzzed with gossip that the three beautiful Khail daughters were poisoned before they could reach the age of inheritance. Few dared question their deaths, for they were only female, of no account, loved only by their mother and brother.

Only Shair Khan and my father were alive to share their father's great wealth. Shair told my father that his sisters had all died of tuberculosis. My father had to accept this as the truth – in 1953, Afghanistan had no scientific methods available to prove otherwise. And any accusations of foul play would be met by dire punishment.

Nevertheless my father believed he would be Shair's next target, so he took matters into his own hands and told him, 'I don't care about money. You are free to hold and control all our father's assets. My needs are few. Provide me with a small allowance only until I can find a government position. I hereby give up my claim.'

I have often thought that my father saved his life with those wise words. Yet he spoke the truth, as he was not a man who desired more than what was necessary for basic life. My father's main concern was his mother's mental state. Mayana and her daughters were closer than most mothers and daughters due to their shared hardships. Their lowly position in the galah had meant they could seek comfort only from each other. All four had been inseparable, even embracing in the same bed each night.

Mayana felt the guilt of the survivor. She hated staying alive while her daughters rotted in the ground. She grieved for her three sweet daughters who had never been allowed one moment's happiness since the day their father died. Their lives had been taken away when they were in their prime, when they should have been cuddling up with their own sons and daughters. Grandmother Mayana felt she had failed her daughters. Now they were gone for ever, and there was nothing she could do but mourn their loss so deeply that her son feared for her sanity.

Chapter 4

My father was welcomed into the highest ranks of society when he returned to Afghanistan. Yet he was strangely uninterested, choosing to live a quiet life instead. He took up residence in the galah, offering what consolation he might to his mother, and his career took the remainder of his attention. His combination of language skills, high education and travel soon resulted in his appointment as a major in Intelligence in the Afghan military. His branch of government was increasingly busy during 1953 as Pakistan had bombed tribal villages in the Afridi area, creating tension between Karachi and Kabul – it appeared the two Muslim neighbours would never enjoy peace. There were stirrings of an alliance between Afghanistan and Russia when a protocol was signed at Kabul. Our government was enthused because the Soviets signalled they were choosing Afghanistan over Pakistan.

There were other notable changes. The Afghan

government was slowly awakening from years of isolation, putting Afghan labourers to work on improving transport facilities, on irrigation projects and in oil exploitation.

On a personal level, talk of marriage surrounded my father. Generally Afghan people marry young, but my father remained unmarried even as he neared middle age. But in 1953 my father was thirty-six years old, and all the family agreed the time had come for him. Shair considered the matter solely his business, and announced that my father's superior education would work in their favour when it came to negotiating for a bride from an influential family. 'I will find my brother the best wife,' he smugly claimed.

My father had his own ideas about the kind of woman he would like to marry. After years of residing in Europe, he had discovered that he took pleasure in the company of women who were educated, women who could be a man's friend as well as romantic partner. He had admired how the English often chose love over family expectations, and he had concluded that he must marry an equal, a woman who would be his partner in every aspect of his life. Of course, my father had to gain permission from his older brother before he could marry such a woman, so he mustered his courage and told Shair, 'Brother, I have decided I will marry an educated woman, someone who will be my equal in life.'

As a man who believed females to be only slightly above beasts of burden, and that the purpose of a woman was for nothing but a man's pleasure and as a vessel to bear sons, Shair was stunned. Never had he heard a man speak like that about women. His own father, Ahmed Khan, had married seven women during the course of his life, and those women had played no role in life outside serving him and bearing his children. Admittedly Shair's father had shown surprising partiality towards Mayana, but Shair had never respected his father for showing his love for his youngest wife, but instead viewed his devotion as an affront to manhood.

Shair's ideas were not unusual. Most men in Afghanistan scorned and mistreated females and nearly all Afghan women lived in subjugation verging upon slavery. To hear his own brother speaking of treating a woman as his equal was almost more than Shair could bear. For the first time he regretted sending his younger brother to Europe.

Shair was so opposed to the idea that, once he gathered his thoughts, he began shouting. 'You will not be allowed to taint our family bloodline with an educated woman! Do you think you will marry a girl who will only speak Farsi? Do you think you will marry a woman who will want to work outside the home? Do you think you will bring a woman into the family who will expose herself to other men? No! No! No!'

My father stood quietly with his new-found calm and determination. Although the ingrained fear of Shair and the habits of his childhood were difficult to overcome, his education and experiences had given him enough confidence to defy his brother on certain topics. He cleared his throat and spoke softly. 'If you will not allow me to marry the woman I want, then I will not marry at all. I will not carry on the Khail bloodline. Our numbers will diminish. I have been obedient to you throughout my entire life. But I will not marry a woman I do not respect. I will not marry a woman I do not love.'

Shair spluttered, shrugging with disbelief, motioning with his hand for my father to leave. He believed my father would soon change his mind, for what man does not desire sons, but Shair waited in vain. My father lived the bachelor's life for a further three years, seemingly content to pursue his military career and to spend time with his male friends.

My father was considered such an excellent catch that most of his friends were eager for him to marry into their families. His best friend, Rahim, was more persistent than most. 'Ajab, I have a cousin who is not only educated and intelligent, but also beautiful,' he said. 'She is so clever that she was accepted at medical school, although she decided she would rather be a teacher. She has a college degree and now has a good position teaching at a girls' school.' After that, Rahim hesitated.

'She is very unusual, Ajab. She doesn't speak Pashto. She speaks Farsi. She has a career. When given the chance, she throws off her veil.'

My father listened carefully. At the time very few women in Afghanistan were educated beyond the most basic level. Most girls were taken out of school after grade six so they could be married. Rahim's cousin sounded completely different. He wondered most how she found the courage to expose her face, because in 1956 it was still against Afghan law for a native woman to walk around unveiled.

Rahim hesitated once more. There was something else he needed to tell my father. 'She is of the Tajik tribe,' he said finally.

My father's jaw dropped. 'A *Tajiki*?' My father shook his head in disbelief. 'Rahim! Do you want my brother to kill me with his bare hands? He would never allow me to marry a Tajiki woman!'

The Pashtun and the Tajik were the two dominating tribal groups in Afghanistan and there had always been bad blood between them. During Afghanistan's long history, it had not been unusual for the two powerful groups to resort to armed hostilities.

Our Pashtun tribe is the largest and most powerful

ethnic group in Afghanistan. It is also the group that historically has dominated the government. While the homeland of the Pashtun is south of the Hindu Kush area, Pashtun are scattered throughout the country. The Pashtun are generally farmers, while a few are nomads, making the black goat-hair tent their home.

The Tajiks are the second largest ethnic group, mainly living in the Panjshir valley north of Kabul, as well as in the north-eastern provinces of Parwan and Badakhshan. Some Tajikis also farm the land, but many are herders of sheep and goats.

The Pashtun and Tajik each had their own way of living, their special cultures defined by an unwritten code. Geographic factors greatly influenced the preservation of the diversity between the two tribes. The two groups do not even share a language, with the Pashtun speaking Pashto, and the Tajik speaking Dari Persian, or Farsi. While the Pashtun rigidly avoid contact with the Tajiki people, the Tajikis are more tolerant of other ethnic groups. Due to their tolerance for diversity and change, Tajikis tend to become more easily urbanized than do the Pashtun.

Certainly no tribe was more intolerant than my father's clan and the more intolerant a group, the more unified they become. Pashtun men feel an over-whelming need to dominate and defend what they know. If any Pashtun suffers harm to his honour, he will be expected to seek revenge by physical retaliation or by insisting upon compensation in money or property. Sometimes a Pashtun man's code of behaviour conflicts with the strict interpretation of Sharia (Islamic) law. When this happens, a Pashtun man will often 'do Pashto', choosing the tribal way over the religious code. To a Pashtun man, nothing is more important than 'doing Pashto', regardless of who might be harmed.

My father was a rare man for Afghanistan, who opposed the ancient tribal codes, perhaps because he had personally witnessed the terrible hurt such ignorance and inflexibility could cause. Still, he was not willing to go to war against his brother just so he could marry a Tajiki woman.

'Forget it, Rahim,' my father replied. 'I have enough problems as it is. My brother will not even agree for me to marry an educated Pashtun girl. He would never accept a Tajik. He really would murder me.'

Rahim knew my father had a valid point. 'Well, she is only half Tajik,' he said, trying to justify his idea. 'But it is the half that counts. Her father is Tajik. Her mother is Pashtun.' Both men knew that in Afghanistan, it is the man's family who are most important.

'Hear my words! Forget it, Rahim,' my father warned.

But Rahim remained so sure the woman was a

perfect match for my father that he kept trying to convince him. After much persuading, my father eventually told Rahim, 'OK. I will look at her. But I will not meet her. I will take one look. One glance only.' My father knew he could not marry a woman of the Tajik tribe, yet he didn't want to cause offence; he truly disliked racial or ethnic prejudice. He had nothing against the Tajik, in fact a number of his male friends were Tajik. It was only because there was such tension between the two tribes that he simply didn't feel up to the all-out family war that intermarriage would lead to. But what harm would one quick look do?

Years later, my father would tease my mother, telling her, 'I realized that Rahim would never stop praising his cousin until I had at least taken a look. After one quick glance, my plan was to make my excuses and leave, claiming that his cousin was too tall or too short, or too heavy or too skinny.' My parents would look at each other with knowing glances, chuckling at what they both knew.

The two friends had set out to drive to Kabul to take that one, fated look. Along the way Rahim told his friend, 'Ajab, I warn you. This cousin of mine is unique. You will be struck by a bolt of love.' My father dismissed Rahim with friendly curses. He couldn't believe he had agreed to travel the rough road from the Khail galah to Kabul only to look at a girl impossible for him to marry.

Upon arrival my father parked his car outside a school gate and, before he could relax a moment, Rahim excitedly shouted, 'There! There! Look on the top step. There she is.'

My father exhaled in irritation, then leaned forward to take a hurried look at the woman Rahim was pointing out. My father blinked, then squinted. First he noticed that the woman was dressed in a chic green coat, an unusual garment for any woman living in Afghanistan. Then he observed that the woman was tall and thin. Then he noticed the woman's shapely legs. They were exposed from the knees down, perfect legs with delicate ankles. The woman was so fashionable that she was wearing silk stockings and high heels. This was highly unusual in a country where women's bodies were more often cloaked by the burqa. As the woman moved closer, my father was able to see her face, for she did not slip on a veil until she actually left the school grounds. She was beautiful, with light skin and extremely dark eyes that set off her shimmering brown hair.

Suddenly one look was not enough.

My father caught his breath, terrified to find himself mesmerized by the woman on the steps. She was having a conversation with another female teacher, and laughter rang out between the two women. The beauty had a nice sense of humour too, he thought to himself.

My father was a man who had been subjected to little happiness, and much sorrow. He believed he had seen it all but suddenly he was a man renewed, startled by the level of attraction he was experiencing for a woman he had never met. He did not believe in love at first sight because his education and sophistication barred such ideas. Yet he was fighting the greatest urge to walk straight up to Rahim's cousin. He had never wanted anything more in his life. He yearned to look full into her face, to find out her thoughts on everything.

My father was a worldly man who had met and romanced a number of women during the years he lived in Europe. But he was no longer in Europe. He was no longer living in a relaxed society where men and women socialized easily. In Afghanistan a casual meeting with the beautiful schoolteacher would create a scandal, possibly causing men of her family to seek violent retribution.

Frustration rippled throughout him. He didn't know what to do.

He realized he was considered a catch in Afghanistan, in a position to have almost any woman from any good Pashtun family. Now, he wanted a woman impossible to have.

That woman was Sharifa Hassen. She was from a

wealthy family held in high regard in Kabul. In fact, her father held influence with the royal family, and had been at one time a top adviser to the former king. Her family appeared modern and happy compared with my father's conservative family. She was an unusually ambitious girl. She had been one of the first women to enrol in medical school, although she had switched her major to education. After graduation, she postponed marriage to assume a position teaching history and geography at the prestigious Malalai High School, built specially for girls in the early 1920s with French cooperation. And that is where my father first saw my mother.

'Arrange the marriage,' my father choked.

Although jubilant to be proven right, Rahim said nothing as the two men drove away from the school grounds.

During the long drive back to the galah, my father experienced a roller-coaster of emotions, exhilaration and terror. He was energized because he had made up his mind that he would marry Sharifa Hassen. He was petrified because he knew his uncompromising brother would ruthlessly fight against a union linking the Pashtun Khail family with an educated Tajiki woman, an unthinkable combination in Shair's bigoted mind. In fact, there was a good chance Shair Khan would murder his brother to avoid such a scandal.

Over the next few weeks my father visited Sharifa's father and brothers, although he didn't ask for her hand in marriage. He was impressed by the Hassen men, finding them intelligent and thoughtful. They were men whom he felt a connection with, unlike his own brother, who was a cruel, ignorant man.

My father knew he could not postpone the confrontation with his brother much longer. It was inappropriate for him to continue calling on the girl's family without expressing his purpose, so he gathered his courage to visit his brother. He stood quietly on one of the many colourful tribal rugs in the grand suite, waiting for his brother to complete some paperwork. Finally Shair looked up, his cold eyes in an unsympathetic stare. 'What?' Shair shouted, as impatient as always.

My father knew if he hesitated his courage would disappear. 'My brother, I have found the woman I want to marry. She is as you said. She only speaks Farsi. She is educated. She works as a schoolteacher. She shows her face to people who aren't part of her family.' My father paused before adding the most damning bit of information, 'She is of the Tajik tribe. Her father is closely linked to the royal family.' Then my father did something so unlike him – he lied. 'I have already told her father.' My father watched as Shair Khan's face reflected his formidable anger. Shair's face paled, then reddened, then paled again.

His dark eyes sparked with rage. He clenched his fists before slowly rising to his feet.

My father braced himself.

Shair cleared his throat as he moved from behind his massive desk and walked in measured steps, the whites of his eyes streaked with red. His angry face was only inches from my father's face. The two stepbrothers locked eyes.

The staring challenge felt endless, but to my father's surprise Shair Khan broke his gaze first, shouting over his shoulder for his special servant to summon his main wife, Nina, and his favourite daughter, Seema. Nothing more was said between Shair and my father until the two women rushed in.

A fuming Shair snarled, 'My brother Ajab has assumed my position as head of this family. He has gone behind my back to ask an unsuitable woman to be his wife.'

The women were still as stones, never having heard of such impertinence in their life. They probably assumed that Shair had ordered them to appear so they might plan my father's funeral. Pashtun men had been sent to the grave for lesser offences.

Shair sneered. 'Because my brother has moved forward with something that is none of his business, I am forced into an impossible situation. Our honour is at stake, so the family must continue the process. But I refuse to be involved. Instead, you' – he nodded first at Nina, then at Seema – 'and you, will approach the family and complete the obligatory arrangements.'

Nina and Seema trembled at the responsibility. Such an important marriage was normally arranged by the head of the tribe, but now Shair was delegating the mission to women. They knew that if their efforts did not please him they would be blamed.

The two frightened women crept from the room and my father followed. The heavy wooden door slammed with an echoing crash behind him.

Nina's lips were quivering and her hands were trembling when she cornered my father to ask, 'Ajab, who is this woman?'

'Her name is Sharifa Hassen. Her family is well known in Kabul.'

Nina's face was red and her voice became high-pitched. 'You are a troublemaker, Ajab! And now you are bringing us in! How could you go behind your brother's back on such an important matter?'

My father shrugged. How could any man explain love?

In adulthood my father rarely felt fear, and he had become nearly oblivious to his eldest brother's threats and actions. Yet on this matter he felt a cold sense of dread because of the lie he had told. He had *not* yet asked Sharifa Hassen's father for his daughter's hand in marriage. My father knew that the Khail name would be dishonoured if he asked for a woman's hand in marriage and was then turned down. Shair was a man who fretted incessantly about his honour. My father's ruse had accomplished his goal but, should his deception be discovered, the consequences would be dire.

My father only knew one thing: that he was going to marry Sharifa Hassen, one way or another, even if he had to take his bride and his mother and flee Afghanistan.

Nina and Seema made the necessary inquiries to locate the father of the schoolteacher Sharifa Hassen. A meeting was organized. Without acknowledging it, the Hassen family understood quite well that my father had not been visiting without a purpose. They knew the Khail heir had his eye on one of the Hassen daughters, although they were unaware which one.

They were soon to find out, when Shair's wife and daughter arrived for their visit. The Hassen family reacted with extravagant hospitality, presenting carousels of sweets and fruit. The families exchanged pleasantries before raising the real business of the day. In Afghanistan, marriage is considered much too important to leave to the bride and groom, as it represents an important alliance for families with great wealth.

Nina was the first to speak, saying that she and her daughter were there to represent the Khail family, to ask that the Khan's younger brother Ajab marry Sheik Hassen's daughter, Sharifa.

Sheik Hassen smiled gently and replied, 'I will be pleased to meet with Shair Khan to discuss the matter.'

Nina had dreaded such a response. It was a great insult to any father when the man representing the groom's family did not personally appear to discuss the proposed marriage. Nina cleared her throat and continued. 'That is why we are here, Sheik Hassen, to negotiate the marriage contract. My husband Shair Khan is involved in certain important matters at the moment, which makes it impossible for him to meet with you.'

Sheik Hassen was too stunned to speak. To hear such a thing was the same as being spat at. He composed himself, however, for Nina was a mere female, a woman who was only doing her husband's bidding. 'Madam, please tell your husband that when he has freed his schedule I will be most happy to welcome him into my home. We shall finalize the arrangements at that time.' His meaning was clear. Sheik Hassen would not allow the marriage to proceed without speaking to the head of the Khail family.

Nina and Seema reluctantly returned to the galah, bearing their bad news with trepidation.

My father was unfortunate because Sheik Hassen was not only well connected, a man accustomed to respect, but he was also a stickler for protocol. But it was lucky no one had revealed that my father had claimed to have already asked for Sharifa Hassen's hand in marriage. That lie remained hidden, preventing a violent clash between Shair Khan and my father.

Nina and Seema went unpunished for the failed mission. Despite Shair's haughty anger at the news, secretly he was pleased. By refusing to meet the most basic requirements of marriage protocol, he had guaranteed a negative response from the family of my father's chosen bride. Now he could move ahead with what he believed to be a more appropriate marriage for his younger brother.

Shair summoned my father. 'Have you heard that Sheik Hassen will not agree to the marriage?' he softly asked with a false show of sorrow. He sighed and waved his hand about in a gesture of resignation. 'There is nothing more I can do. But do not worry, my brother, I have selected a young girl from our tribe for you, the beautiful daughter of a respected general. Your union will bring great advantages for our family.' When Shair noticed my father's worried frown he added, 'This girl meets your requirements, Ajab. She can read. She can even write, a little. But she has no interests other than to be an obedient wife and a good mother.' Shair Khan was so delighted he actually smiled, an expression rarely seen by my father.

My father was not so pleased. For days he had been waiting for the news that his wedding date was set, that the beautiful woman he had loved at first sight would be his wife. He slowly returned to his private quarters, where he found his mother waiting. He told her what had happened and tears formed in his eyes. Mayana could not bear to see him so upset. She had lost all her children but this one son. She had been unable to help her poor daughters, but she decided she would risk her life for her remaining child. His happiness meant more to her than her own life.

Without thinking through the consequences of her actions, she rushed to confront the Khan, the man who had made her life and the lives of her children a misery. She had no appointment, and she knew the mere sight of her face drove Shair Khan into a murderous frenzy, yet she bravely strode into the private quarters that were forbidden to her. Her unexpected appearance stunned everyone who was there.

Without speaking, she lifted her chador, her black cloak, from her body and placed it at the Khan's feet. Loud gasps were heard from every corner.

There are certain codes of behaviour in Afghan society. For a woman to display her chador in this way represents total submission. In her passion to protect and bring happiness to her son, my grandmother had evoked *nang* (solidarity), *namuz* (honour) and *ghairat* (protection of honour by any means).

By reacting thus, an Afghan woman exposes her vulnerability. While the man is free to murder the woman if he so chooses, only a man without honour would do so. He is also free to ignore the woman, to turn away and refuse to accept her offer of peace, but such a man loses face in our culture.

No one spoke. No one moved. The Khan had never expected his hated stepmother to turn to this ancient code against him should he harm her or refuse to grant her son's wish. Shair Khan sat so still and the silence was so complete that it had a noise of its own.

My grandmother later told her son that she braced her body for the blows she thought were coming, but her stepson did nothing. Finally Shair Khan stood and leaned down to retrieve her chador. He moved forward to drape the black cloak over my grandmother's shoulders and bowed head.

'You are free to go,' he said softly.

My father and his mother waited together, and they were jubilant when Shair Khan summoned his brother to accompany him to visit Sheik Hassen in Kabul. They had a high-stake marriage contract to negotiate.

However, further hurdles awaited my father. The

differences between the two tribes, the Pashtun and the Tajik, were causing problems. For the Pashtun, and most especially the leading family of the Khail Pashtun tribe, the amount of dowry offered to the bride's family must match the worth and the status of the head of the tribe, which in this case was Shair Khan. He was one of the most important tribal leaders in the entire land, so the dowry offered to my mother's family was significant.

The opposite was true for the Tajik tribe. They followed Prophet Mohammed's teachings that the wedding dowry should be modest. A large dowry would insinuate that a father was selling his daughter to the highest bidder. Sheik Hassen refused to accept more than thirty Afghani, otherwise he would be insulting himself and his daughter.

There was a stand-off, for both men were proud and determined to maintain their honour, and both were accustomed to being obeyed. Neither was prepared to compromise on the dowry.

Just as it seemed the negotiations would fall apart, Shair Khan impatiently stood up and excused himself, ordering his wife and daughter to handle the matter of the dowry.

The women agreed for the dowry to be thirty Afghani.

Sheik Hassen had triumphed.

The wedding date was set. Within a few months,

Ajab Khail, a long-time bachelor aged thirty-nine, would finally wed. Sharifa Hassen, his bride, would be twenty-seven at the time of her marriage, an old maid by Afghan standards.

While my father was visibly thrilled that he would marry the woman of his choice, my mother was less pleased. Her own educated mother had passed along her ideas about marriage, and they were not favourable. As a child, my mother was aware of the pervading evil that kept females helpless in the face of male power. She knew that marriage for Afghan women meant total submission to the husband. Should Ajab Khail reveal a different face after they were married, no one would step forward to help her. She would be her husband's property.

My mother's opposition to the marriage created discord within her own family. She argued with her three brothers, who were excited by this unexpected opportunity for their family to be linked with the wealthy Khail family. Her brothers argued that Ajab Khail was a unique match for her. Her life would be different from other married women, they said. Ajab was highly educated and sophisticated and they had heard first-hand from their cousin Rahim that he wanted his wife to be educated and to be his equal in marriage.

Still my mother was hesitant. Already her sisters were teasing her, warning her that such a conservative Pashtun tribal family would require that she wear a traditional veil, leave her job and speak in Pashto, a language my mother had never learned. So when my father accompanied Nina and Seema to arrange the final wedding plans, my mother's younger brother Walid took her by the arm to go with him and peek through the keyhole so she could see her groom for herself. My mother said that although the man who wanted her was very handsome and appeared distinguished in his military costume, she remained unconvinced.

Mother was miserable. She was living a dream life in Afghanistan. Behind the walls of the Hassen villa, females were considered humans with wishes and desires too, and she feared she would lose this after she was married.

But her father had promised Ajab his daughter's hand so there was nothing she could do. Despite the fact she was from a progressive family, all Afghan girls were expected to marry *someone*. Already my mother was considered far too old for most Afghan men looking for a bride. My mother felt helpless in the face of overwhelming opposition to her desire to remain single, and had to give in at last.

And so the big day finally arrived.

The year was 1957, a fateful year. It was when Afghanistan and the Soviet Union signed a pact. Soviet 'technicians' started pouring into Afghanistan,

and the Soviet government sent $25,000,000 worth
of military equipment into my country.

But my parents were unconcerned about the
gathering Soviet menace because they were too preoccupied with their forthcoming wedding.

The two families agreed the wedding would take
place at the Khail galah. The Khail family waited for
the Hassen family to arrive. The men were gathered
in one area and women in another, for they believed in
sexually segregated weddings. When the much anticipated caravan of cars finally arrived at the galah, the
Hassen family spilled from the vehicles. Suddenly
loud music rang over the gate and walls. Khail
women crowded the windows of their apartments
while their men waiting in the courtyard exchanged
puzzled looks. What was happening? Was that
singing? Were they hearing *music*?

Shair Khan thought he had controlled all aspects
of the wedding to be held in his home. While there
would be music and dancing later in the evening,
according to his instructions the gaiety would be
segregated, men dancing with men and women dancing with women. Never had he imagined that the
bride's family would bring musicians, singers and
dancers.

The Hassen merrymaking was so loud that
even the livestock became restless. Shair's gatemen
opened the galah gate and enthusiastic members of

the family danced their way into the courtyard.
Drums were beating and cymbals were clanging
while women were keeping time to the music by
waving sheer veils and wiggling their hips.

The Khail family were horrified. Ajab was marrying into a family who allowed their women to
uncover their faces and to dance with abandon! And
to wiggle their bodies in front of men they did not
know!

Suddenly shots rang out. The musicians threw
down their instruments, the singers ceased singing
and the dancers froze. Screams rang through the
crowd like electric shocks and several people were
trampled while they fought to find shelter from what
they believed was an ambush.

The trembling guests spotted an angry man stalk-
ing around the courtyard, waving a weapon. One of
the Hassen men recognized their assailant, calling
out, 'It is Shair Khail, the groom's elder brother! *Stay
down! He will kill us all!*'

Shair was indeed furious. His guests had no respect
for his family and their traditional customs.

Someone in the crowd shouted out that here
music, dancing and singing were forbidden in mixed
company. A few lucid guests began separating the
men from the women, ordering the women to enter
the women's quarters. There they would celebrate the
wedding with the Khail ladies, while the men would

make merry in the courtyard. The men were to be entertained by dancers, too, but their dancers were men dressed up as women. In the world of Shair Khail this was the proper way to conduct a wedding.

The ceremony took place without any further trouble and my father was finally married to the woman he had chosen. My mother soon discovered that her brothers had been right, that her husband was different from other Afghan men. He was truly interested in her as an equal partner. The young couple spent many hours with each other, just enjoying one another's company. My mother soon realized that she had nearly missed out on marrying the one man in Afghanistan who would treat her respectfully and would bring her happiness.

My father's family was less enamoured of the union.

My mother was the most educated woman to marry into the Khail family so far, and problems were bound to arise. My parents were expected to live at the galah, and so they did, moving into a large apartment over the main gate that in the past had been reserved for guests.

Afghan couples rarely go on honeymoon, but instead settle into their new life as a married couple at home. After ten days my father returned to his military duties and my mother resumed her career at the Malalai High School.

Shair Khan seethed at the brazenness of a woman under his galah roof defying him by going out to work and earning her own money. As the head of the clan, he forbade her to leave the galah without the cover of a beige-coloured burqa, a hideous outfit my mother hated. The burqa was draped over her head and covered her completely down to her toes. A tiny embroidered mesh over her face was her only window to the outside world. The ancient code of dress was an indignity for my mother, a woman accustomed to wearing fashionable western dress.

My mother's worst fears were coming true. Her enlightened husband was kindly and loving, but he was unable to fully protect her from his more traditional brother.

Her prison became smaller and tighter when Shair Khan discovered she was pregnant. Shair became so incensed that a pregnant woman would still leave the galah that my mother was eventually forced to resign her position at the girls' school and remain behind the walls of the fort.

Things were not going well.

My mother was busy with her pregnancy so she did not complain much at first. Her own mother was so worried for her daughter's well-being that she sent Nanny Muma to live with my mother to care for her during her pregnancy and to assist with the new baby. Muma was an ideal companion for my mother and she fitted seamlessly into our family.

All Afghan families pray for a male as the first-born, so there was grief and anger when my sister Nadia was born on 21 March 1958. Shair, who was the father of nine sons and three daughters himself, was so enraged at the news he refused to congratulate my parents or to acknowledge the child.

The remainder of the Khail household was equally unpleasant to my mother, treating her the same way they had Grandmother Mayana and her three daughters. While my mother was not forced to do housework, she was continually scorned. Thankfully, she was a strong-minded woman who could disregard her husband's insensitive family. She kept herself busy with little Nadia. Grandmother Mayana was as kind as an angel and tried to do all she could to help her daughter-in-law. The four women in my father's life, his wife, mother, daughter and kindly nanny, would always keep a close lookout for each other.

But after Nadia was born, Shair Khan became even more harsh with my father, asserting that the birth of a useless daughter had doomed their relationship. The wives and daughters and servants of Shair felt the shift and they followed their leader, becoming even more hostile.

Servants in the galah were responsible for laundering all the clothes of the Khail family. Suddenly my mother's clothes were returned to her damaged, with holes and tears. My mother owned an expensive European wardrobe and she was determined to find out who was responsible. One day she decided to hide in a corner of the courtyard. While the servants were busy washing clothes, she saw two of Shair's sons sneaking up to the baskets, ordering the fearful servants to identify Sharifa's clothes. They then took out knives and began to shred her clothes.

My father was furious when he found out what was going on, but he knew confronting Shair about his sons would only lead to violence. From that point on, my mother saved her dirty laundry to send to the home of her own mother. No one knew it at the time, but my maternal grandmother's health was failing and Mother only had a few years left to enjoy her own mother.

Later my mother found more ominous signs that she was being targeted. She discovered several small dolls pierced with many pins hidden in corners of her apartment. Although Islam forbids anything to do with witchcraft, some Muslim women are known to tempt fate by trying to reach the dark spirits. Certainly, someone in Shair Khan's household was practising black magic in order to frighten her.

My parents were clearly unwelcome in my father's family home. Soon the stress affected the health of both my parents, and my father's weight plummeted until he began to look emaciated. My parents knew that their living situation was the cause, and that the only solution was to move away from the galah.

Despite their ill treatment at the hands of Shair and his wives and children, when my father informed Shair he was moving his family out to a private house in Kabul, Shair was aggressively opposed to the idea. 'You will be an outcast! No one will respect you! I will never allow a pariah to share in my father's wealth!' he shouted.

But in his heart my father knew that his own life and that of his child were in danger from Shair. He firmly believed that Shair had already murdered all his other siblings, in order that he, Shair, alone would inherit all of Ahmed Khan's wealth. My father decided that, even if his brother did not eventually find a way to kill him, he would rather be a happy poor man than a miserable rich man. That night he left the galah with his wife, mother, daughter and Nanny Muma.

The Hassen family were the opposite of the Khail clan. They were intellectuals, a family who raised their seven daughters to be educated and resilient, and equal to their three sons. They also helped each other in times of need and, after hearing of my parents' dilemma, they rallied round them, assisting them to find a modest but comfortable home in Kabul. They also helped them financially, because my parents lived frugally on my father's military salary. In their new arrangement, my parents became an exceptionally close couple, enjoying their life away from the tense atmosphere of the galah. My father often said, 'Bitterness squeezes the happiness out of any person.'

My mother confided that her most joyful time was the day she and my father moved away from the galah and my father's toxic family. By fleeing Shair Khan's lethal influence, my mother celebrated a rare victory against the woman-hating evil that cloaked the galah and all that lived within.

Maryam, her mother Sharifa and sister Nadia

Chapter 5

My father was a distinguished presence, tall and handsome, a man of learning blessed with the light of intelligent conversation. He had pale skin and large, expressive amber-flecked brown eyes, with a deep cleft in his chin. I remember how he used to walk with his hands in his pockets, a kindly smile on his face. He dressed immaculately, usually wearing a starched white shirt and grey or beige trousers. Father was so serious about his clothes that the women of the family had their individual duties in order to keep him sartorially perfect.

From an early age I was responsible for cleaning and shining his shoes. Although I hated most tasks thrust upon me, this duty never felt like an unwelcome chore. I spent long hours lovingly cleaning and buffing his shoes with small cloths. Hands and arms aching, I shined until his European-styled leather shoes sparkled.

Around the time he returned from work, I would

be watching the front path. Another treasured responsibility was to greet him with a kiss, remove his shoes and socks, then present him with his freshly ironed kurta pyjamas. When he slipped out of his work clothes, I would deftly hang them on a hanger.

I would be rewarded with a kind smile and loving endearments. 'Come, Maryam! You are my heart!' He would hug me tightly then enfold my small face in his large hands to place a sweet kiss on my cheek. While cuddling me he would call out for my sister, 'Nadia, come.' He would cuddle her too, telling her, 'You are my liver!'

I can close my eyes and see him now, pulling me close with one arm and Nadia with the other, proudly exclaiming to those close enough to witness: 'Here is my heart! Here is my liver!'

Although I felt my father favoured me, he loved both his daughters more than his own life. I've often wondered if his inability to protect his sweet and lovely sisters from miserable lives and an early grave added to his fierce love for us.

Father was unlike all other Afghan men. He set a gentle mood for our household, never criticizing or raising his voice to the women under his roof. He was indifferent that he had not fathered a son. Most men in Afghanistan are contemptuous of daughters, claiming that 'The birth of a girl is a curse straight from God himself!' Male children, however, are welcomed as little gods. While other family members and friends fretted over the absence of a son, my father dismissed anyone foolish enough to mention it. He would respond with a wide smile that his girls were his heart and his liver and he couldn't survive a moment without us.

Such an attitude was unheard of in Afghanistan.

Even my mother agonized that she was unable to give my father more children, and went so far as to try to push our father into taking a second wife, acting totally out of character. I recall some of those bizarre conversations when Mother pleaded with him to marry again, trying to tempt him with the idea that another woman would give him a son. As intelligent and educated a woman as she was, my mother still failed to escape the cultural expectations so rampant in Afghanistan. She was ashamed she had only given birth to daughters. She also naively believed that should my father have a son Shair Khan would become the loving brother he had never been.

Rather than celebrate the fact that he had married a woman who would submit gracefully to another woman sharing his affections, my father was horrified by Mother's suggestion. He exclaimed, 'My dear wife. It is primitive for an educated man to gather a harem.'

With my heart in my throat I listened as he told my mother that not only was she his first wife, but that she was his last wife. He declared that he could never love another woman as he loved her. For him, the subject was closed.

I loved my father so much. I was so happy to hear that he was a contented man with his little female family. If I had been asked to share him with another family, how jealous I would have felt.

Mother was different from Father in every way. While Father laughed, she frowned. Her face gained stern solemnity over the years. My childhood friends were frightened of her and they always took care to be on their best behaviour whenever Mother was near. Although she had been lenient with her wilful and mischievous daughters when we were toddlers, her tolerance developed limits after we grew out of babyhood. She did love her two girls but she could be strict and easy to anger.

While I was spoiled dreadfully as a baby, once I became a young lady Mother's expectations of how I should conduct myself underwent a huge adjustment. Any time I disappointed her, she would freeze me with a severe stare. She would ignore me from that moment, refusing to acknowledge me until I gave a proper apology, generally in the form of a long letter expressing my regret for my shortcomings and for the sorrow I had caused her. Only then would she seek me out, opening her arms in a welcome embrace, exclaiming,

'Darling Maryam. Come! Your mummy loves you.'

Mother was a tall woman for the time, six inches over five feet. Her hair was brown with red tints, and so thin that she always teased it high on the top to cover the crown of her head. Her mood always improved when family and friends complimented her appearance, most saying that she resembled the sensuous Italian movie star Sophia Loren. Mother refused to stay up late because she had once read that Sophia Loren attributed her beauty to getting a lot of rest. So every evening at exactly 9 p.m. Mother would say, 'I must bid you all a good night. Sophia gets a lot of sleep and so must I.'

Mother would rise early every day so she could exercise. 'Although Sophia is busty, she maintains a slim figure,' she used to say. I remember how she would place her morning cup of tea on her stomach, saying it was good for her belly to feel the heat. After warming up her belly she would massage the area with her hands. Later I would watch as she selected various fruits and vegetables, cut them in two and then rubbed the juice into her face and neck. 'Daughters, listen to your mother,' she would say. 'A woman's face needs food, too.' The idea made sense to me, although I never thought to ask if Sophia Loren fed her face.

Her desire to emulate Sophia Loren influenced her make-up and dress sense too. Mother claimed that

Sophia never appeared in public without full make-up and beautiful clothes so Mother was extremely particular about her look and never left home without a light powder on her face, her eyebrows fashionably plucked and her lips perfectly lined with her favourite shade of dark pink. She refused to wear flats, and always left the house in silk stockings and high heels.

My maternal grandmother died a year or two before I was born so I do not know if my mother inherited her ways from her own mother, but I suspect this was the case. I never knew how she died but I guess it was from old age. Over the years I learnt that my maternal grandmother detested her husband despite their many years of marriage and his constant attempts to win her love. It was clear that Grandfather Hassen adored his intelligent, forceful wife with a great passion so I was shocked to hear of the unusual love/hate relationship between the two. I had grown up believing that while my father's family was plagued by unhappiness, my mother's family was content. But now I know there are secrets concealed under every family's roof.

Mother once told me that her mother's hatred stemmed from the fact that at just thirteen years old she was forced to marry a man she did not know. She spent much of her youth pregnant, in the end giving birth to ten children – seven daughters and three sons. Throughout her back-to-back pregnancies, she remained curious about the world outside her home and welcomed learning and study. With her high intelligence and avid reading she was unlike other women in Afghanistan. Most of all, she demanded that her daughters be educated and she would walk around their home repeating these words like a mantra, 'The best friend in life is your books. The best friend in life is your books.' Yet her high intellect was a double-edged sword. Being a woman in Afghanistan is extremely limiting and, despite the fact that she came from a family more modern than most, being enlightened just made her more aware of the injustices.

Her husband, my maternal grandfather, was a tall, handsome man who held some of the highest posts in the Afghan government. He was very close to one of Afghanistan's most successful kings, Habibullah Khan, and there were many stories about Grandfather Hassen's exciting life as a trusted confidant of the most powerful man in the country.

Grandfather Hassen was a good friend of the young prince Habibullah before he became king. He then slipped effortlessly into the role of his right-hand man when Habibullah became king after the death of his father, Rahman Khan, who died peacefully in 1901. For one of the few times in Afghan history, a king succeeded to the throne without chaos and the Afghan people were lucky to be ruled by someone who, for once, was well qualified for the position. His father had trained him well in all branches of the government so he was more than ready to be king by the time he reached the throne.

During King Habibullah's rule, Grandfather Hassen was appointed as the Afghan Ambassador to Russia. His high-ranking position required him to live in Russia, but much to everyone's astonishment he refused to leave Kabul. Somehow Grandfather Hassen convinced his king that he could better serve Afghanistan if he remained in the country, and he performed his duties as the Afghan Ambassador to Russia without ever living there.

Under the rule of King Habibullah, Afghanistan avoided any major political drama for eighteen years, but good times do not last for ever. In February 1919, King Habibullah and a group of his men, including my grandfather, were at Jalalabad at the Ghalat-ul-Seraj palace on their way to go grouse hunting. That night the king was shot and murdered in his sleep.

Speculation was rife all over the world as to who might have assassinated the king. The newspapers in London hypothesized that the assassination was ordered by Lenin of Russia, saying: 'Lenin and his friends are known to have attached the utmost importance to propaganda in British India. Their efforts have hitherto been thwarted because the Amir of Afghanistan blocked the way against their emissaries, just as during the war he denied passage to the emissaries of Germany.'

The event held great political interest for the rest of the world, in particular England, Russia and India, but for my grandfather and the rest of Afghanistan the loss was a personal devastation. The country's worst fears came true when turmoil trailed the new ruler. Criticism aimed at the new king came from every corner. Since nothing strengthens a government like a declaration of war, Afghanistan was battling Great Britain within four months. This war cost my father's family most dearly, for this was the war that took my grandfather Ahmed Khan's life.

By the time I was born Grandfather Hassen was losing his memory, so he could not fully share with me his exciting anecdotes about serving a king. I do recall slipping into his room with my cousins and how he would greet us with the greatest pleasure, believing that we were some of his old acquaintances. He happily described the red uniforms of the Gendarmes, saying that he had played a role in selecting the distinctive attire. He would chatter away about the government intrigues that were so important during the reign of King Habibullah. Much to our delight he would sometimes call out to imaginary servants, 'Saddle up my horse! I am going hunting with the king!' We would play along, pretending to hoist a saddle on to a chair and helping him to his feet. Several times he shocked us with instructions to prepare him for a secret visit, declaring, 'Hurry, hurry! Laila the dancing girl is waiting for me.' He actually smacked his lips in jovial anticipation of visiting that dancing girl!

Later when I asked my mother, 'Who is this Laila who is going to dance for Grandpa Hassen?', Mother would put her finger to her lips. 'Hush.' I later discovered that Laila was an exotic dancer who had captured my grandpa's attention. Perhaps Laila was one of the reasons my grandmother Hassen hated her husband so much.

But when my cousins and I were young his exciting talk thrilled us. We would laugh with him and eventually one of our parents or nannies would hear the commotion and call us away before settling Grandfather Hassen back on his cushion.

How I regret not knowing him when he was of sound mind.

I also felt the loss of my paternal grandfather, whom I'd never met. Had he lived, I would have known my three beautiful aunties and a grandmother who walked with joy, rather than one who was broken from a lifetime of sorrow.

I had heard that Grandmother Mayana was once a great beauty, but her life's hardships had destroyed what used to be. The woman living with us seemed old and withered and even hideous to my young eyes. I would sit and stare and try to imagine the legendary beauty who had caused a powerful man to fall speechless at the sight of her face, but I failed to find a hint of it.

Grandmother was so timid and quiet we hardly noticed her when she was around, although she had lived in my father's home from the time he left the galah. As a child I believed that her grief was the reason she rarely came out of her tiny bedroom and was never truly a part of the family. She didn't even take her meals with us, unless guests were at our table. I never questioned why she was always absent, but after my mother's death I asked my father why Grandmother kept herself away from us. I was shocked when my father told me that it was my mother who did not allow Grandmother to share our family life.

It was then I remembered the spark of joy that would light her face when I slipped into her room to sit and chat with her. My time with her was always brief because she would kiss me on the cheek and say, 'Return to your mother. We must not make her unhappy.' Now I know why she encouraged me not to prolong my visits, I'm wounded to remember that never once did she request anything for herself, not even a favourite dish.

My grandmother's life had been set for unhappiness from the moment the Khan spotted her beauty and claimed her for his own. The sad truth is that my grandmother would have lived a much happier life had she been born plain, or even homely.

My sister Nadia inherited her good looks from Grandmother Mayana, and was known to be one of the prettiest girls in Kabul. She was a tall girl with beautiful long hair framing her perfectly shaped face, set up nicely by big sensuous eyes and a delicate nose. Everyone exclaimed over her unusual beauty. Nadia was not only very pretty but she was super intelligent, too, always heading her class with the highest grades.

Nadia was nearly three when I was born. She had savoured being an only child, the full focus of family attention. With my appearance, she suffered the sting of sibling rivalry. When she ordered my mother, 'Get rid of that baby!', Mother laughed, thinking little of her elder daughter's jealous words. After all, she was not quite four years old at the time. But one day when my mother needed to go to the bathroom she asked Nadia to watch her sleeping sister. After returning, Mother was pleased that I was not crying, for I was a fussy baby. She did notice that Nadia was unusually happy, skipping and laughing and springing from one foot to the next.

Mother hushed her. 'Your sister is sleeping.'

Nadia laughed and replied gaily, 'That baby is not sleeping. That baby is *dead*.'

My panicked mother ran into the bedroom to discover that Nadia had piled pillows and blankets on my head and body. As she threw the pillows and coverings on the floor I was gasping for air. From that time until I was of an age to defend myself, Mother kept a close eye.

Thankfully, by the time I was a toddler, Nadia became more protective, but once I reached my teenage years, her jealousy once again overwhelmed sisterly love. She became very controlling and strict, and when I irritated her she didn't hesitate to scratch my face or to slap me. This sibling aggression continued until she turned eighteen. Then for a few years we became very close before our relationship turned sour in adulthood.

Our family life was very complicated.

I have often wondered if my parents ever regretted having a second daughter. I was such an obstinate child that turmoil ruled our home. My wilfulness came early and naturally. For some reason, I refused to accept milk or juice unless it was presented to me in a glass bottle. Nothing else would do. My mother reported that I would squeeze my lips together, with a wrinkled forehead and rigid limbs, rebuffing all efforts to feed me unless the rubber nipple was attached to a glass bottle. My desperate mother, grandmother and Nanny Muma attempted every trick, but I gave every indication that I was prepared to starve, so eventually they would capitulate.

When I reached my first birthday, the situation got worse. After slurping the last drop of milk or juice I would lean back to heave the glass bottle against the wall, where it would shatter. I seemed to derive the greatest pleasure from the sound of breaking glass, while my sister and mother screamed and poor Nanny Muma rushed to collect the glass from the floor. Despite reprimands and spankings, I was never discouraged. At her wits' end, Mother smeared hot chilli pepper on the nipple of the bottle and watched in disbelief as my face reddened and I endured the burning hot pepper on my lips rather than give up drinking my milk from the glass bottle.

Then the price of glass baby bottles went up. They had to be imported into Afghanistan, and my mother was soon spending most of her household money on those expensive items. Finally one of my mother's six sisters intervened. She arrived at our home with a serious face and held out a glass bottle to me, saying, 'Maryam, this is the last glass baby bottle in all of Afghanistan. The king has decreed that babies can no longer drink from glass bottles, so if you break it, that's it.'

My whole family gathered round, watching my reaction. All Afghan people listened to the king, even the youngest children. Perhaps the vexing problem would finally be solved. I clutched the bottle, drank the milk to the last drop, then paused and looked smugly at my audience before smashing the bottle against the large stone fireplace and toddling away with a pleased expression on my face.

I'm surprised my parents didn't beat me then. Somehow they kept me supplied with glass baby bottles until the happy day when I outgrew them.

I had yet another annoying habit. In Afghanistan, family members congregate on the living-room floor to eat their evening meal. Those few hours are the social highlight of Afghan family life. The floor is covered with a large clean cloth, surrounded with cushions. The meal would be set out on the cloth by our male servant, and everyone would help themselves with the right hand, as is customary in our culture. Once everyone had their fill, the same servant would appear with a jug of water, a basin, soap and a supply of clean towels draped over his arm for everyone to wash their hands. The servant would make the rounds, starting with the eldest in the family, finally making his way to me, the youngest.

This after-dinner hand-washing takes only a few moments, but I always took the greatest pleasure in extending the ceremony, holding family and guests captive, for it is improper for anyone to leave the family circle until all have finished. I would insist that my hands were not clean yet or that the soap was not suitable. My poor family would wait impatiently while the servant dashed back and forth filling the water jug or emptying the basin.

This spoilt quirk of mine lasted until one day when my father had taken us for a family gathering at the home of Shair Khan. Although my parents no longer lived in Shair's galah outside the city limits of Kabul, my father had not totally cut his ties with his older brother. Our little family still travelled back for various family events. I remember we had gathered for a big meal. After our meal I started with my routine of washing and rewashing my hands. My own family members waited as usual for the ritual to complete. My father's family was not so patient. Exasperated looks were directed at me. Loud sighs and questioning grunts were heard from aunties and cousins.

My father's irascible brother, Shair Khan, quickly lost his temper. He was not a man who would indulge any child, especially a female. As I sat merrily enjoying my little rite, I was suddenly confronted by his tall figure glaring down at me. My little hands lathered in soap, I froze in place, looking up at what I thought was a most forbidding monster of a man. He had hypnotic eyes, a long straight nose and thin lips. His loud voice boomed, 'You! Satan's daughter! You are finished! From now on, you will wash your hands only once. Otherwise –' he leaned down to make his point, gruffly threatening – 'you will lose your fingers, little girl.'

He was very convincing. I believed him fully capable of cutting off my fingers with his ceremonial sword. He so frightened me I was instantly cured of my very annoying hand-washing addiction. Although my parents did not believe in threatening their children, I'm sure for once they felt grateful to Shair Khan. My father's miserable childhood filled with fear, threats and beatings had made it difficult for him to admonish his daughters, even when he knew he should. My sensitive parents were undoubtedly too tolerant when it came to disciplining their two wilful daughters when we were little, although my mother became stricter when we reached our teens.

And, of course, there was the issue of my determination to be accepted as a boy, which created one drama after another until I was forced to stop the masquerade. I really do not know how my parents coped with me. Looking back, I now know that I was one of the luckiest girls in Afghanistan, a land where females are made to feel unwanted. Although there were female horror stories in our own family, until I was a teenager I was lucky enough to live in a bubble of innocence.

Few other Afghan girls were so fortunate.

*   *   *

I was born in 1960, only one year after the emancipation of women came about with the abolition of the veil and the chador. Three years before that, female announcers began broadcasting for Radio Afghanistan for the first time. During Independence Week in 1959, the wives and daughters of the royal family and wives of other government dignitaries appeared without their veils, signifying a new era for Afghan women. Although the mullahs rose in furious protest, our Prime Minister Mohammed Daoud, father's old friend from school days, threw them in jail.

The 1960s were a very special time when all over the world people began to fight for human and civil rights, and women had gained new freedoms. But my country was so backward when it came to all things female that Afghanistan lagged centuries behind most other countries. Afghanistan remained predominately feudal. Although industry was being introduced, most families still lived as they had for centuries, with most Afghans under the power of clan heads or regional warlords.

Such tribal authority made it nearly impossible for any government to impose change, for tribal law takes precedence over civil law, as does religious law. The Sharia court and the Islamic police have the authority to enforce certain laws, most particularly family law. Yet when tribal law confronts Sharia law, most Afghans will follow tribal law.

Islam asserts that men and women are equal before God, and gives women various rights such as the right to inherit, the right to choose their own partner in marriage and the right to work. But Afghan men have always ignored these rights, instead focusing on the sections of Islamic Sharia law that keep women under the sway of men. For example, in the Sharia court system, it takes two women to testify to equal the testimony of one man. In divorce cases, the man always wins.

With so many laws from too many groups refusing to bend to government laws, it was challenging for any government in Afghanistan to govern properly, and impossible for women to have a voice.

But there were some diamonds to be found in the dunghill. Various Afghan kings proved to be reformers, brave souls attempting to loosen the restraints upon women. No one was more determined than the son of King Habibullah, the ruler so loved by my grandfather Hassen. While his own father had one hundred wives, King Amanullah took only one wife, showing his respect for the female who shared his bed. Once the brief 1919 Anglo–Afghan war was over, he found his kingly footing, encouraging foreign investment and industry. Later he started trying to modernize Afghanistan, encouraging the people to abandon their traditional dress and don European fashions. He encouraged the establishment of a uniform civil law and, surprisingly, was most progressive when it came to the lives of women. He pursued reforms that would suppress the 'wall of purdah' (total isolation for females), abolish the veil, educate females alongside males and prohibit marriage for girls before the age of eighteen. Another surprising reform forbade any government official from having more than one wife.

The king's brave reforms mounted the first serious attack against the evil of prejudice that had plagued Afghanistan, especially its women, for as long as anyone could remember.

The air was tense with female hopefulness as the educated urban elite embraced the king's modern ideas. But things were different in the countryside. There, fevered imaginations conjured up images of wanton women prancing about exposing their naked faces to strangers. Stirred up by tribal chiefs and clerics, the men became so enraged at the image in their minds that they rebelled in a fury. Eventually King Amanullah was forced to flee Afghanistan and seek refuge in Europe. He was too progressive; thus, he was deposed. Hopes dashed, the broken-hearted women of Afghanistan crept back into their homes and pulled their burqas tighter.

The years that followed were more of the same:

paralysing confusion and tribal conflicts. Kings came and went, with one king putting the fear of God into all Afghan citizens when he murdered his enemies by firing them from the mouths of cannons. Another king was an immature nineteen-year-old boy, who, although later to prove himself, was too young at the outset, and whose uncles ruled in his stead. Without a strong king, unearthly chaos reigned in Afghanistan, with mutual hatreds erupting into a dozen internal conflicts going on at once.

But lucky me! By the time I was born and experiencing the life of a young Afghan girl, a sane voice reigned once more. Female freedom once again beckoned. Sheltered by my father, I could have never imagined that the freedom I took for granted was nothing more than a mirage, and that unimaginable oppression and abuse lay in wait for every Afghan woman.

An old enemy still lived in our midst.

Chapter 6

In so many ways my childhood was wonderful. My loving parents respected each other, my guileless grandmother was kindly, albeit sad, and I was shielded from the harsher realities of our world by layers of protective aunties and uncles and cousins from the maternal side of the family. Until I was ten years old, I bounced happily along in my loving family cocoon. Most importantly, there were faint signs that Afghanistan's king was guiding the country with a moderating influence when it came to women, at least in the capital of Kabul. Although my mother had been one of the first women to cast off her veil, such courage had been displayed only at safe places and events, such as in the school where she worked and in the homes of family and friends. Now, for the first time in her life, she was not breaking a law when she appeared unveiled on the city streets.

Mother often related the glee shown by her family members when the long-awaited word came that veils were no longer mandated by law. The Hassen boys fired up their scooters and the girls leapt aboard, parading through the city centre waving their veils while shouting their joy.

My father was fond of repeating: 'My daughters, you are part of the lucky Afghan generation. You will be educated. You will be respected by our society for your achievements.' My parents were so modern that they insisted our education come before all things. Nadia and I were warned that marriage was not an option until we had graduated from college. Even in our day, few parents were so progressive when it came to their daughters.

Our lives felt so secure that we foolishly believed nothing remained to be done when it came to women's freedoms. Tragically, Afghan's future, and my own future, would prove that we were wrong.

Until I was five or six years old, I assumed I was the fifth child of my parents, and that I had an older brother named Farid, and two sisters other than Nadia, sisters named Zarmina and Zeby. The three were not imaginary siblings, but were our cousins. At one time, Farid and Zarmina had even lived with us. Farid even called my mother 'Mother'. Their intimate connection to our little family came about due to a heart-rending story.

A catastrophe struck my mother's older brother,

Hakim, shortly after my parents and Nadia moved out of the galah and into the city.

Hakim was an idealistic man who happened to be a representative of Afghanistan and assigned to the Afghan Embassy in Berlin during the years prior to, and during, the Second World War. When Hakim arrived in Berlin to take up his diplomatic post, he became a shocked eyewitness to a great evil engulfing Germany's Jews. Although my uncle Hakim did not publicly speak out, he quietly used his position at the embassy to provide visas for Jews seeking to flee the country. German Jews were so frantic for their safety they were willing to live in Afghanistan, a country primitive by their European standards. Although the punishment for anyone found helping Jews was death, Hakim used his position at the Afghan Embassy to provide desperate Jews with false Afghan papers. He even helped transport Jews from Berlin across Germany to the Swiss border.

I was always impressed that Uncle Hakim never once tried to seek credit for his humanitarian actions. In fact, he was always notably reticent about the topic, embarrassed if anyone praised him, saying there were many others who sympathized with the Jews and he had not taken the risk alone. However, he admitted to his family once that he was pleased to have saved a number of Jewish scientists who lived to receive accolades in their fields.

Hakim remained in Berlin until after the war, but once it was safe to travel, he returned to Afghanistan. He had been so long out of touch that his family in Afghanistan believed he had been killed during the terrible battle for Berlin when the Russians invaded in 1945, creating many thousands of civilian casualties. The battle had been so deadly that news of the event had even filtered back to Afghanistan. Upon his unexpected return to Afghanistan, the family celebrated wildly, for it was as though Hakim had emerged from the grave.

Brought up in a family where education for women was encouraged, and having lived for years in Europe where women had many personal rights, once my uncle settled in Afghanistan he married an educated Afghan woman who was the principal of a girls' school. Her name was Zarine.

Hakim and Zarine were delighted to have two children, a son named Farid and a daughter named Zarmina. When Farid was four months shy of six years old and Zarmina was three, Zarine became grievously ill with heart problems. Her medical condition was not treatable in Afghanistan, so Hakim's friends in Germany arranged for his wife to travel there to seek the latest treatment.

Farid and Zarmina became listless and sad, small children missing their mother. My mother volunteered to help with them. Each day she would take little Nadia and Nanny Muma to stay at her brother's home to look after all three children.

Finally, after four months, the welcome message arrived that Zarine would be home in time for Farid's sixth birthday. The family was unaware that the doctors in Germany had warned Zarine she must not travel, that her heart was so damaged she might endanger her life if she left the hospital to make the strenuous trip. In those days a number of exhausting flights were necessary for a traveller to journey from Europe to Afghanistan. But Zarine was determined not to miss her son's birthday celebration, so she forged ahead against her doctor's orders.

The extended Hassen family accompanied Hakim and his children to the airport. No one wanted to miss the happy reunion.

When a shrunken and wan Zarine came into view, Farid pushed through the crowd and ran into his mother's open arms. Zarmina quickly followed. Mother and children were laughing and crying all at once while the watching family members wept at the blissful gathering.

Suddenly Zarine's laughter stopped. In a flash her expression altered from the greatest joy to a puzzled stare. Something was wrong. In the next moment Zarine buckled, her little son still enfolded in her arms, and collapsed on the hard floor.

A frantic Hakim ran to his wife, then cried out, 'She is dead! Zarine is dead!'

Zarmina was too young to understand what had happened, but my cousin Farid was distraught, alternately weeping and calling out for his mother. From that time Farid and his sister were at our home as much as their own, where my mother struggled to fill the massive chasm left by Zarine's death.

Their family misfortune is how I ended up with an 'older brother'. My mother's maternal love created a safe haven for her brother's children. Even after Uncle Hakim later remarried, a nice woman named Rabeha, Farid still looked upon my mother as his mother. Uncle Hakim and Auntie Rabeha had a baby daughter named Zeby only six months after I was born. Even after I finally understood that Farid, Zarmina and little Zeby were my cousins, they remained siblings in my heart.

Having an older brother proved advantageous for me. In Afghanistan, brothers offer protection and I would need all the protection I could get.

Farid was my mentor from the time I was a small child. He was nearly nine years older than me, dashing and handsome, and I believed he knew everything. As a result, his sister Zeby and I called him our 'Agha', which means 'Mr Boss'. We were obedient to Farid's every command.

I remember when Farid decided that since I so

badly wanted to be a boy, he would make me one. There was no reason for Zeby to miss the fun, so she joined in too. Farid ordered us to sit still while he applied glue to our cheeks. Then he pressed black sheep's wool on to our faces. Next he gave us two suits of his old clothing that he had outgrown, ordering us to put them on. He observed us walking back and forth, finally announcing that we passed the 'male' test. That's when he revealed a new idea, saying, 'Since I have made you into males, I want you to visit my maternal grandfather. He is so old that most of his friends are dead. He is very lonely sitting isolated in his room.' Farid believed that Zeby and I might pass for some of his old friends and bring some cheer to the old man. 'Play along with him,' Farid ordered.

When Zeby and I were led into the old man's room, he brightened considerably, shouting out, 'Hey, Fazal Khan!' He seemed puzzled and for a few moments studied our small figures, appearing to be in deep thought, before asking, 'Fazal, why have you become so short? Does your wife no longer feed you?'

When the old man made a move in our direction, Zeby and I squealed in fear and ran out of the room, much to Farid's disgust.

When I was around nine years old, Farid reached the age of eighteen. He had grown very tall with thick brown hair, flashing dark brown eyes and a ready smile. It was claimed he was more handsome than the American movie star Rock Hudson. More importantly to me, Farid was free to do as he wished. Farid could wear whatever fashion he pleased, be friends with whomever he chose, drive as fast as he wanted and even smoke cigarettes, all things I longed to do.

Farid felt my dissatisfaction and played along with my fantasy of being a boy. He introduced me to his friends as his 'little brother' and allowed me to accompany him on exciting adventures, such as pretending to be Batman while he drove his car as fast as he could down the streets of Kabul. Once, when we were sitting in the garden, I started complaining anew: 'Farid, why can't I be a boy like you? Boys get to do anything they please.' I paused. 'Boys make everyone happy just by being alive.'

Farid scrunched up his face in thought for a few moments, then replied, 'Maryam, I'll tell you a secret. Girls can become boys.'

I perked up.

'There is an American doctor who has been performing a very unusual operation,' he whispered. 'You go in the hospital a girl and you come out a boy. Just like that! Magic!'

I was instantly ready for the procedure. 'Does this American doctor ever come to Kabul?'

'Yes, I have heard that he does. But before you can have the surgery, you must purchase a penis.'

I felt crushed by hopelessness. I was sure that no man in his right mind would sell his penis, not for any price. Still, I asked, 'Where would a girl find a penis for sale?'

He said, 'This is confidential, Maryam. As you might imagine, penises are very much in demand. That's why they stock them exclusively at the Hamaid Zada department store in downtown Kabul. All you need do is go in and ask.'

Normally I would ask my father to take me shopping, but at the time he was out of the country seeking medical attention for a mystery illness. With my father away, there was nothing to do but convince my mother to take me to the Hamaid Zada department store. Of course, my poor mother had no clue what I had in mind, so she was aghast when I announced to the store clerk, 'One penis, please,' with as much dignity as I could muster.

The clerk's big pale eyes bulged and his lower lip drooped. The poor man was speechless.

I became so adamant that the store sold such items that the store manager was called over. That shocked man laughed nervously. 'There is no such thing for sale in this store,' he said disapprovingly. 'Who on earth would want to purchase such a thing?'

I burst into tears when I finally realized that my

last hope of becoming a boy was dashed. The entire episode had been nothing more than another of Farid's practical jokes. All the same, no prank could cool my relationship with Farid.

Soon my carefree childhood would come to an abrupt end when our family suffered a big shock: my sweet father was diagnosed with cancer. My happy childhood was upended dramatically when we learned that his latest trip to Russia for his baffling medical problems had revealed the worst news. He had bladder cancer.

Our entire family was paralysed with misery. Nothing would ever be the same again. Father resigned from his high-ranking position in the military. His salary ended, although he would receive a small government retirement stipend. My mother would be the sole supporter of our family. Worst of all, Father would spend many months away from his family seeking the latest treatments in Russia since there was no equivalent care in Afghanistan.

My father had been sickly for most of his life, and I'm convinced that stress also lead to his illness, for I have heard that stress can play a role in robbing the body of a healthy immune system, bringing on cancer and other serious illnesses. Certainly, since the days he was a child my poor father had lived with enormous tension.

Nadia and I were left without parents when it was decided that my mother should accompany him to Russia for his first surgery and subsequent treatment. No one knew how long they would be away, or even if my father would survive, for in those days cancer was considered a death sentence. I overheard adult relatives whisper, 'Ajab will return wrapped in his burial shroud.'

I trembled at the thought, my child's heart bruised and battered.

Nadia and I were left in the good care of our grandmother, Nanny Muma and Askar, our family's male servant. Askar had worked for our family since the time my father had been an army officer. Askar was a small man with a full beard and black eyes. He was a very kind man, and had an unusual sense of humour. Like Farid, he could make me laugh when I was feeling down. After living in Kabul for a few years, he stopped wearing Afghan traditional clothing to become very stylish.

In addition, my mother's brothers Hakim and Aziz and their wives lived near by and were there for back-up, but despite our warm extended family, nothing eased the pangs of abandonment. I no longer even had Farid around to bewitch me with his charm, for in our family the children are sent abroad for their university education and Farid had recently departed to India for his schooling.

So miserable that I wept constantly, I prayed to God to bring my parents back. My only comfort was dreaming of receiving a long-distance call from Russia. My father would be on the line, telling me he had been cured and that I should meet them at Kabul airport on Wednesday, the only day that flights came in from the Soviet Union.

Thinking that God himself was sending me the information, every Wednesday I would prepare myself for a trip to the airport.

Disappointment was to be my reward, for my parents were away for nine long months. Then Mother returned alone to Kabul. Our hearts were in our throats, waiting for her to tell us that Father had died and was buried in faraway Russia. Mother assured us otherwise. 'Lose that long face! Your father is very much alive. His health has improved. I came home without him only because I could not abide another moment away from my family. Your father will return home soon.'

Just as I had given up hope, believing that Mother was hiding the truth and that my father was indeed dead and buried, like magic he returned to Kabul. Much to everyone's surprise, my father was on his own two feet, telling us that those Russians had the best medical care and that their miraculous cures had put his cancer into remission.

Never have I known such complete joy!

But my happiness did not last long, for death hung over our home like a sword. My father remained unwell. He did not return to work, but instead slowly padded around the neighbourhood visiting family or old friends.

From the moment my father was diagnosed with a life-threatening illness, I left behind my childish ways. Although I was still a rebel at school, I became the good daughter at home, devoted to my parents, helping with the cooking, shopping and all other chores. But everyone in our family reacted differently to our changing family dynamics, and now my sister Nadia began to act up, complaining endlessly about Mother and throwing temper tantrums over things of little importance, such as Mother's choice of menu for our dinner.

Poor Mother became edgy, exhausted from her full-time teaching job, a husband in dubious health and a daughter who appeared to delight in tormenting her. Many nights Mother would retreat to the bedroom, where I could hear her piercing cries: 'What did I do, God? What did I do to deserve such a child?'

Everything soft about my mother grew sharp edges. As her work load increased and her worries grew, her lips curled and her weight plummeted, sharpening the contours of her nose and chin. Even her once deep, sensuous voice grew shrill.

Our father was home only a few months before his troubling symptoms reappeared and he returned to Russia for more treatment. This kept happening, and soon he was out of the country more than he was at home.

With Father gone, our family life lost its important core.

Then we endured a second shock when we lost Grandmother Mayana. Thanks be to Allah that Father just happened to be home in between his medical treatments when she became ill. Grandmother Mayana never once complained in her life, and kept a ghostly quiet presence in our house to avoid causing problems between my father and mother. I used to pop into her room daily to sit with her. On the day she became ill, I ambled into her room to find her lying still in bed. It was mid-afternoon.

I was startled. 'Grandmother, are you all right?'

She shook her head, whispering weakly, 'Maryam, it is too hard for me to go to the bathroom. It is too hard for me to perform my ablutions and pray.'

My grandmother was extremely pious and never missed her five daily prayers. But I was only a young girl, unsure of what I should do. For some instinctive reason I did not alert my mother, but waited for my father. When he came in I ran to him, crying, 'Something is terribly wrong with Grandmother.'

He rushed to her room, then came out and prepared her a meal of soft foods. He tried to coax her
to eat, but to no avail.

My father called a neighbour, a female Russian
doctor who agreed to come to our home.

I stood in the doorway as she took out her medical
instruments and checked Grandmother's blood
pressure. 'It is very low,' she said, looking at her
instruments. 'Too low,' she said with an ominous
tone. She stared meaningfully at my father. 'She must
eat. She is very weak.'

My father nodded. 'Yes. I will get her to eat.'

The rest of the evening my father and I took turns
sitting with Grandmother. To make us happy, she
tried to eat, but could barely swallow. I went into the
kitchen and made her favourite drink, sweet lemon-
ade, and she sipped at it a little.

The next morning I rushed into her room to check
on her condition.

The desperate expression on her face frightened
me. 'Maryam,' she whispered, 'go and get
your mother.' Never had Grandmother asked for my
mother.

'Mother,' I called out as I ran to her. 'Grandmother
is asking for you.'

My mother stood and stared at me without speaking, then walked slowly into Grandmother's tiny
room. I watched as Mother helped her to the

bathroom, where Grandmother washed herself so that she could make her prayers. Then she collapsed into her bed, closing her eyes. She looked like a corpse.

Mother and I exchanged silent looks, then Mother went to call the doctor. The same Russian physician returned and after a quick examination, told us, 'Her heart is failing. She will live only a few hours.'

I was terrified, suddenly sorry for every moment of my life I had not spent with my sweet grandmother. I rushed to sit by her side, and clung to her withered hand.

Grandmother opened her sad eyes. 'Maryam,' she whispered, 'go to school, child.'

'I want to stay with you,' I replied, my voice cracking.

She nodded slightly before saying, 'Please, child, go and get my special box.'

I knew she kept a big box in her room, but I had never known what treasures she kept in there. I dutifully tugged the box to her bedside.

By then my mother had returned.

Grandmother looked expressively at her daughter-in-law and said, 'Sharifa, when I am dead, look in the box. You will find enough money to bury me. For a long time now I have saved money so my son would have no need to pay for my funeral. Please bury me in Paktia. Sharifa, please take me home.'

Talk of death and funerals was too much for my young mind. I remember I ran out of the room, then turned round in the hallway and ran right back in. I looked at the clock. It was 10.30 in the morning when my poor grandmother took her last breath.

Soon my father came home to learn that his beloved mother had passed away. He ran in to stare at her corpse and burst into loud weeping, crying like a small child. Never before had I seen my father weep. I ran to him and looked into his grieving face. He shuddered violently, and said, 'Daughter, I weep for my mother's sad, sad life.'

My mother was less emotional, but she did say, 'Your grandmother was an angel, Maryam.'

Muslims must be buried within twenty-four hours of death, so within a few hours we were driving to Paktia province, to the small village where my grandmother was born and spent the first sixteen years of her life. There her body was bathed by my mother, with Shair's wife and daughters, wrapped in a clean white shroud and taken away by the men of the family, who put her body in the ground.

I could scarcely believe my grandmother was dead. I had never known life without her peaceful, kindly presence. Our home was a lonely place without my grandmother, despite the fact she had participated little in our family life. Although I was still a child, I felt in my heart that she had not been treated properly in our home. Within two weeks Grandmother's personal belongings had disappeared, and her small sanctuary was redecorated and changed into a formal dining room.

Feelings of guilt crept through me, for I felt I had been neglectful, never thinking to escort my lonely grandmother on walks or paying any special attention to her. When I became a teenager, these feelings persisted. One day I gathered the nerve to ask my father, 'Why was Grandmother always in her room? Why didn't she join us as a family? Why didn't she sit with us and eat her meals? Why did she have to live such a lonely existence even in her son's home?'

My father confessed: 'Your grandmother did eat with us, at first. But your mother pushed for the family to sit at the table and eat with silverware, and your grandmother was uncomfortable. She liked to sit on the floor and to eat with her fingers, in the old way, so I asked your mother to remain with the old way. When you girls were small there was a big row between your mother and myself about this issue. Your mother packed her bags and told me she was leaving. She asked for a divorce. She told me to take my mother and she would take our daughters.'

My father looked at me and gave a sad sigh. 'I told her to go, if that is what she wanted.

'Your grandmother heard the ruckus and came out of her room. When she learned that the fight was about her, she said, "Do not let your wife go, my son. I have lived my life. From this day on I will be in my room and I will never come between you and your wife." '

I felt sick to my stomach, hatred sparking for my mother's actions. Her shameful conduct had created misery for the sweetest woman I have ever known.

My father walked away, his shoulders sagging along with his spirit.

Soon my father was ill again. On that occasion Mother did not travel with him. After losing my grandmother, and knowing my father was gravely ill, my fear caused me to cling to my mother. I began experiencing panic attacks when my mother was away. When she left home on an errand, I would stand on the balcony watching and waiting, silently praying she would not be run down by a speeding car or become ill while she was out. When I finally discerned her outline in the distance, I would run to welcome her back as though she had been away for weeks.

To increase my anxiety, my mother developed a thoughtless habit of greeting me with predictions of doom. 'Your father is going to die, Maryam. He is going to die. When he dies, his brother Shair will come and take you and Nadia to his galah. Shair will marry you to one of his sons if you are lucky and to an old man if you are not. Prepare yourself, Maryam. You will be married off to a cruel man. You will never be allowed to see your mother again.'

I became hysterical at the image Mother planted in my mind. In Afghanistan, the brother of a dead man has full authority over his sibling's wife and children from the moment of passing. Who knows if Shair Khan would have sent his men to Kabul to collect my father's wife and two daughters to do with them as he pleased, but his cruel ways and past behaviour prepared us for the worst.

Mother's fear of losing her daughters was festering in her heart, and she failed to hold those fears inside her. Her thoughtless conjectures so alarmed her youngest daughter that I spent much of my nights sending passionate prayers to God. 'Please, Allah, send Father home! Please, God, heal his cancer. Please, Allah, do not let Shair Khan get me. I am just a child, God, too young to be a wife.'

My mother grew so paranoid she began to believe that Nadia and I would be kidnapped by our uncle even before our father's death. She warned Nadia and me, 'If I am unable to come to school and pick you up, never get in the car with anyone but our driver or your father. Never. Even if your father's relatives try to give you a ride, do not get in the car. Young girls are kidnapped daily in this country. You will be taken away and married to an old man, or sold to a tea house to become a dancing girl.'

We were properly frightened.

One day Nadia and I left classes expecting to see Mother in her usual place waiting to take us home. Mother was nowhere to be seen. Soon we spotted Askar sitting in a taxi. He motioned for us to come to him, calling out, 'Your mother is preparing tonight's meal. She sent me to bring you home.'

Although Askar had been with our family for as long as we could remember, the change in routine made us uneasy. Never before had Askar arrived in a taxi asking us to join him. Nadia and I exchanged cautious glances, our thoughts in union. Had Askar been bribed by Shair Khan? Was our faithful servant no longer faithful? Was he there to kidnap us and deliver us to the galah? Was this the kidnapping our mother had warned us about?

We shuffled from one foot to the other, anything to avoid getting in that taxi with potential kidnappers.

Askar was impatient, calling out, 'Get in the taxi, now! You are wasting time!'

Not knowing what else to do, Nadia and I warily climbed into the back seat of the taxi. Our worst fears came true when the taxi driver drove in the opposite direction of our home.

Askar turned to explain. 'Your mother asked me to purchase some fruit from the market.'

Nadia knew the fruit market was in the old part of Kabul, well away from our neighbourhood. She began weeping. I felt severe pangs of pain rippling up from my stomach. Our mother's terror had taken root in our heads. We were being kidnapped!

Our screams merged as one. Askar and the taxi driver looked at us as though we were demented.

Askar shouted, 'Shut up, you silly girls.' But that only made us cry louder.

Soon we arrived at the fruit market and Askar, disgusted by our behaviour, leapt from the taxi, leaving us to fret over our fate. I glanced at the taxi driver. He was a hard-faced man who had a look about him that was frightening. He, too, jumped out of the taxi and walked over to join some strange men standing in the bazaar. As he spoke, the group of men turned to stare at us, their eyes blazing. We were convinced those men were in on the plot.

I told my sister, 'I need to go to the toilet, Nadia, quickly.' We knew that there was no female toilet in the bazaar. I was bent double by pain and uncontrollable watery diarrhoea.

Nadia grabbed a plastic bag out of the car and said, 'Here, use this.'

I did the best I could, but I messed up my clothes and the taxi as well. Although Nadia threw the bag out of the window on to the street, there was a terrible stench inside the taxi.

When the driver saw Nadia discarding the bag, he marched to the taxi, then drew back, making a strange noise in the back of his throat. 'What do I smell?'

Nadia and I both resumed our crying.

By then I had hysterical hiccups, but reckless with fear I cried out, 'Are you going to kidnap us? Please don't! I don't want to marry an old man! I'm just a child!'

The driver drew back in offended anger. He simmered and fumed, glaring at me while impatiently tapping his foot on the sidewalk. When Askar returned with his fruit, the driver opened the door and ordered us out of his taxi.

'What is going on?' Askar demanded in a bewildered voice.

The taxi driver had worked himself up to a nice fury by that time. He shouted, '*You take these shitting kids out of my taxi! Look what they have done!*' He yelled as he pointed out the plastic bag. '*They have ruined my taxi! Take them out of my sight!*'

Askar was infuriated, too, when we found ourselves stranded in the bazaar without a taxi in sight. It took us more than an hour walking around to locate another cab. By that time, Askar had got the full story from us.

Askar was a servant, yet he was a proud man who

protected his reputation. We had humiliated him in the bazaar, a place he often frequented. When we got home, he yelled at our mother, explaining what had happened and accusing her: 'You have created two crazy kids with your paranoid predictions.'

In defence of our mother, it must be said that Afghanistan was a country where girls and boys were routinely kidnapped to be used as sex toys or to be worked as slaves. Children had no legal or humanitarian rights in my country. Her fears were not totally unfounded.

There was one occasion when I was truly in danger of being kidnapped. It was in 1973, a few months after my father had returned from his latest medical treatment. The holy month of Ramadan had ended, the month when Muslims fast during the hours from sunrise to sunset, to figuratively burn away Muslim sin. The first day of the new month after Ramadan is spent celebrating, observed as the Festival of Breaking Fast or Eid ul-Fitr.

I believe that Eid arrived during winter that year, which was the best time because in Afghanistan schools are out for three months in the winter, rather than the summer as in most countries. Our brutal winters make school attendance nearly impossible. Middle- and upper-class Afghans leave Kabul in the winter to trek to Jalalabad, one of the most beautiful cities in Afghanistan, and my personal favourite. Everyone in my mother's family would make their way to her brother's home in Jalalabad for Ramadan and the festival of Eid.

My small world was ablaze with joy, for my father was home and I was with my cousins celebrating Eid. Although I no longer spoke endlessly about my desire to be a boy, I still kept my hair short and bothered little with the feminine clothes so loved by my sister and female cousins.

My cousin Zeby and I kept busy flying kites. We were still young enough to escape censure for playing boys' games with the boys. I overheard several relatives mention that I was more masculine than feminine and I admit their observations caused my cheeks to flush with pleasure.

During our time in Jalalabad, my parents decided to visit an Islamic shrine about fifty kilometres from the city, close to the Pakistani border. My mother said that we must go to that shrine to pray for all our troubles. The country was in big trouble, she said, as was our family.

Starting in 1969, Afghanistan had suffered three rainless years, followed by heavy winter snows that brought about spring floods. The drought followed by flooding made it impossible for Afghan peasants to raise their crops. A terrible famine had gripped the countryside. Because we lived in Kabul and our government kept such calamities secret, we heard nothing about the crippling drought until a big group of strange-looking American hippies arrived in the city and began to spread the word about people in rural areas having nothing to eat except roots. There were horrible tales of little children dying from starvation.

Although Russian and American humanitarian aid arrived in the country, there were rumours that government officials were confiscating the wheat and other supplies to hold back and sell to the highest bidder. People were becoming more desperate and angry by the day.

Although our economic situation had become tight due to my father's chronic illness, we did not go hungry. Mother said we must pray at the shrine for the poor starving people. She also got the idea that our family would adopt a girl from the famine area after she heard a report that often the parents died first, and children as young as infants were left alone in their mud huts to starve.

Nadia and I got very excited about the prospect of saving a little girl who would become our sister. Mother's plans grew grander by the minute, saying that we would make that girl our family cause, and after fattening her up we would teach her to read and write.

Mother also whispered that while at the shrine she

would pray for my father's health so that he would be cured of his cancer.

I was overjoyed. I believed that the trip to the holy shrine would solve all our problems. The famine would cease, the starving children would be fed and my father's cancer would be cured.

The shrine was packed. After long hours of praying, my parents were satisfied with the visit. They said it was time to go, so off we went.

After all those prayers and high hopes, I was shocked that we suffered bad luck immediately – on our way back from the shrine. One of the tyres on our vehicle went flat and there was no spare. We were on a dirt road in the middle of nowhere, so my father asked the driver to wait with the car while our family took the flat tyre back to the town we had previously passed. We hitched a ride, arriving a few hours later at the tyre repair shop. While the mechanic repaired the tyre, we looked for a ride to take us back. My father, weak from his treatments, found a truck driver who agreed to take the tyre to our vehicle stranded on the road. That driver glanced at me then said that one of us would have to accompany him so he could properly identify the car.

The driver kept staring at me and said to my father, 'OK, you stay here and rest with your wife and daughter, and I'll take your son with me to identify your vehicle.'

My chest swelled with pride. That man mistook me for a boy, making me happier than I had been in a long time. My father was a man who didn't have one bad bone in his body, so he was overly trusting. He thanked the man and said to me, 'Go with this man. You know our car. Once the tyre is on the car, drive back to the city with the driver.'

The truck driver eagerly grabbed my hand and pulled me away from my family. I thought he must be in a hurry.

For some reason my sister Nadia, who was nearly fifteen years old at the time, was struck by foreboding. She tugged on my father's arm. 'Do not send Maryam with that dirty-eyed driver. Something bad will happen.'

My father shrugged, thinking Nadia was overreacting.

About that time a shopkeeper who was watching the incident realized that I was about to be kidnapped; there had been some recent notorious cases of sex trafficking involving young boys, and it was a lucrative business. The shopkeeper ran to my father, who by now was in a taxi with my mother and sister, ready to return to the city centre. The shopkeeper flagged down the taxi, shouting at my father, 'If you leave your son with that driver you will never see him again! I suspect that driver is going to kidnap your son and sell him in Pakistan.'

Nadia panicked, shouting out, 'Father! Go and get Maryam!'

My poor mother froze, her long-nurtured fears of kidnapping coming true.

My father leapt out of the car and ran towards the truck driver, shouting, 'Wait! I have changed my mind. I will make other arrangements.'

The truck driver reacted angrily. 'If you want this tyre to be put back on your car, then leave me to handle it!' He paused. 'If you don't send your boy with me, I won't do it.'

My father shouted at me: 'Get out of the truck.'

The truck driver got out of the vehicle and started to push my father around, putting up his fists. I was startled, but flattered that the man wanted me to be his travel companion so badly. A crowd gathered round the two men. My father called out for someone to fetch the police. Nadia and my mother were screeching for me to jump out, to run away.

I was completely confounded, wondering what was wrong with my family. I was so pleased to be considered a boy, and to be given a boy's responsibility, that I felt angry. My family was spoiling everything! 'Let me go! I want to go!'

Then Nadia screamed over the racket, 'Maryam is a girl! She is not a boy.'

The truck driver was stopped in his tracks, confused, studying my small figure with new eyes. The police arrived at that moment and the truck driver wrestled from my father's grip and bolted like a frightened horse. He quickly disappeared from view.

The agitated shopkeeper counselled my father, 'Do not trust strangers with your children. That driver was looking for fun with a little boy. He would have quickly discovered your child was a girl. He would have killed her or sold her to a dance house.'

My shaken father paid a big fee for a taxi to take us back to our car.

Visiting the shrine had not brought the good luck we had sought. I had barely dodged a grim future. The famine continued, taking many more lives, and creating unrest across the land. The poor little orphan my mother found to adopt had been so traumatized that she was terrified of any stranger. When my mother tried to take the child in her arms, the frightened child ran away and refused to go with her. We later heard she had been placed in a poorly run orphanage along with thousands of other desperate children who had lost both parents.

During that year of 1973, Afghanistan was a hotbed of misery. Not long after our trip my parents received a communication from a mental institution where one of Shair's daughters, my cousin Amina, was kept. Amina was only a few years older than me, but was already married with two children: she had recently been committed to the hospital and they asked us to come and fetch her.

I had known Amina since I was a child. She was beautiful in spirit and in appearance. I had always admired her lively personality and flashing green eyes. Amina was not so lucky when it came to her father. Shair did not allow his daughters to be educated. They were considered property to use as bargaining chips in marriage deals, and he sold them off at a young age. Amina had received no more consideration than had Grandmother Mayana.

When it came to girls, time truly stood still in Afghanistan.

I remember walking into a bleak room where Amina was waiting. The poor dear was no longer beautiful, although I did recognize her glittering green eyes which now flashed wildly. Before I could even smile a greeting, she leapt at me, kissing my cheeks and wailing.

I was uneasy because she was so demonstrative, and evidently could not speak coherently. I asked my mother, 'What is wrong? I can't understand her.'

A sorrowful look flashed across my mother's face when she said, 'Maryam, Amina's husband used his fists to box her ears, so damaging her hearing that her world is now silent. She is deaf.'

I was infuriated on behalf of poor Amina, declaring confidently, 'I would have boxed his ears had he dared to box mine!' I knew that many Afghan men were brutes but I naively thought that if you fought back all would end favourably. I suppose my attitude came from living with a gentle father who had never raised his hand against his wife or daughters.

'So, Amina is not crazy?' I asked, wondering why she had been locked up with the insane. Some of the inmates were screaming so loudly that their cries carried through the walls to where we were.

'No, Maryam, Amina is not crazy,' my mother said with a sad smile, 'although she became very upset when her husband took a second wife. When she protested, he beat her up. She was put here so that no one in her family had to take care of her.'

I heard more desperate female voices crying out for help and shivered. How many of those women were perfectly well, placed there by their dissatisfied husbands, as Amina had been? I was not surprised my poor cousin was desperate to leave that hideous place.

We carefully settled Amina in the seat beside me in the back of our car. I tried not to stare at the sad spectacle my once beautiful, vivacious cousin had become, but it was difficult not to peek at her pathetic appearance. She had been in the mental hospital for six months and not once during those long months had the staff allowed her to take a bath or to wash her hair. She was so rancid that her odour overwhelmed our car, and so filthy that her olive skin was much darker than usual. Her hair was matted into knots. Her clothes were dirty and tattered.

When we arrived home my mother gently led Amina to a private room where she prepared a large bath. Mother allowed me to remain in the room while she helped my cousin undress and bathe.

For one month Amina lived in our home, but she grew more miserable by the day because she pined for her little son and infant daughter, and she worried that her husband's second wife would be cruel to her children. Amina's children would be condemned by the fate of their mother, now considered a woman fit for nothing more than the asylum. No one would protect her children, not even her wealthy father, who abided by the tradition that once a daughter was married, her husband could do as he pleased with her. Besides, knowing Shair Khan's attitude to women, from the day Amina had left his home I'm sure he had never given her another thought.

After a month my parents reluctantly agreed to drive Amina back to the home of her husband and his new wife. His attitude to her had not improved. At the sight of Amina he snarled and raised his hand. He would have beaten her then and there had my parents not given him a warning.

How I hated leaving Amina in her brutish husband's home. But the dear girl was trapped by her love of her little children. We heard later that her life was a miserable succession of abuse and beatings, but nothing would make her leave her helpless children.

While this drama was unfolding, my mother's family received an invitation to attend a big barbecue at the home of Amina's father-in-law. He was a wealthy landowner and everyone knew he had the most beautiful farm near Kabul.

That farm *was* lovely, with streams running everywhere and huge trees shading the grounds. He was proud of his flourishing orchard and insisted that we stroll under his fruit trees to fill our baskets with peaches and apricots.

He declared the barbecue was in honour of the Hassens, my mother's family. I quickly noticed that we were greeted only by the men of the house, and when I asked where the women and girls were, everyone stared at me. Someone whispered that 'his women' were kept locked away in the huge house surrounded by high walls. When I asked why the women were not participating at the party, someone near me muttered, 'Welcome to the real Afghanistan, little girl.' I knew what they meant, that tribal women living outside the cities were rarely, if ever, seen by outsiders, even distant family members.

My mother and her sisters decided they wanted to chat with the women of the family, so after the feast we slipped away from the men to pay them a visit in the big house. We were in for a big shock. When we entered the compound we were met by the man's older daughter, who was surprisingly strong-minded. She told us, 'After witnessing how my mother and my father's other wives are mistreated, I decided that I would stand up for my rights, and that I will never marry.'

My mother and my aunts seemed shocked by such bold talk, but I felt I understood completely for I knew that I, too, would have such a reaction under her circumstances. But then her mother and her two sister wives joined us in the sitting room.

Those poor women looked older than my grandmother Mayana had looked on the day of her death, yet they were the same age as my mother. The most horrifying thing of all was that all three women walked bent double, their faces so near the floor that they groped and stumbled while finding their way into the room.

At first I thought they must be triplets who had been born with the same birth defect. But the eldest daughter asked, 'Do you know what happened to these dear women?'

No one spoke a word.

She said, 'My father did this. Whenever one of his wives was in labour, he would become furious, claiming that his rest was disturbed by their screaming. He would rush into the room and, oblivious to her pain, shout at her to shut up. If she could not hold back her cries of pain, he would kick her in the back until she was silenced.'

My mouth went dry.

The daughter continued: 'Did you know that he killed four or five of his wives that way?'

Mother made a small noise in the back of her throat. I shook my head, no, but could not utter a sound. Now I knew that Amina had no chance, for her husband was the son of a beast. Like father, like son, I thought to myself.

'My mother and these two lived but sustained such grievous injuries to their backs during childbirth that they could never again walk upright.' She barked a sarcastic laugh. 'Now he strikes them in the face for being crippled! He says that the sight of them turns his stomach.'

She gave us a fierce look, as though we were the enemy. '*I will never marry.*'

That's when I was reminded that a division as wide as a country separated the lives of Kabul city women from tribal country women. Looking back, I believe that was the day that a young girl who sincerely loved her country began to hate her culture.

I was haunted by the fate of those innocent women. But there was nothing any of us could do. Our culture demands that men rule. Our culture demands that cruel men not be punished. Our culture demands that women are faulted for every bad thing that occurs in their lives.

As I cried myself to sleep at my father's absence in Russia, undergoing yet more treatment, little did I know that I should have been jumping with joy that he was safely far away in another country, for Afghanistan was entering a dangerous time of instability. Old hatreds within the royal family combined with resentment over the famine disaster were generating a backlash against King Zahir Shah. A government coup was imminent. As a former military intelligence chief, my father might well have been in danger from one faction or another had he been in the country.

I was only a young girl, so I had no inkling that evil's twin was marching into Afghanistan, setting off a chain of calamitous events that would alter the future of Afghan citizens in a most terrible way.

Chapter 7

Amir Mohammed Zahir Shah came to power on 8 November 1933, the same day his father Amir Nadir Shah was assassinated at a school where he was presenting prizes. Zahir was only nineteen years old, but he was immediately proclaimed king after receiving the allegiance of his three uncles, along with influential tribal leaders. King Zahir ruled wisely and went on to lead Afghanistan for forty years. Zahir was the king when I was born, and was responsible for Afghanistan's longest period of relative peace and prosperity. But all that harmony came to an end on 17 July 1973 when I was only twelve years old.

I remember that day clearly. My father was out of the country seeking additional treatment for his cancer. It was early in the morning and I was getting ready for school. Our doorbell rang and when Mother opened the door to see who our visitor might be, she saw my tutor.

He was standing with his head held high and his

shoulders set proudly, looking taller than usual, then he strode into the house to announce: 'Today is the happiest day for all Afghanistan. The era of monarchs is over. We now have a president. His name is President Daoud Khan.'

Mother was not impressed. Her lip curled and she said bluntly, 'How can Daoud be different? He is a royal prince and the first cousin to the king. Same shit, different smell.'

My tutor was horrified by my mother's lack of respect for Afghanistan's new authority. He stammered, 'I am no longer a tutor. I have enlisted in the army.'

Mother gave our tutor the sort of disgusted look she might convey if confronted by a plate of rotten meat. 'Man proposes and Allah disposes,' she announced.

The tutor turned military man mumbled something I could not hear then scurried away.

Fired by hope that the occasion would call for missing school, I bounded about the house foolishly shouting, 'No school! War is coming!'

But it was not in my mother's character to yield ground when it came to her children's education. Not even a government coup would move her. 'You are going to school whether you like it or not, Maryam, coup or no coup.'

And so our routine remained the same. After

getting dressed and gathering my school books, we got into our car for the drive to school. Our route passed the royal palace and there we saw President Daoud, who was standing outside greeting well-wishers. Mother ordered our driver to stop so we might take a better look at the prince who had laboured to destroy his king. While her curiosity was being satisfied, I leaned out of the window to wave cheerfully at our new president. He waved back, probably thinking my mother was a fan. But I did wish him well: I had a vague memory that long, long ago when my father was a student, the same Prince Daoud had saved my father's life after one of Shair Khan's unprovoked attacks. And my memory was correct – it was Prince Daoud who had saved my father's life when he was tossed down the school stairs by his evil brother Shair. After that incident, Prince Daoud and my father had remained on friendly terms.

Despite my childish enthusiasm, the time would come when I would see the truth: that Prince Daoud's bold but reckless action had sealed all our fates, bringing the beginning of the end for peace in Afghanistan.

Daoud had served his cousin King Zahir as Afghanistan's prime minister for much of the 1950s and early 1960s. But after he disagreed with the government of Pakistan regarding a Pashtun tribal region that straddled the Afghan/Pakistani border, King Zahir removed him from the government post, creating a bitterness never forgotten.

The coup might have been avoided had King Zahir been in the country addressing the various troubles plaguing it, but he had taken his wife and various relatives to Europe so that he might undergo eye surgery and other medical treatments. With the king away in Italy, Prince Daoud had staged a coup d'etat, setting up the new Republic of Afghanistan, and proclaimed himself President, announcing: 'The time of kings has come to an end.'

Indeed, Afghanistan had been ruled by its last king after King Zahir was deposed. Rather than return to Afghanistan and fight for the throne, King Zahir opted to remain in Europe. Perhaps he knew the world was changing, and that monarchs were going out of fashion.

Although the 1973 coup was nearly bloodless, most Afghan people were apprehensive, for a disruption in government is a grave business in a country divided not only by mountains and rivers but by religious and tribal loyalties so fierce that men are willing to fight to the death for the slightest insult. But distracted by recent tribulations including famine, corruption and tribal unrest along the Pakistani border, Afghan tribes remained mainly peaceful at the change, waiting to see what advantages the new government might bring them.

Other than the first few days of excitement, the coup of 1973 was to have little effect on our daily lives. Father soon returned from his latest treatment, and for the first time in years felt well enough to seek work. Rather than return to his government military position, he set up a business with a Frenchman he had met on one of his overseas trips, exporting Afghan handicrafts and carpets. My father said models were needed, so Nadia and I posed for his clothing line, which was an exciting opportunity for two teenage girls.

Our little family was thriving once again, with money to spare. I felt brushed by angel wings when my father announced that our family would be leaving Kabul to take a two-month vacation in India, the first time Nadia and I would be taken abroad.

Although since that time I have travelled the globe, that first experience was so magical that I even remember the exact day we left Kabul: 2 January 1974, the year following the coup.

I was so overcome with excitement I failed to sleep the night before we left Kabul. I rested my head on my pillow with my passport propped up at an angle so I could see the travel stamps for Pakistan and India. My imagination spun out of control as I stared at the travel stamps I believed would allow me to travel to America. For some reason, I thought I was going to live in the state of New York.

I was only a child and knew absolutely nothing about New York or America, other than what I had overheard from adults talking: I had got it into my head that New York City was heaven on earth, that everyone who lived there was too beautiful to look at and blessed with riches fit for kings, sitting on splendid silks and eating the most exotic foods off china plates.

It sounded like the perfect place for me.

I was so on edge about the trip that I was terrified something might keep us from our journey. I prayed to Allah all night that nothing would happen to keep us from leaving Afghanistan.

The weather was freezing cold, which is normal for Afghanistan in January. My mother insisted I bundle myself up in an unfashionable coat and I was devastated to be seen in attire less than beautiful. But when my father's cousin arrived in a taxi to transport us to the Kabul bus station, my thoughts moved on to more important matters. At the bus station a crowd of our friends and relatives swarmed around us, chattering with excitement. It seemed the entire tribe had come to see us off. Aunties and female cousins bestowed on us baskets of food to eat while on the trip. Even our former tutor had forgiven Mother her harsh words on the day of the coup and was there with a smile as wide as the Kabul River.

My father had purchased tickets for the family on a luxury bus, so I scrambled on board to select the best seats. The bus driver came aboard, closed the big doors and we set off. I could hear the sounds of our friends and relatives shouting their goodbyes for nearly a city block.

Thankfully the road from Kabul to Jalalabad was a better highway than most in my country. The bus rattled only slightly as we made our way out of the city before twisting up between the treacherous mounds of snow-covered rocks. I studied the sight of brooks rippling through the dry land and bright plumed birds flitting from green bushes.

I gazed at the folding hills which soon grew into mountains, wondering how many travellers had seen the same view for the thousands of years our lands had been inhabited. Soon we were climbing so high we were nearly in the clouds. Mother was so frightened by the dangerous curves that she closed her eyes to avoid seeing the road falling so far below us that it resembled a curled ribbon.

When I was young, Afghanistan had not yet been stripped of its wildlife. We saw gazelles, their nimble bodies leaping high in the air, and I spotted a number of wild greyhound dogs from the road. The highway often followed the river, which grew wider and bluer, bordered by a variety of lush old trees and dramatic rocks. Most interesting for me were the mud forts littering the landscape. Rural tribespeople were vulnerable to surprise attack so their homes were often fortified with four towers built with rifle slits.

I was upset by seeing a donkey that had become lame and been left by the side of the road to die. It was a pathetic sight. In my country, animals that go lame on the march are abandoned to their fate. Afghan people will not kill the animal to put it out of its misery, but instead leave its fate to Allah, who must decide whether it will live or die. I sighed and turned away. There was nothing I could do.

Soon the sun dropped low over the mountains, turning the white snow to a pink glaze and the shadows to bright indigo. That's when Papa announced we had cleared the Afghan border and reached Pakistan. We quickly disembarked from our luxury ride and crammed our luggage and four selves into a taxi so decrepit I was afraid it might break down on the way to Peshawar.

Suddenly the streets were teeming with bustling crowds. Never had I seen so many people all together. Accustomed to a land only lightly populated, I felt disquiet, although once we left our taxi I was fascinated by the train that would carry us to New Delhi. I had never before had the opportunity to ride on a train.

I asked my father, 'How come Pakistan is so much more advanced than Afghanistan?'

My father patiently explained. 'The British develop any country they occupy. They build roads, trains, government buildings, schools and many commercial establishments.'

'Then I wish the British had occupied Afghanistan,' I said with a sigh, knowing that the British had tried and failed a number of times to occupy my country. I was ashamed to see that my country was many years behind our neighbour.

'My daughter,' my father said sadly, 'do you wish to live under another country's flag?'

'No,' I admitted. I was proud that no country had been able to grab hold of and hang on to Afghanistan. Our men were fierce, brave and ready to fight off any invaders. Even the biggest and most well-trained armies in the world could not conquer Afghanistan.

He nodded with satisfaction. 'All right. That is your reward. You are Afghan. You are free. You live under your own flag.'

Free to be poor and backward, I thought to myself, but said nothing more, for it was clear my father was exceptionally proud of the fact that Afghanistan's warriors defeated all invaders.

The train ride to Delhi was memorable. We had a compartment to ourselves, with a bunk bed and a wide seat. I gazed out of the window for hours, seeing a new world that I could have never imagined.

Along the way Mother served us delicious sandwiches and cups of hot tea courtesy of our kindly
relatives.

We slept the night on the train and when I woke up
the first thing I needed was a toilet. That's when I discovered that not everything in Pakistan was perfect.
The toilet on the train was so filthy that no one in my
family could bear to use it. As soon as the train
stopped in Lahore, I was jumping up and down with
bladder pain. Father said the ride to the hotel would
be brief, but in fact it was a 30-minute journey. By
the time we arrived I couldn't hold back a minute
longer and ran inside the lobby jumping from one
foot to the other. The manager checked my father in
as quickly as possible and I dashed to the room to use
the toilet. My misery was finally relieved.

The following day we boarded yet another train to
take us to our final destination, New Delhi. After we
arrived, I begged Papa to take me for a walk. But he
was exhausted from the journey and retired for a
nap. I pleaded so eloquently that Mother agreed to
take me out for a short walk to explore the city.

After walking a short distance from our small
hotel, Mother and I were in for a big shock. We heard
panicked screams and running feet. Too late we saw
a massive crowd of people rushing straight for us.

Mother and I quickly jumped aside to avoid being
trampled. The alarmed crowd zipped past with such

force I felt a brisk breeze. Thankfully we were not knocked to the ground. Mother and I glanced at each other in relief, thinking the worst was over. That is when we realized with horror that the crowd had been running away from an angry bull. Now that bull was stampeding directly towards me! He locked his eyes on to my lone figure before lowering his horns.

I didn't know about the Indian habit of allowing cows and bulls to roam freely in their cities. But realizing I was about to be gored, without looking I leapt into the congested street.

The bull didn't get me but a car did. A moving vehicle was unable to stop in time. One moment I was running away from the bull, and the next I was tossed high into the air. I thought the bull had thrown me with his horns. My body slammed to the dirt road with a thud. Pain gripped every part of me, from my head to my feet, but the wind was knocked out of me so I could not cry out.

An agitated crowd quickly gathered round me, with witnesses shouting, pointing and poking. Although I was the centre of excitement, the scene felt far away, with every image materializing blurry and indistinct, like a black and white television with poor reception. Voices carried an echo, and I found it impossible to hear what was happening. I had a vague notion that some considerate people were gathering my purse and contents, which had flown from my hand and scattered over the road.

Where was my mother? I tried to turn my head but was unable to move. I couldn't see her.

Suddenly a man on a motorbike pushed his way through the gathering crowd. I felt myself being lifted from the roadway. The man commandeered an automobile and shouted at the driver. I had a vague fear I was being kidnapped, but there was nothing I could do. I was injured and helpless, and far away from my parents.

It was only when we arrived at a hospital that I understood I had been rescued by a Good Samaritan. I was lifted from the car and taken inside, where doctors gathered around me. I looked down, horrified to discover my right leg swollen like a tree trunk. Time blurred, but I discovered later I had been rushed into an operating room.

When I came out of the anaesthesia, my mother was hovering over me. Mother had fainted from sheer fright at the sight of her daughter being attacked by a horned beast and finally run down by an automobile. The kind bystanders had revived her enough to escort her to the nearest hospital, where my Good Samaritan had told someone he was taking me.

My injuries were severe. I was bleeding internally on arrival at the hospital. My right ankle and leg were crushed. Skilled Indian surgeons were able to stop the internal bleeding and put my leg and ankle back together with the use of steel pins. I was devastated to be told I would be in a cast for two months, as long as the time we had planned to be in India for our holiday. I spent a week in the hospital and then recovered in a hotel room.

I should have realized then that I was unlucky.

My Good Samaritan disappeared after ensuring I was safe. I never saw him again and my family never had the chance to thank him for his kindness.

My holiday was not what I had planned, but nevertheless I fell in love with India, a complex yet beautiful and exotic land my family would have many reasons to visit, and where one day we would find refuge. In fact, in 1975 my sister Nadia graduated from high school in Afghanistan, and, as other family members before her, travelled to India to attend university. From that time on, my parents and I made several trips a year to visit her. Thankfully, I suffered no further life-threatening mishaps.

When I was sixteen years old my father's evil older brother, Shair, died. From the time he had become the leader of our tribe, Shair had been a powerful presence, hovering like a malevolent spirit over my father and grandmother, and later over my own life. No matter that my parents had fled the galah and

Shair's daily influence when Nadia was only a baby, his baleful existence continued to haunt our family life. Despite Shair's past misdeeds, my father had always tried to maintain a cordial relationship. My mother said little to her husband about Shair, yet she successfully invoked his name as a bogeyman figure to frighten Nadia and me. Grandmother Mayana refused to speak his name, and went to her grave believing he had intentionally murdered her three sweet daughters.

Shair was such an intense force that his family believed him immune to death. But then one day when he had lived over seventy years he was felled by a massive stroke and died quickly.

I can't deny a sense of relief at his passing. No longer did I have to worry about being kidnapped, or being put under his control should my father die from bladder cancer, for Shair's sons and grandsons were not like their cruel father.

After Shair Khan's heart beat its last, my father inherited his brother's position as the Khan of the Khail tribe. But with the passing years and the formation of President Daoud's government, the leaders of the tribes held much less power. In fact, some years prior to his death, Shair Khan had been ordered to leave his ancestral tribal land and build a galah in another area of Afghanistan. President Daoud cleverly worked to separate the khans from their tribes so their power would be diluted.

My father, being a man of modest leaning in all matters, made no effort to claim the fortune then held by Shair's sons. What was left of Grandfather Ahmed's Khan inheritance remained with Shair's sons. Although Papa became the Khan of the Khail, he accepted it only as an honorary title; therefore, our lives changed very little.

President Daoud proclaimed that Shair Khan of the Khail tribe would be honoured by a military funeral. A great procession was held and Shair's body was returned for burial in his tribal land of the Khail.

Relieved to be free at last from the threat of Shair Khan's cruel rule, I was soon to meet a new evil. Even then this evil was creeping up on us like a morning fog. Only this time, women would not be alone in their suffering. Men too would feel a hand at their throat and many lives would be lost trying to free that grip.

Chapter 8

The Russians were coming. Soon they were everywhere in Kabul. They were sent to us under the pretence of offering technical, medical or educational assistance. During this time my family moved from our house to an apartment in Mekrorayan, a modern suburb built by the Russians on the outskirts of Kabul. Papa thought our lives would improve because the new apartment blocks had running water and modern toilets. There was even central heating, a wonderful luxury in bitterly cold Afghanistan. There were swimming pools, basketball and tennis courts.

Our apartment was much roomier than our former home, with three large bedrooms, a modern kitchen and two toilets.

I thought I had gone to heaven with my own room, which I quickly decorated with posters of Elvis

Presley and Tom Jones. There was also room to display my collection of old coins and stamps.

While many Afghans with political connections moved into Mekrorayan, many transplanted Russians also lived there, Soviet professionals of every trade. We found our Russian neighbours to be so nice that we gave little thought to the threat they represented. My family, like most Afghan people, enjoyed and embraced the modernization being brought to us, without giving much thought to the danger of losing our culture and our independence. We soon learned that the Soviet government didn't spend enormous sums of money and time and energy on a country they did not have designs to occupy. The Soviet Union shared a 1,000-mile border with Afghanistan and, like the British of years past, believed they needed Afghanistan in their sphere of influence.

But 1978 held great promise for me personally. I was a senior at the Malalai High School in Kabul, the same school where my mother taught. It was one of the best girls' schools in Afghanistan. It was named in honour of an Afghan heroine, Malalai, a legend in my country.

Malalai was a simple country girl who, like many Afghan women, followed the men of her family when they went to war, preparing food, supplying water and tending to the wounded. Her magnificent act of gallantry occurred on 27 July 1880 when the British army was attacking the Afghan military during one of their many efforts to invade and occupy our nation. Although the Afghan warriors outnumbered the British, the British were equipped with superior arms. With so many Afghan fallen, it was soon clear that the battle would be lost. Malalai shouted at her father and brothers to stand and fight. When the flag bearer fell in battle, Malalai rushed to hold the flag upright. Later, she was shot and killed herself, but she inspired the warriors with her courage.

From that time on she had been a great hero to all Afghan schoolchildren.

I have many wonderful memories of those long ago schooldays, sitting in a spacious classroom with the yellow sunlight streaming through the tall windows. Although our school was for girls only, our courses were the same as the ones for boys. Due to the school's excellent curriculum, the most influential Afghans sent their daughters to Malalai High. Among my classmates were granddaughters of President Daoud and the daughters of various royal princes.

Although I was occupied with the usual high school activities, I spent a lot of time dreaming and planning for the day when I would be leaving Afghanistan to travel to India and enrol at university. My parents insisted I train to become a medical doctor, following in my sister Nadia's footsteps. But I preferred the idea of studying Political Science, believing I was better suited for a diplomatic career.

For a number of reasons, I was one of the more popular girls at my school. Perhaps this popularity was in part because I was daring and rebellious, and teenagers admire such traits in their peers. The undisputed leader of my group of friends, I provided my girlfriends with many entertaining moments.

French was my favourite class that year, perhaps because I was a natural when it came to languages. I may have inherited a talent for languages from my father, who spoke Farsi, Pashto, French, Hindu, Russian, English and Turkish. Mother spoke only Farsi and a little English, and shunned my father's Pashtun language at all costs, until the day she died. So my sister Nadia and I always spoke Farsi with Mother and Pashto with Papa. We also spoke some English, Russian, Hindu and French. I loved French the best; for me, it is the most beautiful language.

I secretly approved of our French teacher, who was cool, and a bit of a rebel, too. Early in the school year she had announced a new and exciting rule. Everyone in her class must speak French and only French. If she heard any of us speaking in Farsi or Pashto, we were fined five Afghani. That fund would go to finance a special field trip to Paghman, a beautiful summer resort about thirty kilometres from Kabul, where we would stay in a fine hotel and enjoy the scenery and delicious food. As the year progressed, many students slipped, forgetting to speak French. By the end of the first term, she had collected ample funds to pay for the field trip, which was planned for 27 April 1978.

The day before our trip there was much excitement in class. Our French teacher hinted that she planned to bend the school rules on the trip, allowing music, dancing and smoking. She even volunteered to supply us with cigarettes. Although almost every senior girl had acquired a smoking addiction, because Afghan teenagers considered smoking to be cool, none were brave enough to admit to the habit to their parents. Never before had a grown-up joined in our conspiracy. We were filled with anticipation.

My friends and I should have realized that trouble was brewing when we left school that day. Normally the school grounds would be surrounded by cars sent by wealthy parents to collect their daughters. On that afternoon there was only a single military vehicle on the school grounds. Additionally, there were two armed soldiers standing guard in front of the school. Several helicopters were circling in the sky.

Due to our excitement about the next day's field trip, we ignored danger signs. Instead a group of us piled into a taxi and ordered the driver to take us to our favourite soda fountain, located in the centre of the city.

Every soda fountain shop in Kabul employed a man who could juggle plates and glasses as skilfully as a circus performer. He was known as a sweets dispenser. The server at our favourite shop was a talented entertainer who jumped about juggling dishes, a delight to a bunch of teenage girls. We eagerly watched as he covered our plates with frozen snow brought down from high mountain peaks, then trickled syrup over the snow. Sweet paste shaped into long strips was added to the flavoured snow. Ladles of cream with a dash of rosewater were then shaken together before being poured over the tasty confection.

We were happy girls that day, perhaps the last happy day of my life in Afghanistan. We chattered about the upcoming field trip, and how we were going to swim in the cold waters and picnic in the lush gardens of the resort. I was doubly excited because my father had agreed for me to drive our family car to pick up my girlfriends the following morning. Together we would go to the school grounds and meet the bus. My father would come by the school later in the day to collect the car.

Although a small number of women in Kabul knew how to drive, few took the wheel without male supervision. I was one of very few Afghan girls whose father allowed her the privilege of driving without directives from a male passenger.

At the end of the day when the taxi dropped me off at home, I was startled to see my mother, sister and Nanny Muma rush from the doorway. Nanny Muma had her hands in the air as though she was expecting to ward off a bullet. Mother was weeping. My sister, who was home on holiday from college in India, had a worried look on her face as she dragged me from the cab, hugging me and babbling, 'You are safe! You are safe!'

Their terrified behaviour panicked me. I cried out, 'What has happened? Is something wrong with Papa?'

Mother screeched, 'Get in the house!'

'Thank God you are alive,' Muma shouted, dabbing at her red, swollen eyes.

By that time I was so upset by the unknown that I began to shake. Surely my father was dead! What else could so distress my family? Just as we entered the front room, there was a deafening boom. The entire building rattled on its foundation.

Mother screamed.

The others ran from the room.

Feeling hysteria rising in my throat, I screamed, 'What is happening?'

Mother was incoherent, so I ran to the telephone and dialled my father's office. His line was busy.

That's when I heard the sound of machine guns near by, followed by thunderous explosions that shook the building.

The telephone rang. Papa was on the line. 'Maryam, thank God you are home.'

My stomach plunged when I heard the noise of gunfire coming down the wire. Was my father's life in danger?

I cried out, 'Who is shooting?'

Mother grabbed the phone from my hands. 'Come home immediately!' she gabbled.

The line went dead.

I was rooted to the spot in shock.

My mother ran down the corridor to her bedroom, screaming, 'Oh my God! Oh my God! Save him! Save him!'

In a matter of a few hours, our once safe world had been turned upside down. I took a chance and redialled my father's number, surprised when the phone was picked up, but horrified when the next moment there was a loud explosion from somewhere in his office. I was sure my father was dead.

I ran to my mother and shook her to stop her crying. 'Mother! What is happening? Who is attacking us?'

'Maryam, my daughter, there is a coup. A *violent* revolt,' she sobbed.

'Where? What?'

'We only know that someone is attacking the palace.' My mother and I stared at each other. Papa's office was located only a block away from the presidential palace.

Never had I been so frightened. From the noise outside, I knew that people must be dying. But my only thoughts were of my gentle father, a man who had been thrust into the military life at a young age, yet had never fought in a single battle.

While my mother, sister and nanny remained closeted in their rooms, I stood by the front door, watching and waiting. I waited for three long hours, wincing at the loud sounds of war coming from every corner, not allowing myself to envisage the destruction being wrought on our beautiful city. Just as my knees felt they might buckle from exhaustion, I spotted my father's car as he came careening down the road.

I ran into the street. The stench of smoke enveloped me. The sound of machine-gun fire rattled in my brain. But none of that mattered, for my father was alive!

When Papa saw me he leapt from the car, rushing to gather me in a bear hug. That's when we heard bullets striking the walls of the houses around us.

My father bent low to the ground, pulling me with him, and we scurried back into the relative safety of our home. My father was quickly surrounded by the others.

Papa told us, 'I was saved by George Perouch.'

George Perouch was the French Ambassador, a delightful man who was a very close friend of my parents and Uncle Hakim and his family. The embassy was next door to Papa's office.

Papa continued: 'There was a brief ceasefire so that the French Embassy employees might evacuate. George ran into my office, shouting for us to slip into the embassy. He thought that everyone who could should withdraw from Kabul with the French. My staff went with the French, but I came home.' He smiled a little. 'I couldn't leave my girls.'

After a few moments of hugs and tears, he went on: 'I fear that Daoud is dead.'

I gave a little cry. I had always loved our president, mainly because he was connected to my father's well-being.

Papa patted my hand. 'The presidential residence has been under siege and has suffered severe damage. By the time I made my escape, I could see that the walls were breached and the palace was ringed by tanks, although the battle was over. No one was firing into, or out of, the presidential residence.' He shook his head sorrowfully. 'I fear they are all dead.'

My heart raced. Two of Daoud's granddaughters were my close friends. In fact, I had seen them at school the day before. They were laughing and carefree, without a thought of danger in their heads. Were those innocent girls now dead? Papa resumed his tale. 'After passing Daoud's residence, I saw some schoolgirls running down a street. They were in grave danger, so I stopped and offered them a ride home, wherever that might be. Can you believe those girls shouted at me, saying, "You dirty old man! Shame on you to pick up young girls."' He sighed. 'I had to leave them to their fate.'

Then Papa remembered that we needed supplies, for who knew how long the fighting would last. He called out for Askar, who appeared like a mirage from the back of the house. For the first time that day I realized I had not seen Askar during the entire episode. Where had he been?

Papa told him: 'Askar, I think there is a temporary lull in the fighting. Quickly, go and purchase all the food you can.' He dug in his pockets and passed Askar a wad of money.

I was struck by envy that Askar would be seeing what was going on outside. When my father and mother retired to their room to further discuss the shocking events of the day, and Nadia and Nanny Muma returned to their respective rooms, I found the car keys and slipped from our building into the family car. I intercepted Askar who was only a block or two away. When he expressed alarm at my unexpected appearance, I lied. 'Papa told me to come and pick you up. We can bring back more groceries in a car.'

The streets were not as calm as Papa had hoped. There were ongoing street battles. We saw dead and wounded people littering the area. But armed with my teenager's false sense of indestructibility, I drove through the streets without fear, although I saw people running in panic and heard the sound of explosions and bullets zipping through the air. Instead, I felt mounting excitement.

I saw brown roiling smoke rising into the sky over the presidential palace. What terrible things had happened there? Where were my friends? Where were the women and children of the royal family? Without our moderate-minded president, what would happen to Afghanistan?

There was pandemonium at the market. Shoppers shouted and pushed while hurling food into shopping bags. Askar and I began to grab, too, although we were luckier than most since the merchant knew my family well. That kindly soul began stacking bags of rice, cans of dried milk and other canned goods, toilet paper and other items in a pile, before helping us to load it in the car. When Askar and I tried to pay for our goods, the stall owner refused our money, shouting, 'Go! Go! We will settle later! Go!'

We raced to return home because the violence had

escalated, and there were moments when I thought we wouldn't make it. It was the highest adrenalin rush of my life. When we reached our building we nestled the car as closely as possible to the front door and made haste to unload the provisions. I was proud of myself, expecting a heroine's welcome. But instead, I was met by a wall of fury from both parents, shrieking wildly.

My mother was squealing, 'Maryam! Maryam!' I could see that she was wavering between wanting to hug me in relief and slap me in anger.

My sweet father's face was distorted in angry rage. 'Maryam! How could you? We are in the middle of a *revolution*! Have you lost your mind, *spi zoia*!' My father rarely cursed, and now he was calling me a 'son of a dog', one of the harshest expletives in our Muslim world.

I fell to the floor, wrapping my arms around his knees. 'I am sorry, Papa. I am sorry. I was not thinking.'

Neither of my parents made a conciliatory move towards me. It would be days before they dropped their brusque manner with me.

On that first night of the revolution, Mother, Nanny Muma, Nadia and I slept in the living room. My father and Askar slept in a small room in the back of the house. Gun battles and explosions plagued our sleep. We heard tanks rumbling down the street in front of our home. This violent rebellion bore no resemblance to the bloodless revolution of 1973. This was a serious business. With every new sound of carnage, my mother and sister would wail. For some reason I was calm and coped best, managing to snatch some sleep in spite of the noisy disruptions.

The following morning mine was the only rested face at the breakfast table. My father had the radio tuned to Kabul's main government station, which blasted forth only cheerful music. Finally, around ten in the morning, a voice with a Pashtun accent speaking Farsi interrupted the music, telling listeners: 'Afghanistan has been freed from feudalism and imperialism. Afghanistan is now the free republic of Afghanistan. Afghanistan is for the people of Afghanistan.'

Once again, the happy music began. I took a deep breath before scrutinizing the worried faces of my mother and father. My mother spoke first, her voice filled with repugnance. 'The Communists are going to turn Kabul into a suburb of Moscow. We will be ordered to share our home. Your father will be told to divide up his profitable business. Private lands will be confiscated and given to people we have never known. These God-hating Communists will even outlaw Islam.'

A religious woman, Nanny Muma gave a small

cry before placing her hands over her mouth.

I was saddened into silence. For the first time in many years, our family had a lot to lose. Just when Father was making a good living, the Communists had come to take it all away. It was not fair! I could tell by the expression on my father's face that he was thinking much the same thing but he said nothing, although he grunted deep in his throat.

Just then the music from the radio stopped and the same voice announced, 'I am the Republic of Afghanistan's Minister of Defense, Major Aslam Watanjar.'

I almost laughed. It was too good to be true! Watanjar translates as 'to die for one's country'. What a clichéd symbolic name for a man who wanted to give the impression he was a patriot. Later I was surprised to learn the man's name was indeed Watanjar, an ironic coincidence.

Before we had a chance to discuss his message, another voice, this time speaking Pashto, interrupted the major. The new announcer said, 'My fellow citizens. Justice has arrived for both men and women, who will be treated with equal respect in your new Afghanistan.'

While that message would infuriate nearly every man in the country, it would be sweet news for female hearts, yet none of us could seriously believe there would be real change. As male Afghan foetuses grow arms and legs in the womb, their little brain tissues are already busy sprouting prejudice and discrimination against women. Who could change the attitudes of such men? Not even the Communists would be successful on that point.

If we had had any doubt that the Russians were the force behind the coup, the gist of the message that the people of Afghanistan were now equal erased any doubt. Everyone in Afghanistan was to be on exactly the same level. There would be no wealthy and there would be no poor. Everyone would be educated. The first goal of the nation would be to abolish illiteracy, even though most families did not allow their daughters to attend school.

Certainly universal education was a fine goal, but unlikely to succeed, Afghan culture being what it was.

The Pashto speaker ended his speech shouting, 'Long live socialism! Down with imperialism! Down with America!'

We spent the day sitting in front of the radio, our only lifeline to news of the coup. Before the day was over, an announcer informed listeners that 'President Daoud has resigned from his post due to health reasons'.

My father clasped his hands together, looking to the heavens, and exclaimed, 'If only that is true.'

Later that evening we heard more sobering news

when the official radio reported, 'The homeland has been liberated from the yoke of Mohammed Daoud's dictatorship. The time of fraternity and equality has begun. Daoud is gone for ever. The last remnants of imperialist tyranny and despotism have been put down. The national revolutionary council is looking after your rights. Now, for the first time, power has come into the hands of the people.'

We were distraught by the tone of the message, believing that the president had been killed. But what had happened to the rest of his family? The worst was feared after such a violent uprising. Many women and children lived with the president at his palace. President Daoud had a wife, daughters and daughters-in-law, with many grandchildren, some only toddlers. There were also many officials and other presidential employees. Where were all those people now? Nothing had been heard from any former official or member of the royal family since the beginning of the coup.

I had heard the story of Prince Daoud more than once, although I had given him little thought over the years. He was born in Kabul, and his father, who served as the Afghan Ambassador to Germany, was assassinated in Berlin in 1933. The prince had been taken under the wing of other members of the royal family, and was educated in France. He returned to serve in important positions in the

Afghan government, over the years serving as Minister of Defense, Minister of Interior and Ambassador to France, and he was appointed as Prime Minister in 1953. During his decade as Prime Minister, he often turned to the Soviet Union for military aid and opened up a rift with Pakistan over disputed territory. This probably led to his dismissal as Prime Minister. Ten years later, as we have seen, he led a quiet coup against his cousin and brother-in-law, King Zahir, and deposed him when the king was in Europe. This time he declared a Republic and assumed the office of President.

In 1974, President Daoud requested and received military aid from the Soviet Union. Overnight it seemed that Kabul was crammed with Soviet political advisers, physicians, teachers and arms experts.

Two years later, our President Daoud finally 'saw the reality' and, too late, tried to distance himself from the Soviets. And that is when his real problems began. He travelled to Moscow in 1977 for a meeting with Leonid Brezhnev, when Brezhnev pressured Daoud to expel all NATO or US experts.

Whatever else happened during that meeting, it is thought that President Daoud came away even more convinced that he must reverse his earlier sympathies and pull our country far away from Soviet influence. This set off a chain of events that would result in a puppet Soviet government, an armed invasion by one of the most mighty militaries in the world, the near total destruction of Afghanistan and the deaths of many thousands of Afghan citizens. As a final indignity, the death knell for Afghanistan would come with the rise of the Taliban and the devastating actions of Saudi terrorist Osama Bin Laden.

It was our good fortune that we had no way of knowing Afghanistan's ill-fated future during the week of the 1978 coup, or that our family life would be destroyed for ever. We were only one of many thousands of helpless Afghan families who were praying that the chaos and violence would quickly pass and we could return to our normal lives.

If only our prayers had been answered.

Chapter 9

It was no surprise that our much anticipated senior class field trip never occurred. Like most Afghan citizens our little family hunkered down at home, waiting to see what might happen. Several days later our new government announced that children should go back to school. We did as we were told. Upon my return I made a careful survey of all those I knew. The only missing students were members of the royal family. Although we kept hoping they would soon return, none of those vivacious girls was ever seen again.

A rumour went round Kabul that the coup d'etat began on the orders of Hafizullah Amin, who had been put under house arrest by President Daoud after Amin gave a rallying speech for the Afghan Communists. President Daoud did not murder his opponent, as previous rulers might have done. Instead, he was lenient, even allowing the prisoner Amin to entertain visitors. That benevolence was a dreadful blunder, for, it was whispered, Amin's visitors hand-carried the plans for a coup from Amin to his followers. It was only years later that we learned what happened that day. The carefully planned rebellion was started by mutinous soldiers at Kabul International Airport. The rebels mowed down military units loyal to President Daoud until they had battled their way into the city centre.

Hearing about the armed disturbance, royal relatives fled their individual residences to seek refuge at the palace. Perhaps the family believed they would be safe if they clung together, when in fact some might have survived had they spread out over the city, or even left the country.

When the palace came under attack by the anti-government forces, the frightened family sought protection by gathering in a large reception room where the doors were secured and faithful employees manned the entrances, prepared to defend them.

President Daoud told his family he would never relinquish power. Even if he had the opportunity to capitulate, he would not. Before the day ended, the entire family was murdered, other than two princesses who were wounded in the mayhem and taken to a hospital, where they later died.

Muslims must be buried within twenty-four hours of death, and generally even a harsh enemy will allow proper burial. Yet there were no bodies presented for laying in their graves. The fate of our royal family remained a huge mystery, and thirty years would pass before the truth of that day would finally be revealed, that all were murdered and their bodies dumped in a mass grave.

Soon we learned that our new president was a man named Nur Muhammad Taraki. His Prime Minster was Hafizullah Amin, the man who was rumoured to have planned the coup. Those two set about conferring with Soviet officials to determine the fate of all Afghan people.

Within three months of the coup, the new President Taraki announced a programme of reforms, one that would obliterate our traditional culture. In December, President Taraki travelled to Russia to sign a Soviet–Afghan Friendship Treaty, a twenty-year treaty of 'friendship and cooperation', which involved Soviet military intervention. Soon afterwards, spontaneous revolts spread throughout the provinces. There were periodic explosions in Kabul. The people of Afghanistan were angry and quick to make their opinions known.

I was stunned by the rapid changes that came over our personal lives. The school curriculum was quickly changed. Suddenly our history classes had nothing to do with Afghanistan. Instead, we were taught about the glorious Russian Revolution and the outstanding achievements of Communist rulers.

School drama events no longer had any connection with traditional Afghan legends, such as the Stone Dragon or the Holy Grave of the Bride and Groom, folklore known by every child. Now everything put before the malleable students was steeped in propaganda. Our songs were no longer the traditional ones of passionate Afghan poetry. Instead, we were ordered to sing our appreciation of the new socialist government. I remember one silly song about prosperity under Russian rule. There were others that denigrated America and England.

Our school became a showplace for our Russian invaders. Parades of visiting dignitaries marched across the border to Kabul to be shown that Afghan schoolgirls were models of communist youth.

With each passing day, our lives became more bizarre. And with each passing day, I became more angry. I remembered that on my first trip abroad, when I was distressed by Afghanistan's lack of modernization compared to Pakistan and India, my father had told me, 'Maryam, you live under your own flag.' But now, our new government changed our beloved Afghan flag to resemble the Soviet one. I was living under an alien country's flag.

A bubbling volcano of rage was building inside my patriotic heart.

The sister of our new President Taraki was a newly employed teacher at my school. Although I did not dislike her personally, I could not accept her close association with our new communist regime. She was a fervent supporter of all that my family and I hated. She pressured all the girls in her classroom to join the communist party youth group. While some of my friends compromised their beliefs and joined, I refused. Since I was a leader in the school, she made me a personal case, counselling me to join, sometimes whispering veiled threats. 'Maryam, if you do not join the youth group, your chances of being selected for higher education will be endangered.'

Such threats only made me more stubborn. 'No, thank you,' I replied with a calm voice even as my fingers itched to scratch her face.

'Maryam, this will reflect badly on your family.'

I looked at her without speaking. I knew I was making the right decision. I am not a person who can pretend to go along with something I dislike just for a few benefits. If the Communists would not allow me to leave Afghanistan to travel to college in India, then I thought I might slip across the border without official permission.

My decision to refuse to enrol in the youth group was considered subversive, yet I never regretted it. I heard from other students who had joined that they were put under unrelenting pressure to spy on their own families, to report any anti-communist remarks they heard even from their own parents. They were compelled to be present at mixed-sex party meetings, gatherings which were offensive to our culture.

While I had played with boys prior to reaching puberty, once I passed into my teenage years I was no longer allowed to play with boys in the neighbourhood, or to attend mixed-sex events. Although I was pleased with one aspect of the communist rule – that women would be treated equally at the workplace, that women could vote and that women would gain some legal rights – that did not mean I was comfortable mixing with boys I did not know. The Communists were moving in the wrong direction for conservative Muslim Afghanistan.

Like many Afghan people I became more religious after the Communists came to power. Before their arrival, I had taken my religion lightly, feeling secure in my faith. But with so many changes being imposed upon us, I, like many other Afghans, clung to my Muslim faith with a new determination. During Ramadan, I fasted diligently, never eating or drinking during the daylight hours.

During Ramadan a Polish television crew appeared at our school. Before the crew arrived, we were briefed by our teachers to praise the new government. It was a sham. Everyone I knew resented and even hated the new regime.

I was in a foul mood even before the television crew arrived.

Since we were seniors, we were scheduled to be interviewed first. We were led to the courtyard of the school and instructed to sit in a circle. The Polish film crew surrounded us with blinding bright lights.

I saw that one of the young men on the crew was eating an apple. In the past I would not have noticed or cared that a non-Muslim ate during Ramadan, but on that day I was struck by a great fury. I longed for the power to sentence that stupid man to a good flogging.

Never one to temper my reactions, I exclaimed in Farsi, 'Shame on you, you idiot! This is Ramadan and you stand there eating an apple! Where is your respect for our religion?'

Several of my classmates giggled. One whispered, 'Maryam, your loose tongue will get you into trouble.'

'They are too dumb to understand Farsi,' I replied haughtily.

Just then the young man tossed the apple to the ground and said in perfect Farsi, 'I am sorry. You are right.'

I was startled and embarrassed.

When the interview began and the cameras started to film, the apple-eating Polish guy presented himself as the host of the television show. He turned to me. '*You*,' he said, 'how do *you* feel about your new government?'

The blood rushed to my face as defiance overcame common sense. I glowered at him, 'You should know. You are from Poland. You are a puppet living in a puppet state. How do *you* feel?'

I heard a rumble of displeasure from the people standing around us but my anger had been building for months. I was on a roll. 'Don't forget that we are Afghan. We never bow to another flag. We will never be a puppet state,' I snarled. 'Unlike you, we will drive our oppressors out.'

I heard gasps, but no one uttered a word until our stunned principal found her voice. She screeched, 'Return to your classroom! *Now!*'

The lady principal was new to Malalai High, having been sent as a replacement for the kindly head teacher we had known and loved for all our high school years. This new puppet principal knew nothing about us, not even our names. We hated her.

Once we were seated in our class, she stalked into the room, her face as red as the apple the television host had been eating. She marched up to me, her voice threatening, 'What is your name?'

Still brash, proud to have shown some spunk, I told her, 'I am Maryam Khail, daughter of Ajab Khail. We are proud Afghans.'

She grabbed a piece of paper and a pen. 'Who was standing beside you?'

For the first time I felt a small wave of regret.

Although I had been bold from childhood, often committing daring deeds and then taking painful punishment with silent pride, my friends were different. I lied. 'I do not remember who was standing beside me.'

The teacher began interrogating my classmates. One frightened girl was easily broken into supplying the names of my best friends.

The principal squealed in her irritating voice, 'Stay here. Do not exchange a word. I will be back.' She went out, slamming the heavy door with a loud bang.

A few quiet minutes passed before my girlfriends started to rebuke me for behaving in such a stupid manner. 'Maryam, we are in trouble now because of you. The KHAD [Afghan version of the KGB] will be informed. They will arrest everyone in our families!' Some of the girls began to weep.

Although I felt terrible that my friends had been drawn into the affair, I did not regret expressing my true opinion. In fact, I felt the better for it. I felt myself a real patriot, a staunch fighter against the invaders.

While I was sitting smugly in the classroom, the principal was reporting me to the authorities. Luckily for me, she happened to reach a government ministry headed by a man who had been a friend of my father for many years. The minister was stunned to hear that Ajab Khail's daughter had created a firestorm of controversy at the most prestigious girls' school in Kabul. He encouraged our principal to leave the matter in his hands, and told her he would see to it personally that I would be punished. He asked that she not notify the KHAD security officials.

My parents knew the whole story even before I arrived home. Once again I walked into a furious confrontation. My mother was yelling while my father asked me to tell my side of the story. Finally Mother slumped into a chair, weeping softly.

'Maryam,' Papa said with clenched teeth, 'Maryam, you will get us all thrown into Pulecharkhi.'

'Pulecharkhi?' I repeated robotically. Under the Communists, Pulecharkhi had become one of the most dreaded Afghan prisons, notorious for torture and murder. Many of Afghanistan's best and brightest were disappearing into Pulecharkhi, never to be seen again.

'Yes. My friend at the ministry told me that without his intervention, our entire family would have been arrested. While we have avoided imprisonment, we will now be placed on a watch list. Everything we do and say will be scrutinized.' He clicked his tongue in resignation. 'You have put us into very serious danger, Maryam.'

Just as Papa said, our family was targeted. Soon the Russians closed my uncle Hakim's cement factory. Farid's family fell into dire financial trouble. My father's business had suffered a major setback too since it was nearly impossible to export goods; also, his French partner had great difficulty going in and out of the country, although that brave man continued to push against all barriers.

Eid, the celebration at the end of Ramadan, seemed a funeral rather than a festival that year. During Eid the family gathered, and while the little children played, the adults discussed ways we might flee the country. I overheard my father say, 'There are smugglers who will take us across the border into Pakistan. From there we can go to India.'

Uncle Hakim said, 'No. Just last week I heard of a family who hired such a smuggler. As soon as they entered an empty area, the men of the family were bound while the women were raped. No. No. We cannot risk it.' He reflected before resuming telling his ideas. 'I have been thinking. We must use our contacts. Farid is working now to obtain visas for us all.'

I felt a small glow inside. My hero Farid, my dear cousin, he would save us for certain. After attending school for a while in India, Farid had enrolled at a good college in Iran. But that country was in the throes of revolution too, and the increasing tension there had caused him to seek refuge in Bahrain, where he had acquired a good job. Yes. Farid would save us all.

'Thank God Farid was out of the country when all this started,' Uncle Hakim sighed. 'We must be patient. We must wait to see what Farid can do for us.'

During such a family meeting, Uncle Hakim placed his arm around my shoulders and led me away. 'Maryam, I can see that you are very tense and angry. Your mother told me about your outburst at school.'

I looked at him and nodded, knowing that I was in for a lecture. Yet I loved my uncle Hakim and knew that he was a wise and good man, and more courageous than most. He had even stood up to the brutal Nazis.

'Maryam, you must keep your mouth shut. When I was in Germany, I saw that it was the young who were most eager to speak out against the Nazis. Do you know what happened to them?' He snapped his fingers. 'They vanished, Maryam. They disappeared, never to be seen again. Of course, we found out later than Hitler and his thugs killed everyone who dared to disagree with their brutal policies.'

He leaned in closer, and for the first time in my life I saw fear in his eyes.

'Maryam,' he warned, 'the only people as ruthless as the Nazis are the Communists. These people will not hesitate to execute our young people, even a young girl like you. But before they kill you, they will torture you. You know such an outcome would suck the life out of your parents. You must promise me, Maryam, to hold your tongue.'

I promised him I would. If Uncle Hakim was frightened, there was good reason for me to be careful.

But I knew this would be a promise difficult to keep.

Chapter 10

Sadly for our family, Uncle Hakim's warning was prophetic. Our family soon lost two of our most intelligent and gentle cousins.

Due to Shair Khan's unpleasant conduct, we had always been much closer to my mother's family than to my father's family. Yet there were some Khail family members we grew to know and love. Two of the most special were young cousins, a dedicated physician named Sabor, and his older brother, Mohammed, who worked at the Ministry of Justice in Kabul. Because they were older, we called them 'uncle', which is a sign of respect in our culture. Both were married to their cousins. Sabor was the proud father of a six-month-old daughter, while Mohammed was the joyous father of four young children.

Sabor was a tall man whose persona exuded kindness. He had large expressive eyes and bore a remarkable likeness to the Hollywood movie actor

Clark Gable. Although Sabor was so modest that he blushed when receiving compliments on his fine appearance, he was proud of his perfectly groomed beard and moustache.

Sabor was the hardest-working doctor in the country, and his dedication to Afghanistan's poor meant that we saw him infrequently. He would generally pop by once a month, his hands and pockets loaded with fresh fruit. Secretly I wanted sweets and gum, but he made it a point to tell me that such delicacies were damaging to my health. Sabor was years before his time with his insistence on a good diet for a healthy lifestyle.

Despite a lack of sweets, I greatly enjoyed Sabor's visits. He was always interested in every detail of my young life. He would regale us with stories of the most interesting titbits of hospital life or remarkable medical cases.

Sabor's older brother Mohammed was also tall, with a thin nose and full lips. He was carefree and happy-go-lucky, and quick to tease us younger kids. He would laugh at his brother's strict principles and would slip us pieces of chocolate and other forbidden goodies. We were so close to Mohammed that when our father was out of the country, he assumed some of Papa's duties, often picking us up from school and treating us to an ice cream or a walk in the park near to our home. Every Thursday evening Mohammed would take our entire family out to dinner, to the fanciest restaurant in Kabul, which happened to be located in one of the former palaces. Afterwards he would indulge us youngsters by taking us to the movies.

Little did we know how limited our time would be with those two lovely men. Soon after the Communist-led coup, there were reports of young men from influential families being arrested without cause or explanation. Rumour was that thousands had been detained, never to be seen or heard of again. Although we were relieved that Farid was safe living out of the country, we worried about the remainder of our male cousins, whose ages ranged from fourteen to forty. Anything might happen to them under the new repressive regime.

Then one day we heard the terrifying news that the secret police had raided the hospital where Sabor worked. Without explanation, gentle Sabor was led away. Later that same day, other KHAD officials walked unannounced into Mohammed's office. He too was seized and arrested.

Everyone who knew those two kindly men loved them and couldn't believe they would do anything wrong. Now we suffered horrifying visions of their imprisonment in Pulecharkhi Prison, possibly undergoing torture.

In Afghanistan, as in many Eastern countries, it is

not who you *are*, but who you *know*. So all the men in our family started calling on their government contacts to find out why two such gentle and innocent men had been arrested. But the Soviet style was very different from our ways. No one could turn up any news. Sabor and Mohammed were far beyond our limited reach of influence.

We grew more frantic with each passing day.

With the disappearance of my gentle cousins, the volcano in my heart began spewing fury. I so hated the Communists that I was finding it difficult to be civil to our Russian Mekrorayan neighbours, good people who really had little to do with our troubles.

We happened to have two other cousins who were in high-ranking positions in the military. Thankfully they had not been targeted by the new regime, and in fact were able to help our family regarding various minor official matters. One of the cousins had blue eyes and the other had green, so the younger kids in the family jokingly called them 'the blue uncle' and 'the green uncle'.

Some time after Sabor and Mohammed had disappeared, the telephone rang and the voice on the other end told me, 'I am a commandant in the army.' The voice paused, then added, 'I am one of your uncles.'

'Are you the blue uncle or the green uncle?' I asked, playfully.

'I am the blue uncle,' he laughed. Then he turned

serious. 'Tell your father to be home tonight because I must see him. I will arrive at nine p.m.'

When my father walked into the house, I ran to deliver the message and I could see he was pleased.

That evening our doorbell rang at the time given. I dashed to the door expecting to see my 'blue uncle', but instead I was greeted by the sight of a stranger in military uniform. Behind him stood two other soldiers, both carrying machine guns. There was a fourth army officer standing to the side of our porch. None wore a friendly expression.

'What do you want?' I demanded. I realized the voice on the phone had not been my uncle at all. I had been tricked.

'We are here to see your father.'

Hearing the conversation, my father came out of the living room to join me.

'Sir,' the officer ordered. 'You must come with us.'

My voice grew loud. 'Why are you taking my father?'

I was ignored.

Papa had a puzzled look on his face. He had not belonged to the military since his cancer was diagnosed. He was not in the government. He was no longer a young man.

By this time my mother had arrived on the scene. She was so frightened by the sight of armed men she couldn't squeak out a single word.

The officer barked at her: 'Gather your husband's medication. He is coming with us.'

We stared at each other, thinking the same thing: they had a file on my father or they would not know of his illness or of his medications.

Mother took a moment to catch her breath before walking rapidly from the room.

My chest felt so tight I could barely breathe. I looked at my papa. He was wearing a resigned expression, yet his hands were trembling. Never had I loved him more. At the worst moment of my life I was helpless. The armed men were watching us. We were at their mercy. They could massacre us all and there was nothing anyone could do.

My hatred of the new government went up a few notches.

Just then Mother came rushing out of the bedroom with Papa's pills. She was also stuffing a change of clothes and a few cigarettes into a small bag. Thankfully she still had her wits about her, packing items that might provide him with some relief if he was held as a prisoner for more than a few hours.

The leading officer nodded and one of the other soldiers took my father's bag. They began to lead him away. Finally I found the strength to breathe and to scream all at once. I clutched at my father, terrified I would never see him again, that he would disappear, just as Sabor and Mohammed had disappeared.

I had no shame. 'Don't take him,' I begged, my voice breaking. 'He is a sick man.'

One of the soldiers pulled my hands away from my father. I realized then that we were dealing with men whose hearts were made of stone.

My mother cried out, 'Please don't make her an orphan. Don't!'

We were powerless. All I could do was watch my father's back as he walked away to the military vehicle. He was pushed into the back seat and driven away, perhaps out of our lives for ever.

Mother collapsed, but I quickly collected myself and ran to the telephone. I dialled the number of the Minister of Agriculture. He was a family friend and had been a long-time recipient of my father's good graces. Papa had been responsible for his scholarship to a European university, where he obtained a PhD My father had also helped to arrange his current post in the government. I was not shy to remind him of these facts, saying, 'Please. My father did you many favours, and he did those favours with a good heart. Now he needs a favour from you.'

If the minister was shocked by my impudence, he didn't show it. I'm sure by then every Afghan citizen holding a government post had become accustomed to this kind of desperate plea.

He said, 'Maryam, there is nothing I can do tonight. But I will act first thing tomorrow. I promise.'

We were frantic at the thought that Papa had to spend one moment in prison. Close family and friends came to the house to sit with us. No one could sleep. We paced and wept, terrified at the thought that Papa was undergoing interrogation and torture.

The doorbell rang unexpectedly around two in the morning. We stumbled over each other to answer the door. I was stunned to see the Minister of Agriculture standing there, smiling at me. He stepped aside and Papa moved into view.

My mother and I were screaming and crying. We were mindless with joy.

Papa was smiling broadly. 'I was about to be taken for interrogation, and who pops in the door? My friend.' He patted the minister on his shoulder.

Our fear did not leave us after we learned the reason for Papa's arrest. Members of the Khail tribe had recently started an uprising against the Russian regime.

In the new Afghanistan, everyone was considered guilty of *something*. After Shair's death, Papa had become the symbolic head of the Khail tribe. He was so well loved and respected by Khail tribal members that he was suspected of being the one who had called for the rebellion. Nothing frightened the new regime as much as tribal rebellion in a country populated by fierce tribal warriors.

Had the minister not saved Papa, he might have died during interrogation, because torture was popular with the new government and Papa's health was not sound. Papa would have been unable to tell the interrogators what they wanted to hear, because the Khail uprising was news to him, although I suspect he was secretly pleased about it. As for me, I was bursting with pride. Our Khail tribesmen were upholding our cherished honour. But later we learned that the Khail tribesmen were targeted for annihilation by the regime. Many thousands were arrested and sent for detention or worse.

My anger was mounting.

The most horrible news came when the government published a list of names of those arrested since the coup. There were thousands of names, including Sabor Khail and Mohammed Khail. There was no specific charge against Sabor and Mohammed, who had never broken the law in their lives. They were arrested only because they were two educated and accomplished men belonging to an influential tribe. Long before the coup, the Communists had made plans to eliminate everyone deemed to be part of the intelligentsia. They would leave no men alive capable of plotting or leading a rebellion against the regime. Many of our young men were shipped to Siberia, to be worked to death. Others were murdered according to the whim of their interrogators.

By the side of their names, the Khail brothers Sabor and Mohammed were listed as having 'died in prison of natural causes'.

Dead? *Dead?* There is no word to describe our family's despair. We .could not imagine those two handsome and friendly young men dead. Although our family pleaded for the return of their bodies, our pleas went unanswered. Later, through a friend in the government we finally learned how they died. Sabor and Mohammed had been interrogated by one of the most vicious brutes in the new regime during their months of imprisonment. Both brothers had suffered horrible injuries under torture. Neither ever confessed to working against the regime, because they were innocent. Then one day they were taken from their cells. My cousins were giddy with relief, thinking the nightmare was finally behind them. They believed they were returning to their wives and children. Instead, they were taken for a ride on a Soviet helicopter. While on the helicopter they were cruelly taunted, told that their lives were not worth a single Soviet bullet. Over a barren area they were tossed out of the helicopter, their perfect bodies broken as they landed on the rocks of the land they had loved.

The image of their final moments was too horrible to bear.

I was so angry I had no tears. For the first time in my life, I felt myself capable of murder.

One fateful day, Papa gave me permission to drive to collect a girlfriend so that we could treat ourselves to an ice cream. On the way I had to pass over one of Kabul's main bridges. Just as I was approaching the bridge, I saw two Russian women walking across. They were laughing and talking as though they didn't have a care in the world. Suddenly my fury rose. I thought to myself: those two bitches must surely know that their men are imprisoning and killing young Afghan men. Perhaps it was one of their husbands who had tossed Sabor and Mohammed out of the helicopter.

I was gripped by a mad courage, and focused on those two Russian women as if they were the source of every Afghan sorrow. I jerked the steering wheel round and floored the gas pedal. The car engine roared as I bore down on the women. They heard the roar of the engine and glanced behind them to see a car swerving wildly at them. One of the women nimbly grabbed the railing and heaved herself up and over into the river not far below.

The second woman attempted the same agile ploy but she was a bit chubby and lost her footing and fell down on the bridge. I could have run her over as she was spinning around on the ground, but at the last minute I found I did not have a murderer's heart. I wrenched the wheel to the left, veering away from her. To make good my escape, I pressed the gas pedal and tore away. In my rear-view mirror I could see the woman on the bridge jump to her feet to stare after me.

I felt no regret. Rather, I enjoyed a surge of exhilaration. When in conflict with pure evil, all is fair, I told myself. My cause justified the means.

I took a few deep breaths and calmly drove on to collect my girlfriend. While eating our ice cream, she commented that I seemed more relaxed than she had seen me since the coup. I was tempted to tell her about my murderous morning, but something made me hold back. My spirits were lifted for days to come.

Approximately a week later my father came home visibly upset. He shouted, 'Maryam, someone saw our car on the bridge. They are looking for a young woman who was driving our vehicle. What happened? What did you do there?'

I'm sure the blood drained from my face, but I didn't answer.

'Maryam, you are in big trouble this time! I was told that the girl driving my car was going to be charged with a serious crime.'

My mind was racing. I should have known that my stupid act would be traced back to our door. I was one of the few Afghan girls who drove in Kabul.

Someone probably gave a good description of our family car, and the fact it was being driven by a young woman. Perhaps they even memorized the number plate, which was *S 54189 Kabul*. Remembering Uncle Hakim's warning, I began to fidget, becoming increasingly uneasy. What would be the consequences?

When my father saw the expression on my face, he knew I was definitely guilty.

'Maryam,' he repeated with a snarl, 'you are in *big* trouble.'

I bit my lip but still made no reply. I couldn't bear to confide the truth of that day, knowing it would make my father even more upset.

My gentle father, who had never raised a hand against his wife or his daughters, grabbed a chair and came at me with it raised high.

Terrified, I dropped and rolled under the dining table. I screamed when I heard a thunderous crash. My father had broken the chair against the table top.

I held my breath, thinking that any moment he would pull me from underneath the table and give me the beating of my life.

Just then my mother ran into the room. 'What? Ajab? *What?*'

My father told her: 'Maryam committed some kind of crime in our car. But she refuses to tell me what she did.'

My mother screamed. 'Dear God! Why do I have a child like Maryam? Why does Maryam want to kill us all?'

My father stalked away.

I crept to my room and closed the door, avoiding contact with anyone.

To my profound terror, a team from the KHAD secret police arrived at our home later that afternoon. I tiptoed out into the hallway near the sitting room to listen.

The KHAD were polite, but I knew they would not be courteous for very long.

I held my breath as they informed my father that one of the wives of a high-ranking Russian general had been walking on the morning in question, out with a friend on a stroll. An assassin driving my father's automobile had tried to murder both women. The two women had escaped, but both were being treated for minor injuries and psychological trauma. Now the general meant to find the person who had tried to murder his wife. He was determined to make an example of this culprit.

'The vehicle was yours,' they told my father. 'Who was the woman? Was it your daughter, Maryam?'

My father's voice was low, but calm. 'You have the wrong girl. Maryam would not have done such a thing. I am not even sure she had my car on that day.'

The KHAD security officials finally left, but not

before they told my father: 'You must bring your daughter in for questioning tomorrow morning.'

After seeing the KHAD security men to the door, I heard my father call a high-ranking acquaintance, the Minister of Planning, another good friend who happened to be in the government. Father told him, 'I must meet with you. *No. Now.*' He put the phone down and dashed out of the door.

Trembling, I crept back to my bedroom. I cursed myself for lacking self-control, for putting my poor father through such anguish. Perhaps my entire family would be put to death because of my outrageous conduct. And I hadn't even killed the women. I was not a very effective freedom fighter, I admitted to myself.

My father was away for more than three hours. When he returned, he discussed the situation with my mother. My father was too angry even to look at me, so Mother came into my room to tell me what to expect.

Papa had confessed the truth to his friend that his stupid daughter had lost her mind and tried to run over a couple of Russian ladies. Knowing I would be put to death if KHAD had confirmation that I was the culprit, my father and his friend devised a viable story, blaming the incident on the wife of my father's French business partner. She had accompanied her husband into the country on a business trip. On the day in question, the woman had borrowed our family automobile. She was unfamiliar with our car, and while driving had lost control. She didn't know the language, and was too frightened to stop and offer assistance. My father did not even know the full details of the incident until KHAD visited his home. In fact, he was unaware that pedestrians were involved, thinking instead that his partner's wife had simply run off the road.

The truth was that Father's French business partner had indeed visited Kabul, but the couple had left the country a day before the incident. We had to pray KHAD would not look up their travel documents and check the date they departed Kabul. Of course, this meant that my father's partner and his wife could never again travel into Afghanistan, at least not as long as the Communists were in charge.

I had made a big mess of everything.

My father's friend at the ministry was so disgusted by my behaviour that he warned my father that never again would he cover for me. If I got into any more trouble, I would have to deal with KHAD on my own. I was properly warned.

My mother cornered me and spoke some harsh truths to me. 'Maryam, you are a headstrong, stubborn and wilful child. You are naive, immature and show a complete disregard for the sanctity of life, not only for the lives of strangers, but for the lives of your family. You are a terrible disappointment to me, and to your father.'

I knew in my heart that my mother was right but I thought it should count for something that I was idealistic and had acted out of patriotism. Russians were occupying my country and murdering my friends and relatives, and Afghans are known for their fighting spirit. I was a true Afghan. I only felt bad about endangering my family. For that reason I offered a sincere apology to my parents, and to the minister who had helped us.

When I apologized, my mother nodded, but said nothing.

My father's reaction cut me to the core. He stared into my eyes for such a long time I believed he would never speak. Finally he said, 'Just get out of my face.'

The following day my poor father had to return to the KHAD headquarters. He went alone. 'I can't trust you not to try and assault the officials I must pacify,' he muttered.

We became increasingly nervous because Papa did not return for the entire day. He was kept for many hours, the officials questioning him over the same points time and again, trying to trip him up.

Although Papa was not a warrior spirit, he was extremely intelligent and knew he must remain calm and focused if he was to convince the KHAD that I was innocent, and that the driver had been the

French woman now out of their reach. The KHAD were not looking for a fight with the French government, although we heard later that the general had pushed to make an international incident out of the episode, but miraculously they finally let the matter go.

I was saved, once again.

But never again did I feel happy in my country. From that moment my parents treated me like a leper. Every privilege was taken away, and they had devised a strict punishment regime. I could not see any of my friends outside school. Never again was I allowed to drive. The maids at our home were given a long vacation and I was told that I would be doing all the housework. I had to rise at five every morning and clean before school. After school I was taken to my father's office where I had to do the filing. Other than during school hours, my parents refused to let me out of their sight.

My life was a great misery.

Nevertheless, I graduated from Malalai. Surprisingly, despite the fact the Russian teachers had me marked down as a rebel, I was offered a scholarship to attend Moscow University. But I so hated everything Russian that I turned the scholarship down.

My parents were in double despair, worried about my behaviour and also disappointed that their youngest daughter would not attend medical school.

The Cuban Ambassador to Afghanistan was a family friend who offered to arrange a scholarship to a university in Havana. I felt happy with the offer until my parents told me that Cuba was a puppet of the Soviet Union, and that I would receive a communist education there.

I could attend Kabul University, but my parents were determined to get their insurgent daughter out of Afghanistan. They knew that, if I remained, I would be unable to restrain my hatred for the regime and I would end up in prison, or worse.

I loved the idea of studying in India where Nadia was still a student, although it seemed impossible for me to join her there. Once the Soviet Union took over my country, they no longer allowed travel to non-communist countries other than for officially sponsored business.

Thousands of Afghan people fled the country illegally, travelling by car or by foot over the mountains into Pakistan or even Iran, but such a trip was a dangerous undertaking. Many people were caught and returned to Kabul to face prosecution and death as traitors. My parents said that such a journey was out of the question.

The decision was made that I would spend the year at home learning English, and so I enrolled in an English language course. Then one day, several months after my crime, my father told me that I had been a model of good behaviour. Due to my repentance, I would be allowed to have lunch alone.

I was so weary of constant supervision that I was overjoyed over a simple free lunch. I walked from my father's office and went into the nearest restaurant, the Sitra, which served delicious kabobs and burgers. Never have I been so happy to be alone. After finishing my meal, I casually strolled back to my father's office. I found myself walking past two parked official Russian automobiles. Driven by an instinct I cannot explain, like a robot under orders, I walked close to those vehicles, opened my purse and slipped out my Swiss army knife, which was always in my bag. I looked around to see that no one was watching before slashing the two tyres of each vehicle on the side of the pavement.

A sweet release of pent-up anger swept through my body. I returned to my father's office, humming.

I was not the only Afghan citizen to feel thus. With every passing day, Afghanistan heated up even more with unrest and violence. In February 1979, the US Ambassador to Afghanistan was kidnapped and killed. In March there was a mutiny by Afghan soldiers stationed in Herat. In August there was a military revolt in an army fort near Kabul when a rebel group attacked the government forces there, resulting in a major military battle. In September further chaos erupted when President Taraki was overthrown in a coup. Hafizullah Amin became President, announcing that his rule marked 'the beginning of a better socialist order'.

Later in September a general amnesty was announced. The government thought it would placate angry citizens who hated the socialist government, but they were wasting their time. The Afghan people had endured enough. They were finished with the Communists. That's when our Muslim neighbours and friends – Pakistan and Saudi Arabia – began to arm our Afghan rebels. Since the Soviet Union was America's enemy in the middle of the Cold War, we learned that America and England were also lining up to help us, and also China. We wept with joy that such big, important countries were taking our side.

I was elated, finding myself praying for war, knowing that was what it would take to purge my country of the Communists.

During this time, our family luck also changed.

At the end of October 1979, the new president Hafizullah Amin made it known to the educated elite that he would allow some people to travel to India for medical treatment. He did not make a public announcement, so the offer was never open to ordinary people. He would grant a special three-day pass to those who were truly ill. All you had to do was to pay the government 25,000 Afghani dollars (500 US dollars).

We received a telephone call from one of our cousins still working in the government. He knew that our entire family was afraid of what violent act I might next commit that would get everyone in the Khail and Hassen families imprisoned or killed. He also knew that I had expressed an interest in attending medical college in India.

His advice was: 'Use Maryam's accident in India, when she injured her leg, as your medical reason.' He named two relatives who had good relations with the authorities and suggested: 'Tell them to escort Maryam to the President's headquarters tomorrow where she can give details about her injury and fill out a passport application for India.'

The following day my cousins escorted me to President Amin's headquarters, where I was presented with an application form on which I had to write why I needed to travel to India. After writing my tale of woe, I turned in my application and waited. At two that afternoon I found myself facing the Afghan President. Unbelievably, our head of government insisted on speaking personally with every person who made an application for a medical visa.

I told the President that I needed yet another operation to correct my ankle. I handed him my money, and a medical statement signed by an Indian orthopedic surgeon that I had had in my possession since the days after my accident several years before. Thankfully it was undated, and indicated that Maryam Khail had undergone several operations to correct the injuries received after being threatened by a horned cow and then run over by an automobile, and that she would need another operation. I also requested that my father be allowed to accompany me, since I was a young woman and no Afghan family would allow a female to travel alone.

As I finished my little speech I looked up to see President Amin smiling impishly at me. I so hated President Amin for what he had done to my country that I was surprised to find him extremely handsome and charming. He had large brown eyes that twinkled with mischief. His silvery hair was thick and very deftly fashioned. He was dressed impeccably.

He looked at me with appreciation in his eyes and began to flirt with me. 'Ah! Maryam Khail. Are you really going to India for surgery? Or are you going to act in Bollywood?' He grinned widely.

I was taken aback. I was a young girl still in my teens. For me, he was an old man, albeit a handsome old man. I managed to force a smile at his little joke, replying, 'I don't believe I am ready for the movies quite yet, Mr President.'

He chuckled, then without further ado he signed my form with a flourish. 'You are going to India!'

As soon as the form was in my hands, I walked away. I heard him call out to me as I exited his office: 'When you come back to Kabul, come and see me.'

Our president's conduct really was unseemly. I didn't answer.

Although I was joyful to be leaving, I was also sad and apprehensive because my poor mother would be left alone in Kabul. Also, several cousins had put in their application for leaving Afghanistan. Only one cousin, Layla, was granted her request. Another cousin, named Mona, was refused. Many family members would have to remain in Afghanistan and suffer whatever the future held for our beloved country and its trapped citizens.

There were a few more hurdles. Papa and I had to pass a criminal check, but we were unconcerned because of the protection of our friends at the ministries. Within a month we were issued our passports and our visas from the Indian Embassy, and booked our flights on Air India.

Never once did I believe I was leaving my country for ever, yet leaving without a planned return is more difficult than I imagined. Once all the arrangements had been made, the reality set in. Soon I would be leaving the land I loved, not knowing what the future might bring to my country or to my beloved family. And there was the question of when Mother would be allowed to join us. Freedom would be joyless without Mother.

That's when Papa told me that I could only pack a small bag so that we could keep up the official illusion that we were returning.

I was always a collector of little treasures. My heart felt heavy when I was warned that I could not risk taking my coin or stamp collection. For a long time I sat on the edge of my bed rummaging through my rare coins, my rocks and the scores of model cars I had saved since my tomboy childhood. I spent many, many hours poring over my stamp collection, given to me by Grandfather Hassen, who had passed on to me many rare and valuable stamps.

I was sad when I realized that the stamps and the coins were irreplaceable. As I hid them away in my room, I made a vow. 'I will be back. I will not lose these precious family treasures.'

With a big sigh I packed a few clothes, along with my diary, which had become as dear to me as a close friend. The following morning I went into our garden, scratched out a small pile of Afghan dirt and wrapped it carefully in a small cloth. I would carry the beloved soil of my country with me when I departed.

I couldn't even say goodbye to my friends and

family, for my parents no longer trusted me and worried that gossip about our plot to leave Afghanistan permanently might reach the ears of the officials. Only Mother's brother Omar and his young daughter knew we were leaving, and that was because they had graciously agreed to drive Papa and me to the airport. Mother would accompany us as well, but would return alone to our empty home.

December the twenty-seventh, 1979, arrived on a Thursday, the beginning of the Muslim weekend. Uncle Omar and his daughter arrived early. When we locked the door to our apartment behind us I felt nauseous, but said nothing, brushing away my tears. There were few words spoken on the short journey to Kabul airport.

The airport was more crowded and noisy than I could remember. We could barely shoulder our way through the swarming multitude. A large number of Afghan citizens seemed to have paid for a special medical pass to leave the country. That's when I realized the reason President Amin involved himself so personally with the medical exits. No doubt his pockets were bulging with the fees paid.

Our president was a thief; albeit a charming thief.

The family gathered in the waiting area and stood around while Papa and I settled into two seats. Our luck turned bad when two plainclothes policemen approached us. They checked our papers and passports as well as my medical documents before asking my father, 'You are leaving, too?'

My father's voice was very controlled. 'Yes. My daughter must have her follow-up surgery.'

The taller of the two agents looked at me with a smirk, saying, 'Take care of your injured leg in those high heels.'

I didn't respond although I was silently cursing myself for being so stupid as to wear shoes unsuitable for someone with an injured ankle and leg.

The two sat beside us, trying to find some reason to arrest us, I assumed. Praise Allah that our Air India flight was called a few minutes later. I began kissing and hugging my mother and uncle and cousin. Mother was weeping, which set off Papa and me too. Who knew when we would see her again?

As we left the waiting area I felt the eyes of the two policemen on me. I did my best to fake a limp, but I never was a great actress and I am sure they saw through me. But they made no move to stop us.

When Papa and I settled in our assigned seats, I began to weep in earnest. Despite everything, I loved my country. My great sorrow was linked to the feeling deep in my soul that I might never return.

Papa too was stricken by the emotion of the day. 'Daughter, I wanted nothing more than to live and die here, the country where I was born, the country where I should die.' He forced back a sob. 'This is a ghastly twilight to my life.'

He turned his head to look out of the window and I followed his gaze, wanting a last memory to treasure. We were both startled suddenly to notice numerous Soviet planes offloading tanks, armaments and personnel. Russian soldiers were running all over the tarmac. What was happening?

I gasped, and my father's complexion turned sallow.

Something very significant was about to happen in Afghanistan. Were we witnessing the Russian giant arriving to occupy our land by force?

My father began to shiver. He tightened his lips and turned to gaze intently out of the aeroplane window until we had lift-off. Throughout our two-hour flight to New Delhi, my poor father never spoke another word.

Chapter 11

For years New Delhi had been a place where our family vacationed. We had always arrived in the city in a happy mood of anticipation. But our mood was grave when we arrived on 27 December. Our first stop was to see Mr and Mrs Delep, a Hindu couple who had put us up on our vacations, who were startled by our unexpected arrival. But they were such good hosts that they had an elaborate Indian lunch prepared almost instantly. While we ate, Papa began to tell them about the bad times that had come to Afghanistan. They reacted with sympathy to our desperate plight.

I excused myself from the room so that I could discreetly retrieve the bag of Afghan soil from where I had hidden it in my bra. I walked back into the room and said, 'Papa, look. This is for you.'

Papa glanced at the bag of soil with a puzzled expression before recognizing its significance. He grabbed me in his arms and kissed my forehead and hair over and over.

After our meal ended, Mr Delep escorted us to the small, furnished two-bedroom house in Greater Klash Colony that we would rent from him. It was near his house, so the couple would continue to take care of our needs.

Hoping that the morning would bring an explanation of the Soviet military activity at the airport, I went to bed almost immediately, and slept soundly only because I was physically exhausted.

Early the next morning, Papa woke me with loud shouts. 'Maryam! Wake up! Maryam!'

He was listening to the BBC, his favourite radio station. 'Maryam! I can't believe it. The Russians! It was an invasion! As we were leaving, daughter! Afghanistan has just been occupied.'

I couldn't believe what I was hearing. 'What did you say?'

'They are all dead. The Russians killed President Amin and his entire family.'

'Dead?' I repeated in disbelief. It was impossible to imagine him dead. Although I hated him for bringing communism to my country, and had wanted him out of office and out of the country, he was not a man I would wish dead.

Of course, our first thoughts were of Mother and all our relatives. They were in danger. It was unbearable.

Then Nadia burst through the door. She was in

medical school in Bangalore, but Papa had called her upon our arrival and she had taken time off to meet us in New Delhi.

Papa explained to Nadia all that had occurred since she was last in Kabul. That's when I learned something I had not known before. Mother had insisted that Papa accompany me, rather than herself, because Papa was in danger of being arrested. A friend with high government connections had passed on a warning that the communist regime was putting in place a plan to exterminate all military officers who had formerly been loyal to the royal family. It made no difference if the officer was long retired. It was probable that Papa would have been arrested and executed if he had stayed.

It was imperative to get Mother out of Afghanistan as quickly as possible. First Papa tried the legal route, posting a letter to his friend in the ministry explaining that his cancer had returned, that I was undergoing surgery, and that Mother was desperately needed to take care of both of us. The minister wrote back giving us the bad news that Mother had been refused permission to visit us in India. He promised to continue his efforts on her behalf, but Papa knew it was useless. The Russians would not allow all members of one family to leave the country but insisted on holding some family members back as hostages. They believed we would return if they refused permission for Mother to leave.

Now Papa revealed that he had made arrangements for a smuggler to take Mother out of the country if her official permit did not come through soon. He had to bring her out at all costs.

I felt a terrible anxiety, knowing that if Mother were caught when sneaking out of Afghanistan, the current regime might execute her on the spot.

Papa placed a call to Mother in Kabul, telling her, 'You must visit your aunt.' That was their code word for Mother to contact the smuggler.

The smuggler arrived the day of the call, and brought Mother a dress, trousers and matching scarf to wear, a traditional nomadic costume. The dirty outfit was permeated with the stink of human sweat so that Mother would not only look like a nomadic tribal woman but would smell like one too. Mother later reported that the stench of body odour was so strong it made her retch, but she forced herself to wear it nevertheless.

Father had arranged for one of Mother's nephews, a young man named Qaseem, to be smuggled out on the same trip. Qaseem was happy to be chosen as every member of the Hassen family was now keen to flee Afghanistan, as well as many members of our Khail family.

Our homeland was being abandoned by all given the opportunity.

When Mother stepped out of the door, the smuggler's car was waiting outside. She saw Qaseem sitting in the car. He leapt out to greet his auntie and settle her in for the journey.

Mother later told us that at that precise moment she was struck by a frightening premonition. Something told her urgently not to get into that car. She was sure there was grave danger waiting for her on the journey.

Qaseem said, 'Auntie, let's go,' and the smuggler growled, 'Get in.'

Mother pulled back, in a growing panic. 'No! I cannot go,' she told the smuggler. 'I have decided against it.'

The smuggler got angry. 'Get in, I said!' He grabbed her arm and tried to push her into the back seat of the car. 'Get in now!'

Mother slapped at his hands, struggling. 'No! I am not going, I told you.'

The smuggler's face turned red. 'I will not return your money!'

Mother replied, 'I understand. But I cannot go.' She looked at her shocked nephew. 'I cannot go,' she told him. 'I have a bad feeling. This will have a bad end, my nephew, I feel it in my heart.'

Qaseem tried to reason with her. 'Auntie, it is your nerves. Come with us. This is the only way out of Afghanistan.'

But Mother refused, and the driver stomped around the car and slid into the driver's seat. 'I will not return the money,' he snapped, before driving away at high speed, taking Qaseem with him.

Mother was sad that she had allowed her one opportunity to flee to get away, yet was convinced she had made the right decision.

When Mother called us in Delhi, Papa was upset that his wife could alter his carefully laid plans based on a 'feeling'.

For three months Mother remained alone and lonely in Afghanistan while we missed her terribly in India. Before long Papa decided that we would move from New Delhi to Bangalore to be with Nadia, saying that it was silly for the three of us to be separated.

Meanwhile the entire family grew frantic with worry about Qaseem, who had never appeared over the border in Pakistan. He was unheard of from the time he had left Afghanistan with the smuggler. Papa was beginning to realize that whatever instinct it was that Mother had followed, it had been correct.

Some months later Qaseem's worried family received a telephone call from a prison complex in the east of Afghanistan. The smuggler and his clients had been arrested. All had received a beating as well as an eight-year prison sentence. We worried that poor Qaseem would not survive his lengthy sentence because prisons in Afghanistan under the Communists were very harsh. Certainly, my frail mother would never have survived an eight-year prison term.

Papa was never again to ridicule Mother's instincts and premonitions: in fact, he grew to quite respect them.

In Bangalore we found a quaint little hotel that catered for British expatriates. The hotel had a smattering of small guesthouses on the property, and we made one of those bungalows our home. Since Papa was not working and I was not enrolled in school, and Nadia was busy with her medical studies, Papa and I were lonely and bored. Most troubling, Afghanistan was always in the news. Since we had arrived in India, Afghan Muslim rebels had revolted. The Soviet Union had responded by sending in 40,000 soldiers to defeat the warriors.

I knew that for however long it took, Afghan warriors would not give up the fight. Eventually, the mighty Russians would be defeated. It might take one year or it might take fifty years, but Afghans would overthrow the Russian invaders. Afghan people had never submitted to invaders. Obviously the leaders of the Soviet Union had failed to read our history.

The tide was already turning. Due to the ongoing Cold War and the friction between the Soviet Union and America and Europe, the rest of the world focused on the fate of my country. President Jimmy Carter repeatedly warned the Russians of their folly. A special session of the UN General Assembly passed resolution 104-18 calling for the immediate withdrawal of foreign troops from Afghanistan. Foreign journalists were reporting massacres and assassinations.

Afghanistan was exploding into war. Watching the news was a special agony, for the screen would be filled with hordes of refugees, burqa-clad women herding four or five little children each, streaming over the border and into Pakistan to be dumped in tent cities. Were relatives of ours who had once lived the good life shivering in those tents? Not in a hundred lifetimes could I absorb what was happening to my country and to my countrymen and women.

Our chief worry was Mother. Although she had members of her close-knit family near by, we were frantic for her safety. During the month of February 1980 there was a general strike and violent demonstrations in Kabul and other major Afghan cities. The communist militia inflicted heavy casualties on the demonstrators. In April of that same year, Kabul University students staged a huge demonstration, resulting in the deaths of fifty of them. When hearing that story Papa breathed a sigh of relief, saying, 'Praise Allah that we are out of Kabul. You would have been a leader of those demonstrators, daughter, wouldn't you? Then what would have happened to us?'

In June, several tribal groups known as the Mujahedin (a Persian word meaning warriors) united inside Afghanistan. Fighters from neighbouring Muslim countries began to join the fray. People from around the world came to help the resistance against the Soviet army.

That's when we received some rare good news. Uncle Hakim, his wife Rabeha and daughters Zarmina and Zeby had received permission to leave Afghanistan. They were travelling to India and from there to France. Later they might join Farid in Bahrain. Yet our happiness for them was tempered by the fact that with their departure, Mother's little family circle in Kabul was shrinking, making us feel even more anxious for her safety.

Papa had kept in touch with his friend from the ministry and every week or so I would hear him utter a great big sigh before settling at his desk to pen an eloquent plea for his help. Then, unexpectedly, Papa received the news we had longed for. Papa's friend had been quietly working to obtain official authorization for Mother's visa to India. Finally he had won approval for her departure and Mother was leaving Kabul the following day.

Our joy was boundless when Mother came

walking through the airport gate as casually as a
weekend visitor, as though our reunion had not been
a matter of life or death. It had taken us six months
to be together again, the longest six months of all our
lives.

Meanwhile Papa had been busy calling on his
numerous connections, many of which were made
during the time he lived in Europe. He told us that his
good friend who worked for the CIA was coming for
a visit. When the American arrived at our home,
Mother and I were shocked to see that the secret
agent was a tall, attractive female.

After the initial surprise, this made me feel pulled
towards America, a country where women could do
anything. Papa and I were delighted when the agent
informed us that she could have our visas ready by
the end of the week and could arrange our flights at
that same time. We were going to America, or so I
thought.

But Mother was against our settling in America.
She argued: 'They are all gangsters. We will not fit in
with such people.'

Papa told her, 'Yes, some Americans in Chicago are
gangsters, but most Americans are rather ordinary
people.'

'The life will be too tough there, Ajab,' Mother
said. 'You will have to find work as a taxi driver, or
a doorman. Nadia will have to give up her medical

studies. She and I will scrub floors. Maryam won't have a chance. She will remain uneducated. Her job will be flipping hamburgers in a cheap dive.'

I bit my lip to keep from laughing. Mother had seen too many American movies.

Papa and I put our case for moving to America.

Mother and Nadia argued for us to remain in India.

Papa faltered when Mother told him that she had a 'feeling' that something terrible would happen should we leave everything familiar and flee to America.

I, too, had a 'feeling' that Mother was pretending, and using her 'instinct' to convince Papa. But I didn't dare make such an accusation. The most important goal had been reached: our family was once again all together. Anything else, I could endure, although I did believe we were foolish not to exchange living in India for living in America, a rich land that beckoned with luxuriant promise.

Nadia fully concurred with Mother, and Papa was unable to resist his wife and eldest daughter. The decision was made to turn down the American visas and remain in India.

It was the wrong decision. From that moment, nothing went right in our lives.

I loved India from my first day there years before. I had enjoyed every vacation. But once it was decided that India would be our permanent home, I was aware of living in a strange country with foreign customs and languages. My heart told me that India was not the place for my future. I became increasingly listless, finding little to my liking.

For all exiles, the greatest enemy is too much time. We were all lost. Papa and Mother became so depressed that their health was affected. Out of despair they decided to travel to France and visit Uncle Hakim and his family for a month.

They were happier upon their return from the trip, reporting that my dear cousins Zeby and Zarmina were adjusting well. The big news was that Farid had taken a trip to London and while there had met an Afghan girl who had stolen his heart. Farid was getting married!

We were all shocked because the handsome Farid had been a dedicated playboy his whole life, with many girls seeking his attention. Despite our doubts, we were happy if Farid was happy.

My spirits lifted hearing about our family and seeing my parents again after a month's absence. I didn't know the great sadness that loomed in our immediate future.

Within a week of their return, Papa became very ill. He was rushed to the hospital, where doctors found new tumours in his bladder. Surgery followed by other treatments was needed. Once again we lived in fear that we would lose our rock.

Papa was in the hospital for several weeks, and with Nadia in school, Mother and I took turns staying with Papa. I handled the night shift and Mother managed the day shift.

Then one day Mother failed to return to the hospital.

When she didn't appear, we were frantic that she had met with an accident. My memories of a horned cow created specific unease. Anything could happen in a country where cows were allowed to roam free. I was in a dilemma, not knowing whether to stay with Papa, or leave him to hunt for Mother.

Then Nadia burst through the door saying, 'Mother has been taken ill. She has severe abdominal pain. She is undergoing tests.'

Doctors gave various reasons for Mother's discomfort, but none were thought to be serious. I spent weeks running from one hospital bed to the other, until finally both my parents were discharged. Papa recovered rapidly, but Mother grew more pale and ill with each passing day.

As 1981 ended, after seeing several specialists, we received the most dreadful news. Mother was diagnosed with stomach cancer. The cancer had spread. Her condition was terminal. For months she remained in the hospital, but once the hospital had done their best, we took Mother home where I could nurse her. I bathed her. I fed her. I massaged her. I loved her. But despite my care, her condition deteriorated at an alarming speed. She whimpered in pain until the doctor started her on morphine and taught me to give her injections every four hours.

During the spring of 1982, my darling mother became emaciated, with sunken eyes. I would carry her withered frame from room to room in my arms. One night she made a desperate plea. 'Daughter, if you truly love me, then help me to die.'

That bitter night I was tortured by nervous doubt. I awoke early on 11 June 1982, not knowing whether I could go through with it. That morning she stared into my eyes without speaking. Her heart spoke to mine, reminding me of her final request. The hardest moment of my life came when I gave my mother her next injection. I consciously increased the dosage.

Looking intently at me, she gave a satisfied nod. My face would be the last image of her life on earth. She was my mother and she had loved me for my whole life. And I loved her enough to fulfil the most difficult request anyone can ask.

I held her tiny wasted body. We locked eyes for a final moment.

Then, just like that, my mother was gone for ever.

Chapter 12

On 30 October 1982, approximately four months after my mother's death, Papa and I took the heady leap from India to America, the land of my childhood dreams. Although we had longed to return to a peaceful Afghanistan, that dream was impossible. We would have been arrested and executed had we returned to our home in Kabul.

Safely in America, we would have been in bliss but for the troubling situation in Afghanistan. The Muslim Mujahedin insurgency remained locked in a hellish military stalemate against the Soviet troops. After four years of Russian military presence, our country had become a satellite of Moscow: the Communists still ruled our cities while guerrillas controlled the countryside.

When we first arrived, we were met at the airport in Washington DC by Mother's sister Auntie Shagul, her son Nasir, his wife Khatol and another cousin, Razia. Auntie Shagul strongly resembled my beautiful mother in physical appearance and in conduct, so when she smothered my forehead with kisses, her love and warmth consoled me.

Many of Mother's Hassen family members had made the journey to America before us. Due to their unique diplomatic contacts, they had avoided the dismal life familiar to many Afghan refugees, who, having been accustomed to their own homes, were suddenly thrust into a tent city to live in idleness, poverty, bad health and misery. Shagul had setttled in northern Virginia. A few relatives on my father's side had also put down roots in the vicinity.

I was in a hypnotic trance for the first few months, finding my feet in such a safe and comfortable new environment. I was eager to experience everything of the country I had come to know through films and popular music, but I soon discovered it was a land of confusing contradictions. The Americans of my dreams were rich and carefree, living in beautiful mansions, eating the finest foods, in loving relationships, spending their evenings dancing to disco tunes.

But the country and the people were more complicated than that. Very few Americans were wealthy enough to have no worries. Most people I saw lived modestly, or were downright poor, and many were hard-working immigrants who had little time for dancing. That was my first shock.

A second shock came after observing how

American parents and children related to each other. I was accustomed to a culture where fathers rule supreme and expect total obedience. Afghan children did not talk back to their parents. They were seen and not heard. American children were much more self-assertive and argumentative, and could be seen throwing tantrums in public. In the supermarket, I heard kids arguing with their parents over their choice of foods, and in the shops heard their demands for certain toys or fashions. Such cheek was unheard of in my culture.

A third shock lay in store. With my newly acquired short skirts and bikinis, I longed to spread my wings, to be freed from my father's control and our traditional moral taboos. In America the rights of women had found a voice, and I wanted to be a part of that movement. But to my consternation, Papa and other relatives expected me to continue living the life of an extremely conservative Muslim girl, even in the heart of a land that knew nothing and cared less about our traditions. In unison, my relatives decreed there would be no disco dancing for Maryam Khail.

American girls were not only free to dress how they liked, go where they liked without a chaperone and be friends with boys, there was also a sexual freedom in America that no Afghan girl could have ever imagined. Soon after arriving, I met a lovely American girl who was pregnant. I inquired about her husband and drew back in horror to hear she was unwed. Confused, I blurted out, 'But if you are not married, then how could you be pregnant?'

She snapped at me: 'This is America. If you have a problem with it, go back to your own country.'

Papa and I soon moved out of Auntie Shagul's home and into a neat little apartment not far away. I was quickly offered a job at an Afghan restaurant. Although I was a waitress and not a short-order cook, I remembered my mother's biggest fear that America for me would mean an unsatisfactory life of flipping burgers.

The job, in my mind, was a transitional position. I was determined to go to university. I vowed to save my money and buy a car so I could drive myself to university. Meanwhile I worked. I was soon popular with the restaurant's clientele, who were mainly Afghan exiles like myself. I felt quite contented, although the same could not be said of Papa. After the initial stimulation of visiting all his Afghan acquaintances who had settled in Virginia, he became very dejected. His misery had one source. When Mother died, she seemed to have taken half Papa's vitality with her into the grave. He had wept for weeks after her death, his tears acting as a sedative to his misery. Although the tears had ceased, his depression lingered.

My fourth shock came in the form of a glut of

marriage proposals. There were many unmarried Afghan men living in the area, and it appeared that every one of them was seeking a bride. My father's family background and good reputation meant that many men wanted to link their family to my own. Soon Papa was fully occupied once more – in fielding requests for the hand of his daughter.

Papa took the task to heart. He became driven to see his youngest married, and he insisted that I must marry an Afghan Pashtun. It was my sister's fault. Shortly before Mother died, Nadia had confessed a shocking truth. My sister had secretly fallen in love and married a stranger. Not only was her chosen partner a man unknown to our parents, Nadia had broken a number of taboos: marrying a man not of our tribe or of our Muslim sect, a man not even of our country. She had married an Iranian Shiite Muslim.

For those unfamiliar with the two main Islamic sects, they are called Sunni and Shiite. The Sunni and Shiite have been in disagreement since the death of our Prophet Mohammed, who failed to name a specific successor. Those closest to the Prophet disagreed about who would lead Islam. History tells us that a terrible brawl ensued, with each group naming their own favoured successor, and Islam split into two groups over the quarrel. Now, after centuries of bitter quarrelling, the two sects are still divided. Sunni parents sternly object to their children marrying into Shiite families and Shiite families feel no less passionate. People have been murdered for less.

At the beginning Nadia tried to soften the blow by telling my parents that she was in love with a Shiite and *planned* to marry. Only I knew she had gone ahead and married him. However, as far as my parents were concerned, this was almost as bad as a marriage anyway. The shock overwhelmed them. Yet they lived in the hope that Nadia would come to her senses and the marriage would never happen.

Both were distracted from Nadia's illicit love affair by Mother's illness and death. The moment we settled in Virginia, Papa had time to dwell on his eldest daughter's disobedience. Since he was helpless to control Nadia so far away in India, he focused on his youngest child, pondering on the endless marriage proposals coming my way.

I was not consulted, because Papa's heart and head were still in Afghanistan, where choosing a spouse is considered much too important to be left to one's children. I grew frantic. The last thing I desired was a husband. I was only twenty years old, new to a very exciting country, with plans of pursuing my education. I politely asked Papa to wait, to give me a little time. He and Mother had always preached their aversion to marrying before finishing one's education.

But ruled by his Pashtun fears that his daughter would run wild unless she was bound to a husband, Papa stubbornly moved ahead.

My stomach grew knots. I felt myself caught in a great family drama, all the people I loved living for the moment I would be married. I had never missed Mother more, for I knew that if only she had lived she would have stopped the rush for marriage. Mother's goal for her daughters was to see college diplomas tucked in their pockets before watching them walk down the marriage aisle. But Mother was dead in her grave, far away in India. She could no longer protect me.

I was startled when the rest of my family threw their undivided support behind Papa. Suddenly a huge family campaign was unleashed against a twenty-year-old girl. Auntie Shagul quietly reminded me of my familial obligation and duty. 'Losing your mother has been so difficult for your father,' she sighed. 'The strain of living in a new country and worrying about Nadia's unfortunate romance is too much for your father. Don't you disobey him as well.'

I even received a telephone call from Uncle Hakim in France, the conversation drifting to Papa's state of mind. 'Your father is lonely, Maryam. He needs something to make him feel joyful again. A grandson would bring him out of his misery.' I grunted, knowing that I was the one expected to deliver that child.

I knew that my position was perilous when other relatives made my life their business and echoed like a chorus: 'God will see this, Maryam. He will reward you. God will make you the happiest woman in the world.'

Nothing mattered to my family as much but that I marry, and marry soon.

I had always sworn I would never marry against my will. I was too intimate with the details of tragic lives lived by women like Grandmother Mayana and Cousin Amina, and so many other good women. But guilt over my father's grief, and a desire to be a good daughter, created a great conflict with my youthful vow.

For months I swam against the tide, brushing off talk of marriage. I hoped that Papa would weary of interviewing potential husbands. I prayed that something or someone would intervene. I grew more and more frantic with each passing day. My heart lived in my throat, as I waited for Papa to tell me he had selected my husband. Never have I felt so alone, so anguished. Alone against the united will of my family, I felt my resistance wavering.

One day Papa felt ill. He told me he did not believe he was long for this world, and that he would soon be joining Mother. Such talk created a moment of such weakness in me that I finally gave in. I bowed my head, and with a forced smile, trying to feel good that my actions were sure to please everyone, I said, 'Papa. If it makes you happy for me to marry, I will marry. I don't care who you pick to be my husband. As long as you are happy, I shall be happy.'

Papa's health rallied immediately. Suddenly he was vigorous, and organized meetings with several potential grooms by phone.

I felt some relief that I had made my poor Papa so happy, but after he retired for a nap, I retched until I was weak. I cursed myself for giving in.

My obedience won me praise from every corner. I was the good daughter. In spite of my personal feelings, I would do my father's bidding. Unlike my sister, I was faithful to our Pashtun tradition.

For a brief period of time I felt some pleasure and even anticipation. I believed there would be advantages to agreeing to an arranged marriage. Single girls were not allowed to go to clubs. But as soon as I married, I could go dancing. I was so naive that I was stupid. In my stupidity, I failed to see this was the most important battle of my life.

Soon Papa came to me with the news that he had selected a groom, and told me that the man of his choice was a man loaded with every virtue.

My husband-to-be was a man called Kaiss. He was thirty-five years old, fifteen years my senior. He was five feet nine inches tall. He was not ugly. He was not handsome either. He was a Pashtun, and from the same region of southern Afghanistan as our family. Papa had known his father in his youth, although their acquaintance had ended then. It was most important for my father that his daughter would marry a Pashtun.

I was told that the groom was eager to marry the daughter of Ajab Khail, the Khan of the Khail tribe, albeit my father's was an honorary title.

Kaiss wooed my father with exaggerated courtesy and repeated promises. He would be my father's 'son', not his 'son-in-law'. He agreed with all my father's conditions for the marriage to move forward.

'Yes, of course, Maryam must complete her college education. I will make certain of that,' he vowed with a smooth voice as he looked at me with undisguised pride in his eyes. 'I have a good job at a hotel. Your daughter's studies will come before everything else, even the food I put in my mouth.'

Well, at least he is gentle and compliant, I said to myself. I forgot that too many Afghan men will pretend to be something they are not to get what they want.

Nadia happened to be on a rare visit from medical school in India. She had not yet told Papa that she was secretly married to a man whose background was so repugnant to the Pashtun. My sister was in a heated rush for me to marry Kaiss, thinking that the moment of Papa's greatest happiness would be a good opportunity for her to confess to her marriage. Papa would be so exultant with my wedding that he might be less offended by her own.

'He seems very nice.' Nadia smiled at me. 'You should marry as soon as possible.'

'Yes, it will be easy for you to bring an Iranian home once Papa is happy with my Pashtun,' I muttered sarcastically.

'Who are you, Maryam, a princess waiting for your prince charming? You don't have anyone else in your life, do you? For Allah's sake, marry this Kaiss. Get it over with.' My sister looked at me coyly. 'Maryam, if I were in your place, I would make this sacrifice. This is what it is to be part of a family. A good daughter always sacrifices her own wishes for the name of the family.'

I nodded. My sister was right. I was not in love with anyone else. I knew nothing about romantic love. And I was ensnared out of respect and concern for my father. After my mother's death, he had become everything to me, both father and mother. If I backed out after the engagement was announced, my behaviour really would put my father in his grave. Should I cause him such grief, my life would be unbearable.

I would follow the Pashtun way. I would be an obedient daughter. 'All right,' I said to Nadia. 'I will do it.'

I was stupid and naive, ignoring what I had learned in my youth about forced marriages.

My contented Papa conferred with a beaming Kaiss to set a hasty wedding date.

Kaiss appeared besotted with his good fortune and acted as though he had found a great treasure in Maryam Khail. My fiancé's behaviour led me to believe that I would be worshipped by my husband after we were married. Somehow I had forgotten that Pashtun wives are treated as goddesses before marriage, and as servants after.

After the wedding announcement was made, and friends and relatives learned the name of my groom, we were startled when many came forward with fore-warnings. Two friends of the family, both Kabul natives, called to warn my father. 'Ajab. You must call off this wedding. This man is violent, he has a terrible reputation. He is considered dangerous by all who know him in Kabul.'

A burning thought flashed through my mind: the evil I had fled from had followed me to America . . . and now I was trapped.

'Papa?' I cried, wanting him to call off the engagement.

But Papa was offended. He angrily defended Kaiss, the man who had so pleased him with his talk of becoming a son to him. Later, after the two well-meaning friends left our home, Papa reassured me: 'It is their word against Kaiss's word, daughter. And I believe Kaiss.'

But then I heard that when Uncle Hakim revealed the good news to his family, he was aghast when his two daughters screeched in dismay. 'No! He is horrible. He is mean and violent! You must stop the wedding.'

I pleaded with my father. 'Something is wrong! Please, Papa, postpone the wedding until we can at least investigate these accusations.'

Papa, however, was furious that I would believe such malicious gossip about a man who was such a fine catch.

Only after the wedding was I told that another relative living in America had also been alarmed when told of my match by her son-in-law, and had called Auntie Shagul. 'I know that evil man. He is a criminal. He went to prison in Afghanistan for assault. You must stop the wedding.'

My auntie shook her head. 'It is too late.'

'You will save your niece's life. For God's sake, call her father.'

'It is too late.' My auntie never called.

Overcome with misgivings, I was limp with despair on the night of my wedding. Trapped, unable to find the courage to shame my father, embarrass my relatives and anger my groom, I slipped on my beautiful white wedding dress and fashionable head-dress. I looked in the mirror. I looked pretty on the outside, but was mangled by despair and fear on the inside. I wished I had the courage to flee the building, to find a car and drive far away.

But such an action would horribly wound my father. It would surely kill him. I could not do it.

I said my vows, and then I was married. It only seemed to take a moment. After the wedding there was a huge reception in a wedding hall. Kaiss strutted about like a proud peacock, accepting congratulations from well-wishers, while I hung back, regret washed with fear.

Kaiss and I soon left the wedding for our new home, which was in a high-rise apartment building next to the hotel where he worked.

For some reason none of the women in my family took me aside to prepare me for what I needed to know about the wedding night. Kaiss jumped me the moment we walked into his apartment, ripping at my clothes and pushing me into the bedroom. Never having been intimate with a man before, I was stunned and frightened by his assault. Kaiss was so rough with me that first night of married 'bliss' that I ended up in a hospital emergency room.

After I received medical care, I wept like a child. 'Take me home to my father,' I spat at Kaiss. I hated married life as much as I had feared, and after only a few hours.

Kaiss drove me home and I rushed inside to see Papa. I sat on his lap, weeping. 'I want to stay here, Papa,' I pleaded.

Papa asked, 'What on earth is going on?'

'Her stomach hurts,' Kaiss said in a funny voice, rolling his eyes at my father's puzzlement.

Papa did not know how to deal with such a sensitive matter. He needed his wife to handle such a delicate female problem.

Papa pushed me away lightly. 'Go home, Maryam. Go home to your husband.'

My shoulders slumped. I had nowhere to turn. I was in a nightmare, a nightmare of my own making.

Kaiss smirked and lead me away. We returned to his apartment, where he attacked me again as soon as the door was closed behind us.

My marriage to Kaiss was a merciless struggle. My husband was mean and brutal. My daily life was a miserable round of housework, restaurant work and rape. There was no more talk of moonlight dinners or disco dancing. My husband worked, ate and raped his wife. That was his life. I sometimes bore the secret and frightening thought that perhaps my father's eldest brother Shair Khan had been reincarnated into Kaiss.

Soon it was time to enrol at college. I longed for the change, to attend school with like-minded peers, to better myself and get away from my husband for a few hours.

But my husband laughed at me and said, 'Certainly not. You cannot go. I do not want a career wife. I want a wife just like the wife my father had – a wife who obeys me.'

It was like a body blow. I saw all his prenuptial promises suddenly evaporating. 'You promised my father that I would be allowed to get a college degree,' I stammered.

Kaiss sneered. 'Of course I promised. I had to come up with a good package. A good salesman gets you to buy the product he is selling. I was the product. I had to sell myself to your pathetic father to get his daughter.'

I would not submit to the beast another moment, I told myself. I would not. 'I will go to college,' I said. 'You can't stop me. This is America.'

Kaiss sprang at me, grabbing my head with both hands, squeezing my skull until I waited to hear a deadly crack. 'You do not talk back to me. Understand? Talk back to me again and I will make you regret it.'

I stumbled from the room. My life was becoming the mirror image of Grandmother Mayana's miserable existence. I was no different from my cousin Amina. I was even more pathetic than her because I had no innocent children to bond me to my beastly husband. I was living the life of bondage I had sworn never to endure. I was stupid, stupid, stupid! I had been deceived by dreams of happiness, of perfection, dreams of dancing the night away. My mind raced, plotting how I might flee Kaiss and file for divorce.

Circumstances intervened within a few weeks when I started feeling nauseous. I vomited constantly. Nothing would stay in my stomach. I needed a doctor but Kaiss refused, relenting only when I was unable to move from our bed.

The doctor relayed what he thought was good news. 'You are not sick. You are pregnant. Congratulations.'

I glanced at Kaiss, thinking the news might make him happy. Perhaps he would change and would now become the kind husband he had presented himself to be, if only I gave him a son.

Kaiss shrugged indifferently. The doctor said that I must have monthly check-ups, then his face turned a shade of light red. After we left the clinic, Kaiss began cursing. 'That greedy son-of-a-bitch doctor. He is not taking my money. You are not going to go to that son-of-a-bitch and open your legs to him every month.'

I remained quiet, yet noted the date of my next appointment, knowing that I must defy Kaiss for the health of my child. The following month when I started to leave our apartment, Kaiss blocked the door. 'You will not go, Maryam. My mother never went to see a doctor. After nine months, she went into her room and gave birth. The next day she was back in her normal routine. You will do the same as my mother!' He gave me a violent shove before returning to slump on the sofa to watch television.

Kaiss never once believed I would defy him. But even as my body nourished my innocent growing child, my child nourished my courage. I nonchalantly sidled up to the door, and then ran out, screaming, 'I *will* go to the doctor!' I sprinted outside and jumped into a taxi before Kaiss could catch me.

For the first time I understood why Amina had returned to her husband's beatings so that she could protect her babies. Although my child was still nestled in my womb and I had not yet seen my baby's little face, my love for my child was already overwhelming.

After my appointment I walked home trembling, terrified of what I had to face. I inched into our apartment, poised to run should Kaiss try to assault me.

But Kaiss walked towards me, smiling. 'We must take care of you. Your father said that if I was good to you, you would give me a son.'

I hesitated, still thinking it was a trick to catch me unawares. 'What if our baby is a girl?'

'If it is a girl, Maryam, I hope it dies in your

stomach. I only want a son.' He lowered his face to mine, glaring. 'Did you hear me? I will only accept a son.'

I nodded, too afraid to disagree with Kaiss's law, yet knowing very well I had no way of ensuring the child in my womb would be a boy.

During the coming months the beatings were less frequent and less severe although our life together was still volatile and frightening.

On 27 January 1984, I came alert out of a deep sleep with sharp back pains. As Kaiss was driving me to the hospital, he was pleading with God: 'Allah! Let it be a boy! I don't care if he is blind or crippled just let it be a boy.' Kaiss repeated his bizarre mantra the entire time I was in the delivery room. I found myself praying to God for a boy, too, terrified that Kaiss might murder our baby if it was a little girl.

Allah helped me by giving me a healthy baby boy. Everyone was relieved and happy. Kaiss was suddenly attentive and loving, proud that he could brag to everyone about his big and handsome son. Papa rushed into my room with tears streaming down his face. I had given him something to live for, he finally had his much longed for grandson.

On that miraculous day one could even love Kaiss.

Maryam's firstborn son Duran with his grandfather.

Chapter 13

When my precious baby burst into the world the thousand hardships and tribulations I had suffered with his father were temporarily forgotten. My love for my son was greater than I had ever dreamed it might be. For the first time since my disastrous marriage, I was in a good place. I held my son Duran in my arms and looked upon his sweet face, perfect eyes and tiny limbs. One bouncing baby boy had cleared the pain out of my life and I was overwhelmed with sheer joy.

I even praised my husband at whatever cost to the truth, desperate to keep him from exploding into his customary thunderous rages that might frighten my little son. All was good, at first. Kaiss was over the moon to be the father of a son, although he didn't feel he had to spend much time with Duran. His lackadaisical fatherly attitude suited Papa and me, for without the tension of Kaiss's presence we had the opportunity to truly share the joys of Duran's babyhood.

And as I stared at Papa's happy face while he held his first grandchild, I justified my miserable marriage. I had not seen Papa so joyful since before his cancer struck, before our country was lost, before Mother died. I had taken a big hit by marrying Kaiss, but Papa was in a good place, and that brought me some comfort. Watching little Duran's baby face, radiant with unpolluted happiness, for the first time I better understood the Afghan women I had known, women who had silently endured their husband's cruelties. Nothing mattered but the child.

Papa was a changed man. He happily shopped for Duran, supplying him with everything my son needed, whether it was the latest model of baby stroller or a symbolic golden spoon. Watching Papa spoil his little grandson brought a special ache of sadness for the joy my mother was missing. How she would have relished being a grandmother!

An abyss still divided Kaiss and me, of course, for I could never love the cruel man who was my husband and the father of my son. But I reasoned that perhaps I could learn to endure him, at least long enough to raise our child. But all too soon Kaiss started to complain about the baby's cranky moments disturbing his sleep. He ruled that Duran and I must spend our days at Papa's home. Little did my unfeeling husband know that the result gave special pleasure for Papa, Duran and me.

But I should have known that the peace could not last, for Kaiss was a man looking for a fight. My troubles began anew after I took little Duran swimming at the apartment communal pool. Careful not to arouse Kaiss's jealousy, an irrational jealousy that often sparked angry arguments, I had begun a habit of leaving detailed notes regarding my exact plans any time I left our apartment.

Within the hour Kaiss appeared at the pool. A shiver went down my spine as I realized that my husband was in a fury. His voice was low and threatening as he ordered me: 'Maryam. Come home. Now.'

Poor baby Duran whimpered at the tempest he knew was coming. Already he was familiar with his father's verbal explosions. Several swimmers glanced at Kaiss and, noting his angry expression, climbed out of the pool and settled warily at a distance. Desperate to avoid a public scene, I bustled to collect our things and do as he said.

Kaiss stalked away. I grabbed our wet towels and picked up Duran in my arms to hurry after my husband. I cringed in shame at the though that I looked the part of the obedient wife, only because I was. When Kaiss slammed shut the door to our apartment, my mind was racing as I hurried to put Duran in his crib. What had set Kaiss off? I had done nothing I could think of to inspire his rage. Yet I knew an attack was coming.

Kaiss slipped behind me, breathing heavily. I thought he was only going to rape me, a frequent occurrence in our marriage. He grabbed my hand and pulled me roughly into the kitchen, backing me against the counter. Was this some new kind of sexual assault he was planning? That's when he opened a kitchen drawer and pulled out one of our biggest knives.

I froze. Knives have always struck terror in my heart.

Kaiss gripped my throat with one hand while he started slashing at my swimsuit with the other. Choking, I gasped as my swimsuit dropped to the floor. I was stripped naked. He placed the sharp edge of the knife firmly against my neck. I knew if I moved I would sustain a serious injury even if Kaiss didn't slash me. He leaned into my face, whispering in his menacing voice, 'The next time my wife wears a swimsuit in front of other men, I will kill her.' I winced in pain when he deliberately nicked my neck with the sharp blade. I felt blood stream down my neck. Kaiss's eyes widened in excitement at the sight of blood.

He's really going to kill me this time, I thought, desperately casting around for what I might do to save myself and Duran.

At that moment my baby shrieked from his crib. He was hungry.

Kaiss slapped me in the face and kicked me in the leg. 'Go take care of your son,' he ordered roughly.

Duran had saved his mother's life.

Holding my hand over the slash wound, I rushed to my baby. He gurgled at the sight of me. I grabbed him with one hand and ran to the bathroom. There I bound a small hand towel around the cut with my free hand. I took Duran into the kitchen and fed him. Then I comforted him until he slept.

I returned to the bathroom and studied my neck with a hand mirror. The skin around my throat was bruised from Kaiss's tight grasp. But the cut was not very deep and the bleeding had stopped. I breathed a sigh of relief, for even had I needed stitches, Kaiss would have never allowed me to go to the hospital emergency department.

When I tried to tiptoe back into Duran's room, where I planned to sleep, Kaiss leapt from behind a door and dragged me struggling to our bed, where he slapped me around some more, then raped me painfully.

The following morning Kaiss awoke in the same foul mood. He got on his knees in our bed, grabbed my face in his hands, slapped me again for a few minutes, then forced himself on me. His only sexual pleasure seemed to come from raping me. I attempted to push him away, to fight back, but when he started choking me I gave up and submitted to his indignities. I must live for my son. If Kaiss murdered me, my little baby would be left defenceless.

Finally Kaiss had to leave me alone when it was time for him to have his shower and prepare for work. Only after he left our apartment did I break down and weep. But I pulled myself together for the sake of my baby, and pushed my intolerable existence to the back of my mind.

Later that day I ran into one of our neighbours, who studied the huge lump on my forehead and the cuts on my lips. That same neighbour had mentioned other bumps and bruises in the past. 'What happened to you?' he asked.

'Oh, I fell,' I replied in a quiet voice, looking away.

'Again?' he asked. 'You sure are clumsy for a young person.'

'I guess so,' I said, embarrassed, and turned away.

His voice became stern. 'This is not right. You must get away from him.'

I blushed red with shame. I walked away quickly, humiliated by my pathetic helplessness. Tears rolled down my cheeks. It brought back a memory of a woman in a similar situation and a long-forgotten face rose in my mind.

When I was sixteen years old, a lovely lady named Jamila who lived next door came running to the front door of our home. I was standing in the sitting room when she came crashing in without knocking. I thought for sure a pack of wild dogs was chasing her. I grabbed Jamila and sat her down in a chair. 'What on earth?' I said. I called out for Nanny Muma to bring a glass of water. 'Hurry!' I shouted.

Ageing Nanny Muma tottered over to us, a glass of juice in one hand and a cold wet cloth in the other.

'Here, here,' Nanny Muma said, her soft voice a comfort.

'What happened?' I blurted, even though I could see she had been beaten up. There had been whispers between my parents about her pitiful situation, but her wounds had never been as bad before. Always Jamila had suffered in silence, making up one pretext after another about tripping over one of her children or snagging her foot on the edge of a doorway, her clumsiness a cover for her bruises and scratches. But despite her excuses, all knew that Jamila's husband was a wife-beater.

This was the first time Jamila had sought refuge at our house. She whimpered, 'He is going to kill me for sure. Can I please stay the night?'

'Of course. Of course,' I told her, wondering what we might do to get her brute of a husband locked up. In those days I was naive enough to believe that all a woman had to do was seek justice to receive justice.

By this time Nadia was away in India in medical school, and we were living in the apartment where I enjoyed my own bedroom. 'You will sleep in my room, Jamila,' I said. 'Your husband will not dare show his face in my room.'

She nodded her relief, but still wept. I studied her face. On the day of her wedding Jamila had been a beauty, but marriage had aged her terribly. With each year of married life her face had coarsened. Now every part of Jamila's face was swollen and her soft flesh was horribly bruised. Poor Jamila had endured a terrible beating.

'What did he hit you with, Jamila?'

'It was my fault,' she cried. 'I walked away from the kitchen when the baby cried. I burned his meal. He was hungry without anything to eat. It was my fault,' she repeated.

'Stop, Jamila. It is not your fault. Your baby has been sick for the past two weeks. You had to tend to her.'

'No ... no ... it was my fault. I deserved a beating.'

I took a deep breath. I so hated how Afghan women would excuse their men. If a woman was beaten up, it was her fault. If a woman was killed, she must have been a prostitute, and it must be her own fault. Nothing was the fault of males. Women bore all the blame.

That night I had lain awake while Jamila wept. I remember my anger at her meekness, at her inability to stand up for herself! Neither of us slept, for poor Jamila wept throughout the night.

The following morning Jamila was having a cup of tea in the sitting room when her husband knocked on the door. Nanny Muma let him in.

He stalked up to his wife and did not appear to feel a single spark of shame at her pitiful appearance.

'OK. Go home, Jamila. The pyjama party is over.'

I was furious, shocked that the brute didn't even apologize despite the fact Jamila's face bore the pitiful signs of his beating.

I was so angry that I snorted, making Jamila's husband notice me for the first time.

'Why are you not in school?'

'I am going to take your wife to the doctor. She is in terrible pain from the beating you gave her.'

'She is going nowhere,' he sneered.

With other women in the room, Jamila found the courage to stand up to him. 'Maryam is going to take me to the women's centre and report you for all the abuse you have done to me,' she burst out with surprising defiance.

Jamila's husband took a couple of steps closer so that he could slap her full in the face. The blow was so strong that her head flew backwards. She dropped her cup of tea. 'Yes? You can't make any reports if you are dead. Now shut up and get home and tend to your children.'

With that he turned round and walked out.

Jamila collapsed, weeping.

I put my arms around her. 'Jamila, let's go. He needs to be punished.'

'No. No. I cannot go. He *will* kill me. Then what will happen to my little children?' With that she pulled herself away from me and staggered out. Over the years we remained close, but she never again sought our help, despite the fact the beatings became even more frequent.

I had always thought myself above the fray, never believing I would become like Jamila. Brought up by a gentle father who never raised his hand to his wife and daughters, I had always felt myself to be powerful, and immune to such aggression. But now I felt as powerless as the poor women I had so pitied. Now I myself was to be pitied by all.

I knew that Kaiss's violence was escalating, and I knew that for the sake of my son I had to get away. Comparing myself to Jamila and Amina and other women in Afghanistan, I reminded myself that I was now in America and that my situation really was different. Here I could get away from my abusive husband. Here women had rights.

I took action. First I approached my father. 'Papa, I know you do not want to hear the word divorce. I know it is taboo for a Pashtun woman. But I stupidly married Kaiss to please you. I married him so that you could at least have one daughter married to a Pashtun.'

Papa looked at me in surprise, leaving me to wonder how it was that a stranger could see my bruises, but my father, who saw me on a daily basis, saw nothing.

Tears streamed down my face. 'This marriage should not have happened. You were warned that Kaiss is a violent man. Papa, it is true: my husband beats me routinely. He hurts me. His violent temper is scary. He will end up killing me, Papa. Is that what you want?'

Papa said nothing, but he got up out of his chair, locked the front door and put his arms around me. My bitter tears suddenly turned to joy. In his own way, Papa was telling me that I could come and live with him. Although the Pashtun forbid women to seek divorce for any reason, my father would accept my leaving my husband.

And then Papa said, 'Daughter, please forgive me for what has happened. This was my fault. I am the one who chose your beast of a husband.'

I wept in my father's arms, forgiving him. It was the first time he had taken responsibility for the agony I was enduring.

Three days later Kaiss burst into my father's apartment, pleading for another chance. 'Yes, I hurt your daughter, Ajab, I admit it. I love Maryam so much that I lose my mind with jealousy. But that will never happen again. You have my word.'

Papa stared at him.

I watched Kaiss, wondering how such a wicked man could seem so charming. My violent husband began to shed false tears. He grabbed my father's hand and began kissing it. 'I beg you to forgive my many shortcomings.'

Just then Duran awoke from his nap and noticed his father. He gurgled in pleasure.

Papa gazed at Duran, then stared at me. His feelings were plainly written on his face: your son needs a father.

I heard my mother's voice whispering in my ear: 'Your husband's strategy is to divide and conquer, Maryam. Walk away, my daughter. Walk away.'

I stared pleadingly into my father's eyes, trying to convey a silent message. He will do it again, Papa. He will do it again.

Papa looked away helplessly.

Kaiss threw himself at my feet. 'I beg you, Maryam. I beg you. I promise, from this day I will treat you only with love and respect.'

Helplessly, I watched two Pashtun men, my husband and my father, ganging up on me.

I was united with every Pashtun woman who had ever lived. We had no rights, no power. We were too feeble to defend ourselves. Grandmother Mayana had always told me that a woman must be obedient, devoted and self-sacrificing to be worthy of her

Pashtun Muslim heritage. Never once had I agreed with her, but for all my fighting talk as a child, now that I was a woman, I was weak, too.

As I knew he would, my father cleared his throat and urged: 'Maryam, go back to your own home. Make a fresh start, daughter. It is the best thing for your son.'

Without one person to stand up for me, I felt my former strength wilting away. Why? I do not know. My Afghan upbringing had stripped me of my sense of self-worth.

With a deep sigh I began gathering Duran's things. Kaiss lifted our son in his arms. I didn't speak as I followed Kaiss from my father's house.

When Nadia next visited us from India on vacation, I had gone back to work. Never at ease leaving my son alone with his father, I got my sister and father to look after him so my sister could enjoy my son's cute antics. One evening I went home to prepare Kaiss's dinner before leaving for work. I was in the kitchen, cooking, when he came in and stood behind me. Suddenly he pinched my buttocks as hard as he could. I screamed and turned around. 'That hurt, Kaiss! Why did you do that?'

'Well, Maryam,' he whispered threateningly, 'I did it because you are wearing tight slacks and your ass looks very sexy.'

Assuming he was trying to compliment me, albeit in a very odd manner, I said, 'Thank you.'

But before I could move, he grabbed a knife and slit my trousers down the back.

I gasped and, squirming, tried to pull away.

He rolled his fist and punched me as hard as he could in my stomach.

I fell backwards on to the floor.

He kicked me in the stomach, screaming: 'Here is my law, Maryam: my wife will not show her butt to other men!' He kicked me a second time. 'God knows how many men thought of sticking their dick in you!'

I pushed away, scrambled to my feet and ran to the bathroom, the one room where there was a lock. I quickly slammed the door and secured the lock.

Panting, I examined my face in the mirror. I didn't remember Kaiss slapping me in the face, but my lips were already swelling. Upon further examination I found a big gash across my back where Kaiss had cut my trousers off my body.

I remained locked in the bathroom until I heard Kaiss turn on the television, then I crept out to dial my boss at the restaurant. 'I'm sorry,' I whispered. 'I am sick. I can't come in tonight.'

I heard my boss exhale loudly. 'Maryam, if the bruises are on your face, don't come in. But if Kaiss just kicked you on the legs and the bruises are not

noticeable, I really need you to come to work tonight.
I am short-staffed.'

I stifled a cry. My charade of a life was fooling no
one. I was a pathetic creature unable to defend herself against one man. Never had I felt so useless. I
began to weep.

'Child,' my boss whispered urgently into the
phone. 'Leave him. Leave him before he kills you.'

For the rest of the night I pretended to behave normally with Kaiss, but the following day when I took
Duran to visit Papa, I called him from the safety of
my father's apartment. 'Kaiss, this cannot go on. I
want out of this marriage. I will take good care of
your son. You can see him any time you want.'

'Maryam!' he screeched. 'Get home where you
belong! *You belong to me!*'

'Kaiss, listen to me. Marry another woman. Marry
a woman who will not complain when you beat her.
Marry an obedient woman like your mother. I will
no longer obey you. I will no longer submit
to your abuse.'

'The only way you will leave me, Maryam, is when
you are dead,' he threatened. 'You can leave me
when we put your body in the ground.'

I felt a cold chill run up my spine, but I didn't give
in. 'On Monday, I will find a lawyer. On Monday I
will file for divorce.' I hung up on him. Although
frightened, I felt more optimistic than I had in years.

I had finally made up my mind to reclaim my life.

Kaiss called my father and, abandoning his charming facade for the first time, snarled, 'Kiss your daughter goodbye, Ajab. Her days are numbered.'

Papa realized too late that he had been wrong about Kaiss. The product he had been sold was fraudulent. From the first day, his son-in-law had deceived him.

The police were notified, but we were reminded that in America personal threats carry no weight with the legal system unless followed up by violence. For the first time I yearned for our Afghan system, a country where physical threats are met with tribal violence.

The following night Papa's phone rang. A close friend of Kaiss's warned him, 'He will kill me if he knows I called you, Ajab. He is going to do something. Take your daughter and grandson and flee.'

Papa protested. 'There is a court of law in the United States. What can this bully do? He will be punished.'

'Please leave, Ajab. Kaiss has hired someone else to do the job. He is serious.'

Papa was befuddled. 'What job?'

'Why are you making me spell it out? I am telling you, your son-in-law has hired someone to kill your daughter! Take Maryam and the baby away. Leave the city. Don't tell anyone where you are going! I am risking my own life by warning you!'

When told of the conversation, I became hysterical. '*A hit man?*'

But Papa was still unconvinced, believing it was an idle threat to frighten me into returning to Kaiss. I knew different. I knew Kaiss. He was a brutal, violent man. He had tried to kill me before. It had all gone too far. My husband and I had reached a stalemate. I could never return to Kaiss. But he would never let me go.

Farid was in the habit of checking in on us every few days and he called from Paris. Papa told him the latest. Farid listened quietly, then said, 'Kaiss's friend is telling the truth, Uncle. Think about it. What does he gain by warning you? The man is obviously worried that he will get caught up in a murder investigation.'

'Maybe he is as crazy as Kaiss,' Papa said, hope in his voice. The last thing he wanted to do was to flee his comfortable home.

'I am coming over,' Farid said.

'From Paris?'

'Yes. Stay in your apartment. Keep the doors locked. I will be there on the first flight.'

Farid was as good as his word. Within twenty-four hours he was in Papa's apartment. My cousin was as wonderful as ever. He looked at me with his familiar, mischievous eyes, and said with feeling, 'Don't worry, *my little brother*. Your *big brother* is here to protect you.'

Farid would never let me forget my childhood pretence to be a boy.

My anxiety swept away any joy I might have at seeing Farid again. 'Farid. He has hired a hit man. He really is going to kill me, and then he'll take my son and flee to Afghanistan.'

Farid soothed me, then made all the arrangements. Duran and I would get away and travel as far as possible without leaving the continental United States. That night he drove me to the airport, where I took my baby and boarded a plane to Los Angeles, California. Farid had close friends and family living there who would meet me and keep me safe.

After closing up Papa's home and packing his personal items, Papa and Farid joined me in Los Angeles. I felt hopeful that everything would turn out well, that I could remain alive to raise my son. We were starting a new life, a life without violence and pain and anger, or so I thought.

Chapter 14

I filed for divorce and, in view of Kaiss's violence, full child custody. I cared nothing for child support. I didn't want Kaiss's money. I only wanted to raise my child in peace and unmolested.

Being so far away comforted me. I began to feel human again, experiencing occasional sparks of happiness. Duran was a merry, robust child and didn't seem to miss his father at all. Soon he was saying a few words, and he picked up on my family nickname, Malo. He tried to say it, but it came out as Mano. The sweetest sound I'd ever heard was my little Duran calling me, 'Mano! Mano!'

Still, the danger was real, and fear of Kaiss meant that we had to guard our address and telephone number, only giving it out to our closest family members. Then one morning my auntie from Texas called. Kaiss had been phoning round all members of my family, pleading with them that he wanted nothing but to make me the happiest woman in the world. He claimed he loved his wife and son so much and missed them so. When he realized that my auntie was weakening, he concentrated his efforts on her and she crumbled to his bogus charisma. Unknowingly duped, she gave Kaiss my telephone number and address. After only a few telephone conversations, she was confident that she alone knew Kaiss's true temperament, telling me, 'Maryam, he is a good man. He will be different. He will be a good husband, now.'

Divorce was so unthinkable in my culture that most family members wanted me to accept my miserable lot as a woman and to endure the abuse in silence, in the way women in Afghanistan had always done.

I put down the phone and ran to my father, screaming, 'Auntie gave him our address!'

At that moment the telephone rang again. I grabbed it, thinking it was my aunt once again. 'Maryam,' I heard Kaiss say in a menacing whisper, 'if you fly into the sky, I will catch you by the leg. If you hide under the ground, I will catch you by your head. *You cannot hide from me!*'

With a frightened gasp I hung up.

The phone rang again. Papa rushed to answer it only to hear, 'Ajab, I am coming to Los Angeles. I am coming to kill Maryam and you. I will even kill my own son if that is what it takes. Do you think I am afraid of the electric chair? I will make history. An Afghan man defending his honour will sacrifice his life for the satisfaction of killing his wife, his son and his father-in-law.'

'If you want to make history,' Papa shouted back, 'go do jihad in Afghanistan! Fight the Russians! Go! But don't ever call here again!'

Papa crashed down the receiver. My gentle papa had never harmed anyone in his life, but at that moment he swelled with warrior energy. Had Kaiss appeared then and there, I am certain that my father would have fought him to the death.

While sympathetic, the police again told us that they could do nothing against verbal threats. Kaiss would have to physically assault one of us before they could arrest him. We were frustrated to discover that America's justice system was splendidly fair for the criminal, but less so for the victim.

My lawyer filed some papers, for whatever good that would do.

Kaiss called again. This time I was surprised to hear he was calm. 'OK, I am giving up. But I wanted to tell you that I did not hit you because I hated you. I hit you because I loved you. I did not want any other man looking at you. Maryam, if I could make magic, I would carry you in my pocket all the time. But I can't make magic. So, because I do love you, I will let you go. I will give you a divorce

. . . on one condition. You will never marry again.'

I responded as he wanted only because I didn't know what else to do. 'All right. I agree. I will never marry again. Why would I? You taught me that marriage is a nightmare. All I want to do is to be left alone so that I can raise my son in peace.'

'All right. Let's agree. Let's work together to be a mother and a father to our son.'

'I agree,' I said, feeling a tinge of relief. Had Kaiss come to his senses? Had he finally realized that America was different from Afghanistan, that American men did not routinely beat their wives?

A week later Kaiss called again, claiming that he must see his son on a regular basis. He was moving to Los Angeles.

I was panic-stricken, but there was nothing I could do to stop him. America is the land of the free. After Kaiss moved to Los Angeles, he shined up his 'best product' and presented his charming face again to my father. Never had a man so devoted himself to the work at hand. He poured himself into the moment. To my horror, my father began to weaken once again to his studied charm, to forget the monster Kaiss had proved himself to be.

But I was not deceived. I knew the real beast behind the mask of civility. I was revolted by his performance.

I refused him visitation without supervision. So I

went along each time Kaiss came to spend time with our son. During our fifth or sixth outing, I was sitting on a bench in front of a drugstore watching my son play with his father. Kaiss looked at me and smiled, pointing at the drugstore behind me. 'Maryam, I need some toothpaste. Do you mind buying me some?'

My guard was down. 'Sure,' I said, as I ran into the store to purchase a tube. When I returned five minutes later, Kaiss and Duran were nowhere to be seen. My heart stopped. I began to dash about like a mad woman, searching for Kaiss and my baby. I cursed my stupidity.

My lawyer could not believe that I was still so naive. He told me: 'The court has not yet ruled to give you full custody. So we cannot claim Duran was kidnapped by his father.'

I was distraught. I blamed myself, wondering if I would ever get my son back. I didn't know where to turn, what to do. I stood guard over the telephone, waiting. An agonizing week later Kaiss called. With a smirk in his tone he said, 'I will give you one day to get back to Virginia. I will give you one day to start living as my wife again. Otherwise, I will slip away and take your son to Afghanistan. You will never see him again.'

I wanted wings so that I could fly instantly to my son. I left my job, my new home and my papa. I was in Virginia the following day. I was resolved to endure every misery to reclaim my baby. Within minutes of entering Kaiss's apartment, even before I had the opportunity to hold my son in my arms, I was raped and beaten.

Kaiss had taken four days off from work. He raped me repeatedly during those endless days and nights. When he went back to work, I was locked in our bedroom and guarded by one of his friends, an Afghan Mujahedin who had travelled to the United States for medical treatment after being wounded in battle by the Russians. He was hard and cruel and without pity. He was a perfect guard.

Most Afghan men are suspicious of females. They believe all women are promiscuous and must be isolated from men who are not of their family or else they will commit the most sexually depraved acts. He accepted my husband's lies as the truth, that I was an immoral woman. He easily believed that I refused to stay home and take care of my son and that I was so untrustworthy that I had to be beaten and locked in our home. Without supervision, I would abandon my faithful husband and our son, to slip out to go dancing and engage in sex with strangers.

The truth was that I lived only for little Duran, who had been traumatized during the week away from his mother. My baby screamed in terror if I just stepped out of his sight. I worried about what had happened to my little son during the time his father was in charge of feeding and changing him. Kaiss was not a patient man. My baby had probably gone hungry, and perhaps was slapped around.

After a month, my jailor, my husband's friend, returned to the war in Afghanistan. Kaiss secured our apartment with heavy locks, and popped in and out at odd times to make certain I was not trying to escape.

The holy month of Ramadan came to us but I failed to maintain my fast for the first time since the Russians had invaded my country. My life of relentless tension and abuse was taking its toll, and I was frail. I lost so much weight that the contours of my bones showed through. I knew that I would die if I didn't get away, but I had to plan my escape carefully or risk losing my baby for ever. I really did not know where to turn. My family all believed me to be fine after Kaiss forced me to telephone Papa to assure him that he was keeping his promise to be a devoted and loving husband. Most likely all were relieved that I was not causing the family dishonour by going through with my demand for divorce.

But change was coming sooner than I thought.

One afternoon during Ramadan Kaiss walked into the kitchen to see that I was preparing some food for Duran and me. Kaiss sneered because I was not fasting. 'Look at you, eating during Ramadan. You are corrupted by the West.'

Not wanting to be punched, I bit my tongue. Kaiss was in a bad mood and his bad moods always resulted in a beating.

'You look hideous,' he shouted, 'hideous and despicable.' He turned to my baby. 'Oh, Duran. Your mother is so ugly.'

I still did not respond. Duran started to whimper, my small child already fearing violence and danger when his father was around.

I said nothing.

Kaiss pushed me. 'Beer. I want beer. Go to the grocery store and buy me some,' he ordered.

'Kaiss, please don't drink beer during Ramadan.'

'Bring me beer, bitch!' He looked like a wild animal when he opened his mouth in a snarl. 'Who are you to talk? You are not even fasting! When I break my fast, I want to break it with some beer!'

I took a deep breath and turned to walk away, muttering under my breath, 'Hypocrite.' I realized too late that I had spoken louder than I intended.

Kaiss went crazy. 'What did you say, bitch?' He grabbed my arm, pulling me back, wrapping his hands around my throat, choking me, shaking me. Everything grew dim. I could hear baby Duran screaming with fear. I tried to pull away, to look at my son for the last time, but all I could see were black shadows. I became hysterical. By talking back, I had cost my baby his mother. Now Duran would be raised by a maniac.

The telephone rang, snapping Kaiss out of his rage. His fingers loosened. 'I will kill you later,' he said drily as he got up to answer the phone.

I was gagging, desperate to fill my lungs with air.

Kaiss said something down the phone, then walked out of the apartment, slamming the door behind him.

I crawled to my baby and held him tight, but I was gagging and retching. Duran began to kiss my face. 'Mano, Mano,' he cried in his sweet little baby voice.

I struggled to reach the telephone. I dialled the police, praying to Allah to complete the call before Kaiss returned. He would really finish what he had started if he knew I had alerted the authorities.

The apartment filled with police officers, with one writing down my statement while another took photographic evidence of my injuries. Others were checking out the rooms to find signs of our struggle. Before Kaiss returned, Duran and I were driven to the battered women's shelter, where I would remain until I could get a restraining order.

I was finally being heard, and the seriousness of the situation claimed the attention of authorities. Kaiss was arrested but was out a few hours later after posting bail. Based on my visible injuries, the judge did approve a restraining order for Kaiss. A hearing was set in two weeks.

At the hearing, Kaiss and his lawyers spun one lie after another.

According to them, I was the abuser, and beat Kaiss regularly.

Kaiss had never threatened to kill me or to kidnap Duran.

Kaiss was a saint. His wife was the real devil.

The judge examined the evidence, including the police photographs of my injuries. I was granted full custody of my son, although to my horror and despair, Kaiss was given visitation rights. I knew then that during the first visitation Kaiss would try to kidnap Duran and flee to Afghanistan. I had to do something or I would lose my baby for ever.

Chapter 15

I returned to Los Angeles with my son, all the while planning how I might seek a change in the custody ruling. My attorney agreed that Duran was in genuine danger of being taken out of America and carried back to Afghanistan. We decided to wait until Kaiss arrived for his first visitation, and at that time he would be told to meet us at the courthouse. We would be legally prepared.

While I had been in Virginia rescuing my son from Kaiss, my sister Nadia had graduated from medical school in India and moved in to live with Papa. I felt as contented as I could be under the circumstances, but I was desperately worried when Kaiss would appear to claim visitation rights.

He arrived on Wednesday 30 July 1986. Nadia and I were cooking dinner for invited guests. Papa was sitting with Duran in the living room. Our building manager knocked on the door, warning us that Kaiss was downstairs, saying that he had come to visit his son.

'Do not let him in,' I ordered, my skin crawling with fear.

I knew that something terrible was bound to happen. My voice breaking, I said, 'Tell him that before he can visit with his son, he must have legal permission from a court in California. We will meet at the court on Monday.'

I knew Kaiss would not give up easily. I warned my sister. 'Nadia, if Kaiss comes to the door, do *not* let him in. He will steal Duran away. We will never see Duran again if that happens. He has threatened to take Duran to Afghanistan. We must be vigilant.'

But Nadia tried to reason with me. 'Oh, come on now, Maryam. You have put the family through so much trouble with this marriage! You are separated from Kaiss. He can't do anything to you now. Don't blow this into something bigger than it is. Let the poor man in. He just wants to see his son.'

I couldn't believe my sister's reaction. Although from the time of my birth we had had a roller-coaster love-hate relationship, now that we were both adults I had believed all that was behind us. Besides, I had told her everything that had happened between Kaiss and me. My sister knew he had tried to kill me. Surely she would stand by me against Kaiss.

To my shock and amazement, Papa agreed with Nadia. 'What can happen, daughter? We are all here. He is, after all, the boy's father.

We are only asking you to let a man see his son.'

'No!' I shouted. Trying to show them I wasn't overreacting, I reminded them, 'The lawyer himself said we should not let Kaiss be around Duran. There is no way. No!'

Nadia pulled me by my arm into the bedroom we shared. 'Look, Maryam,' she said. 'Dad and I were very happy living a nice quiet life out here until you had to come back with your dramatics. Can't you see you are making a big deal out of nothing! What can he do with the three of us here? *Nothing!*'

Papa followed us and ganged up on me with my sister. 'Maryam, we must be nice to him now. If we are kind, he will return the kindness and understanding. And if you won't allow your son to see his father, your son will grow up to hate you. Is that what you want? Do you want Duran to hate you?'

I stared at my father in disbelief, remembering that his life had been threatened by Kaiss, too. What was going on? Evidently during the time I had been in Virginia, my sister had convinced my father I was exaggerating. Finally I spoke. 'I know this man much better than either of you. He does not know how to be kind. He can only be cunning. The lawyer said—'

'Oh, yes, we know about lawyers,' Nadia said dismissively.

'We are living in a democracy,' Papa said as he

started walking out the door. 'Be reasonable. I will go down and bring him up.'

I tried to follow to stop my father but Nadia pulled me back and I fell back on the bed. My sister ran for the door, securing the lock behind her. I could not believe what was happening! I pounded on the door. I shook the handle. I screamed. I listened at the door. I heard voices. I imagined Kaiss grabbling little Duran and dashing from the building, catching a plane and taking my baby far away where I would be unable to find him.

Then the door handle moved and my sister stuck her head round the door. 'He wants to see you. Do try to control your emotions.'

I ran into the room to see Kaiss kissing my son. He smiled warmly at me, and then at Papa. 'I will be moving to Los Angeles to be near my son,' he explained. He looked back at me. 'I want to be your friend, Maryam, nothing more.'

He then turned his full attention to Nadia, his voice a singsong of unctuous pleas. 'If only Maryam would take me back. Even though she tried to have me arrested and put in jail, I have forgiven her. I still love your sister.'

I clenched my fists, enraged by his smooth pretence. Through gritted teeth I told him: 'Never again will I live with a man who beats me.'

'When I hit you, Maryam, it was only because I love you.'

Outraged, I stalked from the room, unable to stand the charade another moment.

Kaiss called out, 'All right. I will not ask you to live with me. But I am moving to Los Angeles to be with my son.'

Papa and Nadia moved as one force, both insisting that he join our invited guests for dinner.

Clever Kaiss recognized he had a friend in Nadia. He redoubled his efforts to ingratiate himself with her and with my father.

When the guests had arrived, with Nadia's backing, Kaiss presented himself as the host, offering them tea and juices. He was such a talented actor that he won them all over. His actions were unbearable. When I couldn't abide the situation a moment longer, I lifted Duran in my arms and went into my room.

Soon Nadia followed me. She sat on the edge of my bed. 'Oh my God, Maryam, he still wants you. Even after what you did. And he is so sweet, a wonderful man. Surely you can give him one more chance?'

'Nadia! You should hear yourself, sister. You want me to give him one more chance to break my bones? You want me to give him one more chance to try and kill me?' I covered my eyes with my hands. 'Don't be fooled by his act, Nadia.' I took a ragged breath. 'Please, be loyal to me, your sister, not to a man who is a danger to me.'

But Nadia ignored my pleas and made it clear she thought I was being hysterical.

I was devastated by my sister's lack of understanding.

The guests soon left, and so did Kaiss. He was wily, now he had detected the weak link in the chain keeping him out of my life. He called Nadia within an hour of leaving. 'Nadia, please let me come back. I am so lonesome in this cold hotel.'

Over my shrieks Nadia left Papa's apartment to go and get Kaiss. They returned within the hour. Papa graciously gave him his bed. I moved Duran's cot bed next to my own, knowing that, if given the chance, Kaiss would steal him away even as we slept.

The following day, on Thursday 31 July, twenty of our friends were having a picnic at Marina Del Ray Park. We were invited. Kaiss pleaded with Nadia to get him an invitation. Fear was working its way through my body. I sensed that something was up, but I didn't know exactly what he was planning. With so many people around surely he didn't believe he could kidnap my Duran. Last time I had let down my guard, but that would never happen again. I would never again leave Duran alone with his father.

Against their protests, I remained at home with Duran, refusing to take a chance or to endure yet another social charade. My son was so precious that day. I felt sad that he had to miss the picnic, and that our friends would not see how cute he was in his sweet little blue shirt with white stripes and his dark blue shorts.

Papa and Nadia returned from the picnic with some of our friends. To my despair, Kaiss was now an accepted family member. Obviously his innocent act had reached Greek perfection. All were raving about the thug as though he was the winner of the world's best husband award. Various family members pulled me aside to whisper compliments about Kaiss. 'Such a wonderful man!' Another said, 'He took over the barbecue.' A third told me, 'He asked me to save the liver kabob for you, Maryam. He told us how much he loved liver, but he wanted it for you.'

I ignored my relatives, warily watching Kaiss as he hovered around my sister in the kitchen. Instead, I sat watching television with Duran, who was drinking a bottle of juice. Family members continued to discuss Kaiss, speaking just loudly enough so that I could hear.

'Maryam is a fool to let him go.'

'Yes, I agree. He still loves her. He wants her back.'

'Even after she had him put in jail.'

I felt I was in the house of the insane. How could my family and friends be so bewitched by Kaiss? They knew his history! On the verge of screaming at them all, I put Duran on the floor in front of the television and said, 'Papa, please watch the baby while I am in the bathroom.' I glanced into the kitchen to make certain Kaiss was still occupied with my sister. Satisfied, I looked at my precious baby and smiled, telling him, 'Mano is going to the bathroom. I will be right back.' My little treasure looked at me and smiled, waving his little fingers: 'Bye, Mano.'

I paused for a long moment, admiring my beautiful son, knowing that nothing in my life really mattered but my baby. I turned to run into the bathroom to freshen up, trying to think how to convince my family of Kaiss's true character. I must find a way to convince them of the utter futility of trying to persuade me to live with a man who was a potential murderer.

I clutched my face in my hands, thinking over my situation, considering what words might make my family and our friends hear me. I was dealing with a misogynistic tradition that stretched back many generations. Pashtun women never complained, and never divorced their husbands.

No one cared that Kaiss had tried to murder me. No one cared that he had also threatened to murder Papa and baby Duran as well. I groaned in desperation, stung by the indifference of those who claimed to love me. It seemed my family would prefer that I lived in utter misery, that I be beaten daily, that I be used as a sex slave by my husband, anything was better than for a Pashtun woman to have sought independence and a divorce.

For the first time in my life I fully understood what Grandmother Mayana had been up against. The utter helplessness of her life struck me anew.

I straightened my back, feeling a fury taking hold. My family was wrong, and it was up to me to set them straight. I was *not* Grandmother Mayana, a woman who bent to submit to men. I was Maryam Khail. I was no longer in Afghanistan. I was in America, a country where women's rights and needs were recognized.

I would handle this matter once and for all. I would get rid of Kaiss. I would break every rule of civilized society by revealing every humiliating detail of the horrors that criminal had committed, from beatings to rape.

I stepped into the living room, my eyes automatically seeking my son, something I always did to reassure myself my son was safe. I couldn't see him. 'Where is Duran?' I asked.

Papa explained: 'Oh, his father took him down to the shopping centre to get some juice.'

My breath left my body. I was paralysed. '*What?* You let Kaiss take Duran?'

Papa waved me away dismissively. 'Don't be silly, Maryam. They only walked across the street. They went to get some juice.'

Without a word I ran from the apartment and down the stairs and across the street, dashing frantically from store to store and then back again. The shopkeepers there knew Duran. None had seen my baby.

I ran back into the apartment. Kaiss and Duran were not there. I started screaming, 'Call the police! Somebody call the police!'

My relatives began pulling on my arms, pleading with me to sit down, imploring me to get a grip on my emotions, 'Control yourself, Maryam. They will be back. Don't worry.'

I shook them off so that I could call the police myself. I listened in horrified silence as I was told they could do nothing. The standing court order allowed Kaiss visitation. Monday was the day we were going to get the visitation orders changed. Monday was three days away.

I lost my mind. I wept. I screamed. I set upon my father and sister, blaming them for getting my baby kidnapped. Despite my warnings, they had under-estimated Kaiss. 'You let that kidnapper into our house. You gave him my son!'

I grabbed my purse and keys and fled the room. I broke every speed limit driving to the Los Angeles International Airport. The miracle was that I did not crash, for my tears were flowing and I could barely see. God was with me on that day for I arrived at the

airport in one piece. Once there I ran inside, dashing
from one airline to another, pleading for the ground
crew to help me. Once they heard my story, all began
scrambling, checking their flights, looking for Kaiss's
name.

Nothing.

I refused to leave, even after being told that my
husband and son had not left LA International, not
unless they had travelled on an assumed name.

I called my father, hoping that Kaiss had come to
his senses and returned Duran to his home.

Nothing.

I remained at the airport all night, thinking that
Kaiss might have hidden out waiting for a specific
flight.

Nothing.

At 6 a.m. I called my father again. But my baby
was still gone. Papa pleaded with me to come home,
but I refused. Finally he drove to the airport to
convince me. I fell weeping into his arms, agreeing
to follow him home. I drove while weeping.

Nadia tried to comfort me. 'Oh, Maryam, he has
done this before. He just wants you back. You'll get
a call.'

'No. This time it is different. I will never see Duran
again.'

I sat on my bed holding Duran's clothes and his
pillow. By now Duran would be crying with fright.

He was a mama's baby. He didn't know his father, only that his father created fear.

I sobbed. I ran into the kitchen. I was going to kill myself. My family scrambled to hide all sharp instruments.

I was tortured by my last image of Duran, his beautiful smiling face, his sweet lips blowing kisses, calling out, 'Bye, Mano!' I cried bitter tears, already missing my son more than I could bear. I wanted my baby back. 'Duran!' I had to have my son back. I couldn't live without him. I had to hold that tiny being my body had made. 'Duran!'

I fell into bed, nursing the grief that threatened to bury me. I knew in my heart I would never see my baby Duran again.

At twenty-six, my life was over.

Chapter 16

Papa pulled strings and used all his contacts trying to locate Kaiss. We soon discovered Kaiss's route out of the country. Just as my premonitions of disaster had warned, Kaiss had carefully planned his escape prior to his visit to Los Angeles. He knew that if he could only ingratiate himself with my family, that a moment would come when I would be out of the immediate vicinity. My folly had come from relying on Papa to watch over and protect my baby. Five short minutes in the bathroom and all was lost.

Devious Kaiss had had a rented car sitting outside on the street. The moment Papa permitted him to take Duran out of the apartment on the pretence of going for a cold juice, Kaiss had dashed to his car, strapped in Duran and driven out of Los Angeles, up through California and Washington State into

Canada. Once in Canada, he hid out in a small village. After a week, he flew to Europe. While there he obtained documents to travel to Afghanistan, the one place on earth where he knew he would find tribal protection and be beyond the reach of the law of America.

I discovered too quickly that the United States government could do nothing once Kaiss left the United States. They had no jurisdiction in Afghanistan.

Sadly, events proved I had been right: only I knew the real Kaiss, a brute raised by a brute. I knew his history only because, during one of the few times Kaiss was feeling affectionate, he had confided something of his childhood to me.

Kaiss's father was an ignorant, cruel man. Kaiss's earliest memories were of a household consisting of a wicked father, two cowed wives and many children. As a child, Kaiss clung to his mother, who was vilely mistreated by her husband. Kaiss's father had such a violent temper that all the children hid when he made an appearance. When Kaiss was four years old, his mother was diagnosed with tuberculosis. His father became enraged at his wife, beating her severely for contracting an infectious disease. The father then hired someone to take Kaiss's mother away from her children to a family farm where she was locked away in a small dark room. The poor woman was fed only once a day, and had to live in that tiny room without access to a toilet. Her disease only worsened with time and eventually she died.

One day Kaiss had a mother, and the next he did not. Without a mother to protect him, Kaiss was often beaten, and so he learnt to be cruel himself. He turned into a tough kid, harming animals and beating up his younger siblings. He was proud to admit to me that he had stabbed a few people over minor disagreements, and once even demonstrated the best way to do the most harm with a small knife.

That was Afghanistan, I thought, one monster rearing a second monster. Would that happen to my baby too? Would his father's cruelty destroy my baby's sweet nature? Would the most loving child in the world grow into an unfeeling tyrant, the same as his father?

My wounds were open and made raw by a family who had met my warnings with smiles even as Kaiss outwitted them all. I was most frightened by the knowledge that Kaiss did not truly love Duran. He was proud to have fathered a son only to brag to other Afghan men about it, but he had never shown any affection for the child in my presence. I shuddered to remember all the times Kaiss had grown so easily irritated at Duran, had shouted at him, had beaten me in front of him, and had, on occasion, even threatened to smack Duran. My son had been saved from violence only because I was there to intercept his father's angry hand.

The truth was that Duran hardly knew his father. He had been living apart from his father most of his life. My gentle papa was his father figure. My frightened son was bound to cry for his mother and his grandfather. When that happened I knew Kaiss was fully capable of battering my tiny son.

My baby was only two years old, too young to comprehend his mother's absence. I knew that my baby was looking for me, just as I was longing for him.

I called Kaiss's favourite relative, a half-sister named Zena living in Germany. She was falsely friendly, and denied any knowledge of Kaiss's where-abouts. She swore to me on the Koran that she would tell if she heard anything. Knowing in my heart that she was lying, I appealed to her own love for her children, but she swore she knew nothing.

I suspected that Kaiss and Duran were most likely living with her. One week later, I arrived in Germany, having flown there as quickly as I could arrange the trip. Thankfully, the German police were most help-ful. They swung into action, preparing documents and accompanying me to Zena's home.

Zena was terrified by the sight of stern-faced police officers pouring into her house. 'What did I do?' she screamed, clutching her bosom. 'Why are you here?'

The officers searched her home but found nothing. They separated Zena and her children, questioning them all individually. A fearful Zena finally broke her silence, confessing to the officers that, yes, Kaiss and Duran had stayed there for several weeks and, yes, both had actually been there on the day I had called to plead for information. She also tearfully confessed that Kaiss was cruel to my son, and that he admitted to her that he had taken him only to hurt me. Then the German police discovered that one week before we arrived, Kaiss and Duran had flown from Frankfurt to Moscow and on to Kabul.

My toddler was now trapped in a dangerous country torn by violence. It was September 1986, and Afghanistan was in a full-blown war. Earlier that year new laws were passed in Afghanistan obliging any male over eighteen to serve in the army. Would Kaiss be drafted and forced to the front? If so, what stranger would be left looking after my baby? I read about major offensives in the Panjshir valley near Kabul, with the Mujahedin warriors fighting the Russians. Soviet and Afghan troops had large numbers of casualties, but my concern centred on the fact that there had been a huge loss of civilian life as well. Most worrying was that during the same period of time Kaiss was flying into Kabul, there had been a bomb explosion at the Kabul International Airport. Over two hundred civilians had been injured and killed. Another troubling report cited a recent Soviet programme where babies and young children were forcibly taken from Afghan parents to be sent to the Soviet Union for ten years of indoctrination.

Afghanistan was no place for my son. Just thinking about the turbulence and danger surrounding my innocent baby would make me lose my mind, dropping to my knees and screeching like the insane.

One day a few weeks after I returned from Germany, I received a large manila envelope in the mail. There was no return address. My body shook with fear at what I might discover in that envelope.

I opened it. Inside was a recent photograph of my adorable son blowing a kiss. At the bottom of the picture Kaiss had written in large bold letters, 'BYE BYE MANO!'

I blacked out, falling to the floor.

Chapter 17

My grief was unendurable.

I nearly lost my mind.

I plastered the walls of our apartment with baby Duran's photograph. I kissed those images repeatedly, muttering aloud, 'Allah, how is my son? Is he hungry? God, is my son cold?'

One day on a routine trip to buy groceries, I saw a little boy pleading with his mother for a candy bar. She said no, and he began to weep. I fell apart, hastening to open a candy bar and offer it to the child. His mother drew back suspiciously, as I began to plead: 'Give him the candy. Please give him the candy. My baby loved candy too, but now he is missing and I have no way of giving him anything.' Looking at her sweet baby's face, I burst into tears and ran from the market. That kind woman grabbed her child and followed me to my car to find me sobbing. She put her free arm round my shoulder and wept along with me.

Unable to control my emotions, I soon learnt to avoid any place that catered to children. At home I talked to myself and slept with my son's favourite blanket and his most beloved stuffed animal. My depressed state led to my skin erupting in raised welts that itched and burned. No medicine could heal me.

Kaiss's threats haunted me, keeping me awake every night. He had always said, 'Maryam, if you get away, I will find out and kill you, but first, I will kill your son. Your last vision will be your dying son.' Had he taken Duran to Afghanistan to kill him?

Even if his father didn't murder him, I feared that my baby would be killed in the war. Nineteen eighty-six never improved for Kabul citizens. Exhausted, emaciated, traumatized refugees poured into the city, resulting in one of the greatest mass migrations in history, doubling Kabul's population to over two million people. Five million Afghan people in all had been uprooted, with four million becoming refugees abroad. The numbers were staggering.

Although I had followed the events of Afghanistan from the moment I fled, once my baby was in Kabul I became even more obsessed with every bit of news. With my baby's photographs hanging on every wall, I kissed his image, weeping and raging while the television reported explosions and shelling and murder and mayhem. There were estimates of over 12,000 Afghan civilians having been killed during the previous months. News reports said that the situation in Afghanistan was approaching genocide. My father's tribe had fought the Russian invaders from the beginning, and I heard that 700 resistance fighters were killed in the Paktia province, my ancestral home.

How would such a tiny boy survive such a holocaust? I had protected him from the moment of his birth, keeping him safe and happy. Who would prepare his favourite foods? Who would keep him warm? Who would read him stories? Who would play hide and seek and make him laugh?

Kaiss was not the sort of man to waste his time on a toddler.

Papa tried to comfort me. 'I am praying to Allah that Duran will be back soon.' He paused and then stupidly remarked, 'But at least you know that your son is with his father.'

I didn't bother to remind Papa yet again that Kaiss was a brutal man who had admitted to his own sister that he did not love Duran. I simply walked away.

Nadia couldn't admit she had been wrong. 'You should have stayed with Kaiss. None of this would have happened had you stayed with your husband.'

'And been beaten to death?' I asked, my voice rising in disbelief.

'He only beat you because you answered back.'

Nadia shrugged. 'You shouldn't have been so disrespectful.'

Nadia was distracted from my troubles because Papa had finally given her permission to marry her Iranian Shiite boyfriend, little knowing that in reality Nadia had already married him years earlier. So with her marriage finally out in the open, her life was just peachy, while mine was unbearable.

I plotted to slip into Afghanistan to find my son, but Papa feared that very thing so he hid my passport, saying he would keep it in a safe place. Nothing could convince him that I should hire someone to slip me into war-torn Afghanistan, reclaim my son and return with him to America. Although I didn't think so at the time, perhaps Papa was right, for those were the days when the war with Russia was in full swing and the borders were closed. Even hardened warriors had difficulty moving about within the country. It was a no-go area. When it came to war-torn Afghanistan, either you were in, or you were out. My son was in. I was out.

Papa had never lost contact with family members or friends who had remained behind in Afghanistan. Now he called on those contacts, enlisting the support of everyone he knew to try to track down my son's whereabouts. 'I will get your son back, Maryam, I will,' he promised loyally.

Eight months after Duran was taken, my father

received an address. We knew for the first time where Kaiss and Duran were living. I dashed to the Los Angeles State Department, naively believing the American government would now send in the troops to rescue my son from his father. Their response was more than disappointing. 'There is nothing we can do,' I was told by the official. 'The United States has no diplomatic relationship with the current Afghan government.'

Accustomed to a country where the leaders often respond to an individual's needs, I wrote to President Reagan's office, pleading with the American president to do something to help me get my son back. I received a form letter with the exact message I had already received from the state department. *The United States has no diplomatic relationship with Afghanistan.*

When I fell to pieces yet again, Papa showed me a newspaper article about a small boy in Florida who had been kidnapped and murdered. 'Why are you showing me this?' I asked, my voice rising in panic. Had something similar been discovered about Duran and this was Papa's way of breaking the news to me?

'Think how lucky you are,' Papa replied. 'At least your son was not kidnapped to be murdered by a stranger. At least he is with his father, Maryam.'

I could only shake my head and marvel at the lack of understanding and the absence of compassion from my own family.

We realized that Duran was still alive when Kaiss sent me a message via my father's friends and relatives in Afghanistan: 'If Maryam sets one foot inside Afghanistan, I will cut it off and send her body back to Los Angeles.'

Friends and relatives living in Kabul continued trying to see Duran. Some of them even took food and gifts for Duran, but they were met at the door by an angry Kaiss who threatened their lives. We did learn that Kaiss had switched his allegiance from his fellow Afghans to become a Russian puppet. He was a food caterer for the Russians, making a tidy sum of money. I tried to see the good in it. At least Kaiss was not at the front, leaving Duran with perfect strangers. And although he was helping the enemy of my country, I hoped he was using some of the enemy's money to take care of my baby.

One woman did get a chance to get to Kaiss and see Duran, only because Kaiss did not know she was my friend. She reported back that I should not worry, that my son was alive, although he cried a lot and called out 'Mano! Mano!' any time a woman came into the room. She was taken aback when she heard me shriek in agony at her words.

I often prayed that my baby had forgotten me, anything to make his life less painful. But evidently Duran was so traumatized that he was still looking for me, even after ten months of separation. Knowing that, my pain increased and I grieved even more. Friends and family whispered their fear it would kill me, and that I would soon be dead.

When I heard that several cousins were preparing my shroud, I knew that I must try to be strong. If I were to die, who would continue to push for the return of my son? Once my epitaph was written, I knew that my son's miserable fate would be mainly forgotten.

That's when I decided I had no option except to go on living.

Chapter 18

In October 1987, I accepted a mindless position working in a video store, checking videos out and checking videos in. My boss had never had such a reliable employee. I became a work robot, arriving early, working at a feverish pace and remaining late without asking for extra pay. The shop became my total preoccupation and the customers became my social life. A number of men asked me out on dates. I said no to them all. Finally one of them probed, 'Are you a lesbian?'

I shrugged, not bothering to explain how a man and marriage had destroyed my life. I had no interest in investing anything in another relationship.

About that time Nadia gave birth to a baby girl. Some joy returned to my life when I gazed on my sister's baby. My niece, Suzie, became a focal point in my life. Although there were moments when I relapsed into my profound grieving, the time had come for my life to start again.

Shortly after my niece was born, a tall Middle-Eastern man walked into the store to rent a movie. I asked for his video card and ID. The ID he presented was of another person, and he then explained that he was visiting his brother-in-law and was there to rent a movie for the family. When he mentioned he was from Saudi Arabia I spoke without thinking: 'Did you bring your four wives with you?'

He laughed easily, unoffended. 'Not all Saudi men have four wives, you know. I don't even have one.'

Soon he was coming in daily and before long he asked me out for dinner.

'Why not,' I answered without enthusiasm.

Many Muslims think of Saudi Arabia and Saudi Arabians as being backward, mainly because of the harsh manner many have towards their women, but my Saudi date was a perfect gentleman, and I found him interesting.

Then he surprised me by asking, 'Do you believe in love at first sight?'

'Definitely not.'

'Well, I do. I fell in love with you the first minute I saw you. Will you marry me?'

I burst out laughing and asked him to take me home.

The following day he returned to the video shop
with another Saudi man. His friend was dark, handsome and moustachioed, with vivid green eyes. 'This
is my friend, Khalid,' he told me.

He turned to Khalid. 'Khalid, this is the girl I will
marry.'

He looked at me again, 'Maryam, I must go back
to Saudi Arabia today, but Khalid will look after you.
Please think about my proposal while I am away.'

I laughed, thinking that Saudi men were surely
quick to fall in love. Perhaps it had to do with their
closed society. Of course, I was never going to marry
again, so his proposal meant nothing to me beyond a
joke.

Khalid came to the video store frequently and
would chat with me. He never mentioned his friend
and neither did I.

The time passed slowly. My life was filled with
only two things: work and mourning my son,
although I became excited when in 1989 the Russians
were defeated and pushed out of Afghanistan, for it
gave me hope that the time was coming when I might
be able to find my way into the country to reclaim
my son. Little Duran was by that time five years old,
still too young to be without his mother. But just as I
was making my travel plans, everything fell apart
again. The moment the Russians withdrew and the
Afghan warlords broke the Russian fetters, they

began to struggle against the Soviet-backed government for control of Afghanistan. One day the warlords were battling the Russians, the next they were battling each other. Soon the country had erupted into civil war.

I unpacked my bags, knowing that Afghan warriors would fight until they were all destroyed together. I carefully followed one major battle after another, from the Battle of Jalalabad, to the fall of Kabul, to the race to control all Afghanistan.

Would my son never know peace?

Khalid the Saudi became a daily fixture, renting so many movie videos that one day I asked, 'How can you do your studies? All you do is watch movies!' The handsome Saudi said nothing in his defence, although he smiled his sweet smile.

Then one day Khalid telephoned and asked my advice. 'Maryam, what is the most romantic restaurant on the beach? I am going to ask a very special lady to dinner and want to take her to the best place.'

I suggested: 'There is a delightful Indian restaurant with the best view on the pier in Redondo Beach.'

That night when I was closing the store, Khalid walked up. 'Maryam, can I ask you to please come with me to this restaurant? I want you to meet this special lady.'

'That's kind of you, Khalid, but no. I am very tired tonight.'

'You must be hungry.'

'Yes, but too tired for an evening out.'

'Please. You said the food was great.'

I studied Khalid carefully for the first time, wondering why he would invite anyone to accompany him on a date with his special lady.

'Please.'

'Oh, all right.' I was hungry and I reasoned that going to the restaurant would save me from having to cook. And Khalid must have a reason for wanting me to meet his friend. He was a very nice man. Perhaps he wanted to get an unbiased opinion of the woman.

We waited thirty minutes for his special date but she never arrived. Finally I said, 'Her majesty is late. And I am starving.'

Khalid stood up. 'Wait right here.' He walked away. I assumed he was going to call his overdue date.

Within a few minutes Khalid returned. He was carrying a long-stemmed red rose and was smiling widely. He presented me with the rose. 'Maryam, you are the special girl I have been waiting all my life to meet.'

I blinked in surprise, thinking the situation was getting ridiculous. 'Khalid, what is it with you Saudis? First your friend proposes to me on our first date. Now, you are telling me that I am your special girl. Is this normal for Saudi Arabia? Do good friends fall in love with the same girl and both propose?' I teased him. 'Is this a national custom I have not heard about?'

Khalid laughed. 'Maryam, I can't speak for my friend. But he is back in Saudi Arabia and just informed me yesterday that he has discovered it is very difficult to bring a wife from another country to Saudi Arabia. I think he has given up. But I, I am here. And I am staying here. I want to see more of you.'

At first I didn't take him seriously. But he continued to call me daily and soon I found that I looked forward to his calls. Slowly we began dating seriously. We became very close.

One day he asked: 'Maryam, why are your eyes so sad?'

Since the loss of my son I had become much more reflective. I discovered that people rarely talk about the things that mean the most to them. Since my baby had been stolen, I had placed memories of my precious Duran in a special place in my heart. Never did I confide my heart's secrets.

Khalid looked so gentle and caring that I looked away. 'One day I might tell you, Khalid, but not now.'

I thought a lot about Khalid that night. He was the

most mild-tempered man I had ever known. I had never heard him raise his voice. He never criticized me. We never argued. If we disagreed on any topic, we calmly discussed it. Khalid respected me. Respect from a man was something few Afghan women ever experienced.

Khalid was the exact opposite of Kaiss.

That is why I fell in love with Khalid.

When I told my sister that I had fallen in love with a Saudi man, her temper flared. 'A Saudi? My God, Maryam!'

'Yes. A Saudi. A Saudi who happens to be the nicest man I've ever known.'

'Do you have any idea of what life is like for women in Saudi Arabia?'

'Tell me, Nadia, how can life for women be worse in Saudi Arabia than it is for women in Afghanistan?'

'Well, it is,' she insisted. 'Do you have any idea of how Saudi men regard women?'

'Better than how Afghan men behave towards their women. Listen, this Saudi man treats me with respect and with love. He is the best man. There is no man in Afghanistan who is his match.'

Nadia studied my face. 'Does Papa know?'

'No. And you will not tell him. You destroyed my life once, Nadia. I won't let you do it again.'

Admittedly, I dreaded telling Papa. Since Duran had been kidnapped, all the happiness had gone out of Papa's life. He would not be pleased I was dating anyone, but to date a Saudi would be particularly unacceptable because Afghan men believed other Muslims were beneath them. Not even the King of Saudi Arabia would be considered worthy of a Pashtun woman.

To keep arguments at bay, I used a trusted girl-friend as an alibi, making it easier to see Khalid.

One special night I confessed to Khalid everything that had happened to me. Without seeking sympathy, I told him about the brutality of my first husband and the abuse I had endured. Finally I told him about losing Duran. The painful memories brought back my fears for Duran's safety because Afghanistan was still hell on earth. Before the confessional ended, I was weeping in Khalid's arms.

Khalid was gentle, wiping the tears from my face. 'Never give up hope, Maryam. You son will come back to you one day.'

That's when Khalid asked me to marry him.

I was happy for the first time in years when I said, 'Yes. Yes, Khalid, I will marry you.'

Chapter 19

Things did not go so well with Papa. I was too nervous to tell him in person, so I wrote him a heartfelt letter and left it on his pillow.

Papa, I have fallen in love with a wonderful man. He is gentle and kind, everything that Kaiss was not. Khalid is from Saudi Arabia. I am asking for permission to marry him. Please do say yes. If you say no, I will marry him anyway. Please tell me soon that you will bless my marriage. Your loving daughter, Maryam

I longed for Papa to smile his approval, but he did not respond at all. A month passed while I was never brave enough to raise the subject. Then my father asked that I drive him to the airport. He was leaving for a three-month holiday in France to visit Uncle Hakim and other family members. When Papa kissed me goodbye, he handed me a fat envelope. His face was solemn. 'Maryam, please consider this letter very seriously. I hope you answer it positively.'

Then he was gone without his usual affectionate goodbyes. My heart sinking, I tucked the letter away in my purse to read it later after I returned to our apartment.

Daughter, if you marry this Khalid, you will never see me again. You will no longer be my daughter. Khalid is a Saudi Arabian. His society is the most conservative in the world. You could never survive in it. In Saudi Arabia, men are given full custody of their children. If you marry this man, and you have children, if he decides to leave you, he will not have to kidnap your children. They will be his legally.

He is only living in the States to finish his studies and when he returns to Saudi Arabia he will abandon you. You will be brokenhearted.

Have you learned nothing, Maryam?

Don't forget, if you want to see Duran again, you must never remarry. You must be patient and wait for your son to be returned to you. I am trying to find a way to seize Duran and bring him back, but if you take a new husband, no one in Afghanistan will help us.

*Most important, Maryam, remember you are
a Pashtun. It is your duty to marry a Pashtun
man. Please do not forget your family history.
My own mother lived courageously under her
brother's harsh rules. She never remarried. She
lived for her children. Unless you remarry
another Pashtun, you, my daughter, must do
the same.*

I wept in despair. How could Papa forget his own
struggle against our culture's antiquated traditions to
marry the woman he loved from outside his own
tribe? How had he so easily slipped back into the
dark ages? Who could be more dangerous, toxic and
dishonourable than the man I had married: a Pashtun
man specially chosen for me?

Truthfully, my anger had been building against my
father and sister since the day Duran was stolen from
me. I felt that my closest family members had made
it possible for Kaiss to kidnap Duran. Without Papa
and Nadia's support of Kaiss's cause, my baby would
have still been with his mother. My anger spiked
anew, and I knew then that never again would I trust
anyone to make personal decisions for me, not even
my father.

I stomped into the kitchen and grabbed a pair of
scissors and cut Papa's letter into many pieces. Then
I called Nadia, who was living temporarily in

Maryland to do her medical residency. I was so angry I shouted at her down the phone. 'I am going to marry Khalid whether you and Papa like it or not! I don't give a damn.'

Nadia was so shocked that I, the 'good' daughter, was so aggressively self-assertive that she didn't say a word.

Khalid and I married while Papa was still in France. We drove to Las Vegas for a real honeymoon. I had fun for the first time in my adult life. I had found true love at last with a wonderful man.

Three months later my bravery had deflated a bit. After Papa returned I could not find enough courage to confess I was married. Instead, I said, 'Papa, I read your letter carefully. And I thought about it. But, Papa, I really love this man. I will never be happy with another. Please, all I ask you to do is meet him. You will like him, Papa, I promise.'

Papa didn't speak.

In the meantime, Khalid was staying with friends while I tried to talk my father round. He soon grew impatient and insisted on meeting my father.

So I announced to Papa, 'Khalid is coming over tonight. Please be nice.'

Poor Khalid was so nervous that he brought his nephew with him. He told me later that to gather his courage he had paused to recite verses of the Koran before entering our apartment.

Papa received our visitors with a cold, limp hand-shake. Then he took his newspaper and sat in his favourite chair, rudely burying his face in the paper.

Khalid cleared his throat and said in a low, sweet voice, 'How are you, sir?'

Papa did not answer.

'Papa,' I said, embarrassed. 'Khalid has very kindly asked you how you are.'

Papa looked up from his paper. 'Which university are you studying at?' he barked.

'The University of Southern California.'

'What is your area of study?'

'Business.'

Papa grunted, and made it clear he had nothing further to say. He stood up, went into his bedroom and closed the door behind him.

I followed. 'Do not act like this, Papa. It is beneath you.'

Papa said, 'I want to catch the news. Close the door when you leave.'

'Papa, you yourself did not marry a pure Pashtun woman. Do I need to remind you of the difficulties you faced to marry my mother?'

'This is different,' he said firmly, as he turned his back to me.

'Different? Why? Because you are a man and I am

a woman? This is beneath you, Papa. I am so disappointed in you.'

The next day, Papa abruptly left California to visit Nadia in Maryland and to help with her two-year-old daughter. As soon as he arrived Nadia broke my confidence, gleefully revealing to Papa that I was already married. Papa sent word via my sister. 'Tell Maryam I will never see her again. I will never speak to her again.'

I am not the kind of daughter who can live without speaking to her father, so I called Uncle Hakim and pleaded with him to intervene. Papa would always hear Hakim even when he would listen to no one else. It soon produced results.

Khalid and I were invited to Maryland for a visit. Although Papa was initially dismissive and rude to my husband, soon he couldn't help appreciating Khalid's kindly ways. Papa finally agreed to return to Los Angeles to live with us. And I returned to school, studying to become a respiratory therapist. I enjoyed my classes and I loved my husband.

Over time, Khalid and Papa became very close, and I felt myself part of a happy family for the first time in many years. But our family circle had a missing piece, and that piece was little Duran, still held hostage in Afghanistan. I fretted that my poor baby would never have known a moment of peace since his father had taken him to Afghanistan. Since that July day in 1986, my son had lived through the Russian war and was now living through a civil war. Despite the fall of Kabul, the city was still under constant rocket fire because none of the powers would admit defeat. The socialist government was fighting until the end. The warlords were the same. Those violent men would fight until the entire country was in rubble. I could barely abide watching news broadcasts showing Kabul in cindery ruins. To my eyes, it appeared that no building had survived intact. Where in that rubble was my little boy? I spent many hours reading the Koran and praying for Duran's safety.

One day Aunt Shagul announced that she had decided to make the dangerous trip into Afghanistan in January 1990 to see one of her daughters, who had been trapped there. While there she was going to seek out Kaiss so she could visit with my son. She was a determined woman and I knew she would get to see Duran, one way or another. I longed to send my son toys and clothes, but I was unable to walk into a children's clothing or toy shop without collapsing, so Papa and Nadia and Aunt Shagul shopped for Duran instead, gathering many items they thought would appeal to a seven-year-old boy. Unbelievable to imagine, my baby would turn seven during Aunt Shagul's visit, as his birthday was on 27 January.

Aunt Shagul arrived safely in Kabul, although the city was under bombardment. She found Kaiss easily enough, as he was still in the catering business. First he had worked for the Russians. When they were defeated, he had worked for the pro-Soviet government until the day they fell from power. His lack of loyalty to any one group meant that he had easily allied himself to whomever was in power. Over time, he had amassed a fortune, or so we were told.

Kaiss's home was extremely grand, large and beautiful. A servant answered the doorbell, but Kaiss appeared almost immediately to discover the identity of his visitor. He remembered Aunt Shagul from family gatherings and he fell into a rage, shouting at her, 'You stay away from my son!'

Aunt Shagul spoke softly, but firmly. 'I only want to see him, Kaiss. I will not make a scene. I give you my word.' Her calm demeanour finally convinced Kaiss to allow her entry into his home.

Aunt Shagul soon discovered that Kaiss had remarried, to a very shy woman sitting silently in the living room.

Kaiss called out for Duran, who came walking down the stairs, a puzzled look on his face.

Aunt Shagul said she gasped because Duran had grown so big, and extremely handsome.

My son looked at his father and quietly asked in English, 'Who is this lady?'

Aunt Shagul spoke calmly. 'I am your great-aunt. I have brought you some presents.'

Kaiss growled in his gruff voice: 'These gifts are from that lady in the picture, the one who was my secretary. Now, take them up to your room.'

Duran quietly gathered his presents and left the room without saying goodbye to Aunt Shagul. He seemed a sad, reticent child to his auntie's eyes.

Aunt Shagul looked at Kaiss. 'He doesn't know about his mother?'

'No. And if you tell him, I will kill you.'

Aunt Shagul looked over at Kaiss's wife. 'Do you have children?'

The wife looked cowed, too frightened to answer.

'No,' Kaiss answered on her behalf, 'she does not. She is here to look after my son. When my son is grown, I will let her have her own baby.' He glared at Aunt Shagul. 'So, you have seen him. The show is over. Now get out. If you ever come back here you will live to regret it.'

Aunt Shagul pleaded with him. 'Kaiss, please, let me have a picture. For his mother.'

He opened the door. 'Get out. I will send you a picture.'

As Aunt Shagul walked away Kaiss shouted threateningly, 'Tell Maryam for me that if she ever comes to Kabul, I will send her body parts back to her father in a plastic bag.'

Some things never change.

Surprisingly, Kaiss kept his promise. After nearly

five long years I finally had a new photograph. My baby was now a young boy, looking so serious and so handsome. I kissed that photograph a hundred times. I had it enlarged. I framed it and hung it in the most prominent place in our living room. I stared at it endlessly. I wept tears of joy at how healthy he looked. And I wept tears of bitterness that my son did not even know I existed.

Chapter 20

The civil war in Afghanistan never ceased. Sometimes I thought the war might carry on for ever. When the Soviets finally pulled out they had left the country brimming with the latest military hardware, which was commandeered by the Afghan warlords, who proved themselves easily more brutal and merciless than the Russians at the expense of the civilian population. A fully fledged civil war erupted when the warlords failed to agree on anything.

We were all frantic for Duran's safety. In an effort to save my son from all the mayhem and madness, Papa wrote to Kaiss, offering to pay for a boarding school in India or any other country Kaiss might choose. He would leave all the decisions up to Kaiss, if only he would take my son out of danger. My father sent letter after letter. But we never knew if

Kaiss read any of my father's heartfelt corres-
pondence, although several of our messengers were
beaten bloody by Kaiss and his men.

There were a number of attempts to steal my son
back by friends still living in Kabul who had learned
of my situation. Some were more serious than others.
One particular friend and his young brother were
determined to right a wrong, and made my son their
cause. They watched Kaiss's house, noting when he
was away and the time that Duran left for school in
the morning.

One morning, perfectly timed for Duran's departure
for school, the two parked their automobile close to
Kaiss's house. When Duran came out, my friend's
brother approached him and urged him to walk over to
my friend, who was waiting in the car.

Just as my mother had frightened me when I was
little about being kidnapped by Shair Khan, Kaiss
had terrified his son that he would be kidnapped for
ransom. When he was approached by our friend poor
brainwashed Duran ran screaming for his life. His
screams alerted his father, who happened to be unexpectedly home, and he came dashing to the rescue.

My two friends sped off, but were spotted and
identified by Kaiss.

That very night Kaiss and a gang of thugs arrived
at my friend's home armed with machine guns. My
friend's brother was beaten senseless, and would have

been shot, but the boy's mother clung on to Kaiss's feet, begging for her son's life. Kaiss demanded to see my friend, but he was not there at the time, so he threatened he would be back and, when he did, that he would kill the whole family. Since Kaiss was protected by those in power, there was no recourse to the law, and my friend and his brother felt compelled to flee across the border into Pakistan.

But that failed attempt bore dire consequences for me, because Kaiss took his wife and son and fled Kabul to an unknown destination. All knowledge of my son's whereabouts was lost.

About this time exiled Afghans first heard about a new group rising from the concrete dust that had once been the grand buildings of Afghanistan: the Taliban. Led by a cleric named Mullah Mohammed Omar, the group came out of Kandahar in 1994. Afghans heard how Mullah Omar and his faithful armed religious students first appeared as defenders of the ordinary people from the corruption and brutality of the warlords after they went to free some girls from a poor family who had been raped on the road to Kandahar.

In the beginning, the Taliban were welcomed with open arms by the Afghan civilians, who were weary of years of ruthless violence and incessant fighting between the Mujahedin warlords.

Papa and I were cautiously optimistic, because the Taliban were religious students (*talib* is Arabic for student, and in Afghanistan is used for students in religious schools, who study the Koran in Arabic). Although Papa never wanted to be ruled by a religious movement, we were hopeful that a pious group of holy warriors would bring peace to the land.

Never did we imagine that the Taliban would spell unimaginable repression, suffering and doom for our poor fellow countrymen and women.

During this anxious time Khalid graduated from college and surprised me when he broached the subject of our moving to Saudi Arabia. Khalid was from a large family, consisting of ten brothers and sisters. I had met several of his siblings who had visited us in Los Angeles. They had made a good impression.

'But we agreed before we married that we would never live in Saudi Arabia,' I reminded him.

'We won't stay long. I just want my family to get to know you.'

'But, Khalid, *Saudi Arabia*?' I didn't want to say the obvious, that no woman in her right mind longed to live in the gilded cage of Saudi Arabia.

'Oh, you will love Jeddah,' he assured me.

I knew nothing much about my husband's country, other than that women were still veiled, and were not allowed to drive, and that Saudi men commonly took more than one wife. Over the years there had been publicity regarding American women trapped in Saudi Arabia after their husbands married other women, or, worse, stories of Saudi men stealing their half-American children, who never saw their mothers again.

Everyone knew that Saudi Arabia was not a woman-friendly country. It wasn't surprising that I preferred living in a country where women had legal rights, as we both knew. Afghanistan, too, was a frightful country for women to live in, and was getting worse for them by the day, by all accounts. Why would I leave the freedom of America for another misogynist country?

Yet I agreed to move with Khalid to Saudi Arabia. Khalid left the choice to me, promising that if I did not want to move, we would not move. His attitude made me trust him all the more. Most importantly, I was aware that marriage had not changed Khalid. Unlike Kaiss, he had not turned from an adoring suitor one day to a beast the next. I could count on Khalid. But Papa and Nadia were opposed to my move, once again trying to tell me what I should do – a mistake, as after the fiasco with Kaiss I had vowed to never again allow my father or sister to make personal decisions for me.

I decided to give it a try. I knew in my heart that

Khalid wasn't hiding any nasty surprise from me.

My family went crazy at my decision. Papa was getting older, and at seventy-seven years recognized that his time on earth was limited. He wanted his daughters near. But I plunged ahead with my plans to move, promising to spend half the year in America.

When we said our goodbyes at the airport, Papa spoke bluntly. 'Khalid, I don't think my daughter will do very well in "no-woman's land" (Papa's nickname for Saudi Arabia).'

Khalid smiled without taking offence.

And so it came to be that I went to live in Jeddah, Saudi Arabia. On the plane, I felt tense when Khalid presented me with a black garment encased in plastic wrap, explaining, 'You will need to wear this when we reach Saudi Arabia.'

I slipped the black light-weight cloak and scarf from its packaging, shook it out and examined for the first time the obligatory disguise, called an abaya, worn by all women in Saudi Arabia. Everything was black. Considering Saudi Arabia's blistering climate, I knew I would look a ghoul, a sizzling hot ghoul. Although the costume was styled very differently from the pleated pastel burqas worn by many Afghan women, the intention was the same, to hide women behind a curtain. My mother had broken Afghan law when she refused to wear the burqa. I had never worn it myself other than once when I played a trick

FOR THE LOVE OF A SON 349

on relatives and friends as a young girl and had pretended to be a beggar asking for the price of a ticket to the movies. This of course sparked a sermon from my aunties, who thought a beggar woman should use any alms given for food rather than for frivolous entertainment.

If mother had been alive, I'm certain she would have ripped the outfit to shreds rather than allow her daughter to submit to this backward tradition. I sighed. What was I getting myself into?

An hour or so before our plane landed in Jeddah, I noticed that the chatty, animated Saudi women on board became very quiet as they donned their abaayas and scarves. Some went so far as to cover their faces with a black veil. The atmosphere on the plane was transformed as soon as the lively women transformed themselves into black shadows.

At Khalid's behest, I threw the abaya over my dress and loosely draped the scarf over my hair. I shrugged, thinking I was luckier than the Saudi-born women, because I could always leave if I found the place too oppressive. At least, that was my plan.

Chapter 21

I arrived in Jeddah on 29 October 1994. Jeddah was a surprisingly beautiful city, homes and buildings shaded by swaying palm trees and situated on the Red Sea. Khalid's family was as I remembered, friendly and very pleased to welcome me to their country. I was not unhappy.

Nevertheless, despite the fact that I loved Jeddah and made many new female friends, and adored my husband's family, I would be lying if I claimed that Saudi Arabia was a friendly place for women. Although I had grown up in Afghanistan, a country well known for harsh discrimination against women, here there were so many 'rules against females' that it was difficult to remain in high spirits.

Not being able to drive was exasperating, although Khalid was happy to take me anywhere I wanted to go. Also, after arriving in Saudi Arabia I made the upsetting discovery that I would be unable to travel anywhere without a written letter of permission from my husband. Leaving Saudi Arabia would not be as simple as I had imagined. Should Khalid have a personality change and start wanting to control me, I would be trapped. It was also difficult to find a job as a woman, although I was an experienced professional in my field, respiratory therapy. Nor was the social life what I was used to, as at parties women mixed with women only, and men socialized separately with other men.

The list of restrictions against women was endless.

When men have all the power, many men become extremely cruel to women. Saudi Arabian men were no different from other men in that regard.

Even some men in Khalid's family were guilty of cruelty to women. One of my husband's cousins had married more than twenty wives. Since Islam only allows a man four wives at one time, that man kept himself busy divorcing and remarrying. His first wife was his first cousin. In Saudi Arabia, marrying one's first cousin is considered insurance against divorce since many men will avoid creating discord in the family by divorcing a close relative. Khalid's much-married cousin was extremely wealthy, and during Ramadan he gave his wives cash as their Ramadan gifts. One of the younger, more attractive wives received a larger cash gift than the older, plainer wives. To give one wife more than the others is taboo in Islam, whether in gifts or personal attention.

Jealous wives often quote the Koran when squabbling about this point. All four wives started bickering, so incensing Khalid's cousin that he announced he was divorcing all four of his wives at once.

He divorced wives number two, three and four, but when he faced his cousin, wife number one, to say the words 'I divorce you', she fainted. When her husband saw her sprawled on the floor, he took pity on her and didn't have the heart to divorce her after all. When she heard the good news, she forgot she was faking a faint and leapt up screaming her joy. 'Thanks to Allah! Thanks to Allah!'

'So,' I said, 'this means you are the only wife now?'

She laughed loudly. 'No, Maryam! He quickly married three more women. My husband is a man who needs four wives. I have accepted it.'

She was so cheerful about it that I laughed along with her, but in truth I felt like crying.

I knew that Khalid desired children, and that he would make a wonderful father, but I was so apprehensive after the loss of my first son that I didn't believe I could conceive. Besides, I was living in a country where children are considered the sole property of their father and the mother has no rights. Although Khalid was still the loving man I had married, I knew that nothing in life was ever guaranteed, and it worried me.

Then one day out of the blue Khalid said,

'Maryam, no matter what might happen, I would never take a child away from you.'

I looked at him gratefully, but made no promises.

It didn't help that I was aware that some of my American girlfriends married to Saudi men were suffering terrible indignities. One was an American named Linda who had met and married a Saudi man when he was attending school in the United States. After Mohammed acquired his degree, the family moved back to Saudi Arabia. By this time Linda and Mohammed were the parents of two children. Shortly after I met Linda, Mohammed returned to their home with a Saudi woman. Linda thought the woman was a relative, until Mohammed tersely told her that she was his new wife, and to make her welcome.

Linda was so stunned she couldn't speak. Mohammed had never behaved in a way that would lead her to believe him capable of such boorish behaviour.

The following day she called me in tears. 'Maryam, please come over. Bring packing boxes. I am leaving him.' Linda believed that all she had to do was hire a divorce attorney and leave Saudi Arabia with her children.

Khalid felt so bad for Linda that he drove me to various stores to collect boxes. When we arrived at her home, Linda was out of control with despair. She had called the American Embassy to seek advice and was told that she had two options. She could leave the country, but she would lose her children. The Saudi government would not allow her children to accompany her. Those children belonged to her husband. She had given birth to them, but according to Saudi Arabian law she had no parental rights. Her second option, she learned, was to remain in Saudi and to share her husband with a second wife. Unwilling to leave her children, Linda remained in that miserable situation. The new wife turned Linda's previously loving husband hateful and malicious.

Later in the year a second friend named Joyce had a similar experience, when her husband too surprised her with his second wife. Joyce's husband Ahmed was even more ruthless than Mohammed. At the same time he took a second woman, he removed his children from Joyce's care to live with his brother in another city. Joyce was allowed to 'visit' her children only once a month. She was too fearful to ask for a divorce and leave Ahmed after he warned her she would never see her children again.

Such stories intensified my own continuing sadness over the loss of my son, although I would have felt myself in heaven if I had had the opportunity to see Duran at least once a month.

Khalid made me happy when he found me a lovely little three-bedroom townhouse by the Red Sea. The view was extraordinary, and the sound of lapping ocean waves incredibly soothing.

That's when I became unexpectedly pregnant. Khalid was overjoyed. He was so different from Kaiss in every way that I soon found myself excited. Khalid insisted on going to the doctor with me for every appointment. I discovered the sweetness of enjoying a normal pregnancy with a loving husband.

Of course, Saudi Arabia being what it is, everyone around me wanted my child to be male. I remember one of Khalid's female cousins asking, 'How is that healthy baby boy that is growing inside your stomach?'

I wrinkled my nose and laughed. 'This time, I would like to have a healthy baby girl.'

'No! No! No! Don't say that,' she hissed, superstitiously waving her hand around in the air as though she wanted to erase my words. 'Maryam, don't ever wish for a girl! Girls are no good. Wish for a boy. Having boys is the only way for you to get respect from the family.'

I had to bite my tongue to keep from making a retort.

Other things about living in Saudi were beginning to annoy me. One day Khalid called the cable company to come and put up the TV dish at our new home. I was sitting in the living room while our maid was tidying up when the man arrived. Khalid raised his voice to me for the first time and ordered, 'Go into the bedroom at once, Maryam, and stay there until I call you.'

I was embarrassed that our maid had heard my husband speak to me in a rude tone. 'Why?' I asked.

'Because I said so.'

We had our first argument after the cable employee left. 'Why is it OK for the maid to stay in the room but I am kicked out?' I demanded.

'Because she is a maid, Maryam. It would not be honourable for you to be seen by a stranger in my house. You are my wife. It is that simple.'

The next time a repairman came to the house, I decided to prove a point. My modesty protected by my abaaya and scarf, I deliberately sat in the living room. But Khalid pulled me by the arm and marched me to our bedroom. I was furious when he locked the door.

Khalid's mother and sisters were on his side. 'The maid is nobody. It doesn't matter if a strange man sees her. You are a wife. You are somebody. You must be respected.'

And that was that!

I didn't want all-out war, but I was not too happy about it. The following day, however, I forgot my anger at Khalid when I discovered the heart-stopping brutality occurring next door. When our doorbell rang I answered it. The visitor was Sarah, our next-door neighbour, a twenty-three-year-old Saudi woman who had a four-year-old son, Ali. I welcomed her in my home, despite my surprise, because up till then she hadn't sought me out. Saudis do not mingle easily with their neighbours, and are content to seek companionship within their family units. But I was happy to meet her and I had a special affection for little boys who reminded me of Duran. I spoke poor Arabic but she spoke passable English, so we managed to communicate.

The month was July and the humid heat in Jeddah was unbearable. I quickly understood that Sarah and her son were hot, thirsty and hungry. Since they had just moved in, and rental houses in Saudi Arabia are not equipped with refrigerators or stoves, I thought nothing of her request for food and drink, and was happy to present them with snacks and drinks.

After the two of them satisfied their hunger, they left.

Later that day I prepared some sandwiches and filled a thermos with ice and water and walked over to the neighbouring house to deliver the refreshments. When I rang their bell, Sarah's husband answered. He shook my hand, which caught me off guard, because Saudi men make a big point of avoiding touching women not of their family. The husband was pleasant to me, and speaking in fluent English he told me he was an air force pilot and had received his training in France.

I felt very pleased to have such nice neighbours.

The following day Sarah and Ali returned. Ali ran straight to my garbage can and began digging around in the trash. I assumed he was going through an inquisitive stage and thought nothing of it, until I saw him pulling some stringy meat off a discarded chicken breast and gobbling it up. Sarah started pointing to her mouth, also asking for food. I quickly got a few things on the table and watched while they wolfed down the food and drank two big glasses of cold juice before they abruptly left.

Late one evening when I was having trouble sleeping, I thought I heard a cat howling. I looked out of the window but saw nothing.

The next morning I heard the noise again and looked out once more. I was stunned to see it was Sarah making the strange howling sounds. She was banging on a second-floor window and I heard her calling my name through the glass. 'Maryam!'

I opened my window and shouted, 'Sarah? What is going on?'

The poor woman began to weep. 'We are locked inside. My husband is away. We are hungry. We need food,' she cried. 'My son will die without food. Can you throw us some through the window?'

What on earth?

All homes in Saudi Arabia are surrounded by high walls. Large metal gates secure the grounds. I walked out of our garden into the street and tested their gate. It was locked. I assumed that the front door was locked too, or Sarah would escape rather than cry for help from an upstairs window. I gathered some food from my kitchen then ran up the stairs until I was above the walls on the same level. She opened her window as wide as she could, and I began tossing her bread and cheese, although most of it fell into the garden below.

Khalid was away on a business trip, but when our gardener came to work, I urged him: 'Come! I need you to break into my neighbour's house. There is a woman locked inside. Her son is hungry.'

'Madam, I cannot,' he told me in a shaky voice, looking all around as though searching for an escape. 'I am a poor Indian who is in this country working to support my family. If I break into a Saudi home I will never get out of prison and all of my family will starve.'

I understood migrant workers from India and other Asian countries were frequently ill treated in Saudi Arabia. I took matters into my own hands. What would the Saudis do to a pregnant Muslim woman married to a Saudi? Nothing, I told myself. I took a hammer from Khalid's small tool box, carried a chair outside and pulled myself up to the top of the wall separating our houses. Remembering I was six months pregnant, I was extremely cautious as I lowered myself to the ground on the other side.

As I thought, all the doors to the villa were locked, so I took the hammer and bashed in a large window at the back of the house. After clearing away the broken glass, I crawled in through the window and was hit by an airless heat. The air-conditioning was turned off, although Jeddah was a hot, humid city. I called out for Sarah, following the sound of her voice until I reached a locked upstairs door. I smashed the padlock on the door and released Sarah and little Ali. The room smelled putrid.

The three of us fled to safety to my home.

I felt their hot foreheads. After being locked in a small house without air-conditioning for two days, both were feverish. I insisted they take a cool shower while I prepared a big meal.

They devoured the food.

'Sarah, I must call the police,' I told her.

Sarah started weeping. 'No! No! He will kill me.'

Before I could respond, Sarah's husband burst through the front door without the courtesy of ringing the bell. He lunged for Sarah, slapped her two or three times around the head and started dragging her away by her hair. Ali was screaming.

The violent scene brought back for me horrible memories of the many times Kaiss had beaten me while my terrified son looked on.

I shouted, 'How can you lock your wife and child

in the house to starve? What is wrong with you?'

He turned on me and snarled, and I saw the previously polite man had turned into a beast. Then he pushed and kicked his screaming wife out of my home.

I was furious. When Khalid came home I rushed to tell him the story. He was aghast that I had become involved in such a private matter between husband and wife. 'Maryam, this is Saudi Arabia. Men can do what they want when it comes to their wives and children. No one will interfere. Man makes his own law at home. It is considered a private matter, even by the security forces. He can kill her if he likes. No one will protest.'

I nodded, knowing he was speaking the sad truth. Although Saudi Arabia is rich and Afghanistan is poor, when it comes to the treatment of women, the two countries are very similar. Women are helpless in Afghanistan, too.

I was awake most of the night, my thoughts with Sarah. She was living the same nightmare I had once endured, although her situation was even more dire. At the most dangerous moments, I had been able to run from Kaiṣṣ to my father's home. Sarah had no such escape route.

The next day Sarah surprised me when she came back to my house and banged on the front door. She was screaming, with blood running down her body. Her husband ran in behind her. I moved as fast as a heavily pregnant woman can and grabbed the only weapon I saw, a big kitchen knife.

I returned to the living room, where that beast was continuing to beat Sarah. I held up the knife and screamed: 'I am calling the police!'

The air force pilot gave me a glance then started laughing at the sight of a pregnant woman in a night-gown holding a long knife over her head. 'Go on, call the police! I will dial the number for you! The police chief beats his wife too.'

I was frightened, but stood my ground.

'This is not America,' he taunted. 'Stay away from my family or I'll tell your husband to beat you too!'

Later in the day, Khalid refused to get drawn in. 'Please, Maryam. There is absolutely nothing we can do. No one will tell a husband not to beat his wife. No one. Not even his wife's family.'

Once again, my sad thoughts drifted back to my own family. My sister and father and aunties and uncles and cousins had pleaded with me to save my marriage at all costs, even if it meant I was returning to a life of physical violence and abject unhappiness.

What was wrong with the world?

Khalid pulled me to him. 'Listen, you are pregnant. You are about to give birth to our child. This man might try to harm you. You must stay away from the situation.'

I wanted to do as my husband asked, but I could

not. The following evening when we went to my mother-in-law's house for dinner, I brought up the subject again. I pleaded with my sisters-in-law to tell their husbands, one of whom knew the police chief in the city. 'If you don't, I will have to do something myself, even if it means Khalid gets angry with me.'

To keep me from getting involved, one of my brothers-in-law contacted the police chief. The following day police arrived at my neighbour's house. When the police told the air force pilot that they had received a complaint, he was so furious he divorced Sarah on the spot as the police watched on. He told her he never wanted to see her again. Surprisingly, he did allow Sarah to keep her son, and sent her and Ali to live with her father.

Before Sarah left the neighbourhood she came round and hugged me. 'Thank you, Maryam. I will never forget you. You saved my life.'

I was happy until Khalid told me Sarah would not be allowed to keep her son after the age of seven, at which time Saudi men traditionally take control of a son's future. But I reasoned that at least Sarah had him for a few more years. And anything might happen. Had Sarah remained married to her violent husband, the man would have killed her for certain. Ali would not have had a mother.

Chapter 22

The Taliban first came to the notice of the West in 1994. Within two short years they had overrun Afghanistan and taken over power. In November 1996 the Taliban imposed its own law, which was based on their interpretation of Sharia law, but more strict than any imposed anywhere in the Islamic world. Papa happened to be visiting us in Jeddah at the time, and after reading the laws in the newspaper, Papa expressed fury, saying that the Taliban's interpretation did not agree with accepted Islamic scholars.

The basic message of the decree was simple: there would be no joy or freedom for anyone living in Afghanistan.

Most of the edicts focused on former female freedoms. Women were to remain in their homes. Other than physicians, females would not be allowed to work outside their home, nor would they be allowed to attend school.

If it was imperative for a woman to go out, she must be covered head to toe in a shapeless burqa, even her eyes covered with a thick veil, and if so much as a foot showed underneath she would be flogged on the spot by the religious police.

Women were no longer allowed to wash their clothes on the banks of rivers, something women of Afghanistan had been doing since the beginning of time. Since most homes were not equipped with a washing machine, the problem of keeping clean became considerable.

Dancing, even at wedding parties, was forbidden. Music was banned everywhere. If music cassettes were found, the owner would be arrested and imprisoned.

Female doctors were not to treat male patients. Female patients could only go to female doctors, leading to terrible tragedy when sick women could no longer get any medical help at all. (Later, female physicians would be banned from work.)

No taxi drivers were allowed to transport women not properly veiled. If a woman was found out alone in the street, her husband was liable to be beaten or imprisoned.

When the law was first passed, Afghan men had only a month and a half to grow a beard. From then on if any man cut or shaved his beard, he risked going to prison.

The popular pastime of building and flying kites

was prohibited. All kite shops in the cities were to be closed and anyone caught making a kite would be imprisoned.

Photography was considered idolatry. Television was banned. All cameras, photographs, films and portraits were to be destroyed.

Even laughing out loud in public could earn one a prison sentence.

Almost immediately we found ourselves watching news footage of Taliban men beating up burqa-clad women. For what was never clear. The Taliban appeared to despise women for the simple act of existing.

Although women in the Afghan countryside had never ceased veiling, city women had been wearing western-style clothes for years. Few were accustomed to the claustrophobic traditional burqa, layered with many yards of pleated fabric, hooded with only a small embroidered screen for the eyes. Even underneath the burqa, the law said women should dress modestly, although we all hoped that Taliban enforcers would not crouch down to peek under the women's skirts.

I was happy that my fashionable mother had not lived to see this day. Surely she would have been one of the first women to suffer a beating from the religious police for clicking her fashionable high heels on the Kabul pavement.

Stories leaked out of the country from family members and friends. While some relatives or friends were humiliated at the hands of the Taliban, other incidents were life-altering and even life-threatening.

One cousin reported that the new restrictions were being put into place without warning. Often Afghan citizens would find themselves beaten or arrested for an action they did not even realize was against the law.

All females over the age of puberty donned the burqa speedily enough, but few women realized that shoe styles also caught the unwelcome attention of the Taliban. One day my cousin walked with her husband to the market. She wore her shoes, a white pair she had often worn before without incident. Without warning, a red-faced bearded member of the Taliban swooped furiously down on the couple, screaming threats. They were paralysed with fear, not knowing what they might have done. Soon the man made it clear that he had become incensed after spotting the tip of a white shoe from beneath her billowing pale blue burqa.

My cousin said she believed he might execute them both on the spot. She prayed to Allah to live to return to her little children, who would be on the streets if made orphans. But thanks be to Allah they weren't killed, although he pummelled her husband with his fists and then attempted to stamp on her toes.

Thankfully my cousin was nimble enough to jump away in the nick of time. The incident meant she could no longer go outside her home, because her white shoes were her only shoes.

A male friend had the audacity to wear a pair of blue jeans, which the Taliban considered a sinful import from the West. He was attacked by a group of men. Thinking he was about to be robbed of the last money he had to buy bread, he fought back. He was quickly overpowered and pushed down on the side-walk, and his jeans were ripped off his body. He was truly frightened then, believing he was going to be raped. But the men left my friend in his tattered underwear while they lifted him from the ground and tied him backwards on some poor farmer's donkey. They had a lot of fun parading him around the city as an example of a man polluted by the West. My humiliated friend never did get his jeans back.

The world had gone mad.

Other more horrifying stories were even more upsetting.

Another former schoolmate defied the Taliban by having a small school in her home, as school had been forbidden to girls. She was only teaching her own daughter and nieces, along with two neighbour girls, but you might know the Taliban became suspicious when they witnessed four girls walking together. They followed the girls to her home and stayed outside to observe several more girls arriving, one of whom had a book clutched to her chest.

Members of the Taliban burst in, destroying her few pencils and books before arresting everyone, even the children. The women's prison was a horror house, without heating even in the winter. Their only food was dry bread, a thin soup and water. My poor friend was beaten with a whip every week and kept imprisoned for two years, and never in that time was she allowed to see her children, who had been released after a few weeks.

Her health was broken, and within a year of being released from prison, she died from cancer. The fate of her two daughters remains unknown because her husband was murdered by the Taliban over some minor transgression or other.

Yet another dear friend, named Nooria, who had worked so hard to rise above terrible poverty, was also destroyed by the Taliban. Prior to the Russian war, her father had died, making it necessary for her mother to become a servant, washing clothes and cleaning houses so her daughter could attend school. Nooria was the head of her class and her dream of supporting her mother finally became a reality after she received her degree and found a job as a teacher in a girls' school.

The day she began work, she told her mother that she never again had to wash another person's dirty underwear or clean another woman's house. Nooria never once missed paying the rent or buying the family necessities. She was very proud to be able to support her mother.

Nooria decided not to get married, because she feared a husband might forbid her to support her mother. But Nooria's sister did marry and had five children, all greatly loved by Nooria and her mother. Tragically, during the war with Russia, her sister's home was bombed. Nooria's sister and husband, and two of their children, were killed. Nooria adored her sister's three surviving children, so she took them into her home to support them. She felt that her sister's children were like her own, and loved them fiercely.

After the Russian withdrawal, the country was plunged into civil war. But still Nooria managed to keep the family together. Then the Taliban gained power. One of their first acts was to close schools for girls. Then they banned female employment. So many men had been killed during the recent wars that Nooria's family was only one of many households who had no adult males to support them.

With no man in the house to act as a breadwinner, and the Taliban banning all women from employment, suddenly Nooria's little family was facing starvation.

While the Taliban would not allow women to work in respectable jobs, they did often turn a blind eye to prostitution. With three starving children to feed, Nooria became desperate. She did the unimaginable for a respectable Afghan woman. Nooria sold her body. Since she was a virgin, she received a high price for her first time. But soon her fee declined, so she had to take many customers per night. Since she was not allowed to go out without a male, she was forced to take her sister's twelve-year-old son with her as guardian when she called on her clients. The poor child would have to wait outside in the cold and listen to the sexual activity of his beloved auntie.

That's what the Taliban brought to Afghanistan.

Despite the tragedy of many Afghan female lives that I was aware of when I was growing up, never could I have imagined that Afghan women would reach even greater depths of misery.

My grief was multiplied when I thought of my poor son, still a prisoner of his father, and living in the mad world of the Taliban. How I wanted my son out of that hell-hole!

Yet despite all this gloom, far away from my country in Saudi Arabia, I finally found some joy to fill my life.

Maryam's second son, also called Duran

Chapter 23

On 31 March 1996 at 7.40 in the evening, I became a mother again. I gave birth to a beautiful baby boy, and promptly named him Duran. Everyone in my family and in Khalid's family was opposed to my decision, claiming it was bad luck to name a second child after a lost first child. Only Khalid supported me. 'Maryam should name this baby whatever makes her happy.'

Duran was a perfect baby, although I was an imperfect mother, panicking at every little whimper, rushing him to the doctor for the slightest sniffle. After having the driver break the speed limit three times in one day to get to the hospital, the doctor sat me down for a stern talk.

'Maryam, babies cry. Duran is fine. You are the one I am worried about.'

That's when I admitted: 'I'm sorry, doctor, but my first son was kidnapped when he was a toddler. I haven't seen him since. That is why I am so easily panicked over the well-being of my baby. Nothing bad must happen to this baby. I would not live another minute.'

Although Duran's birth had brought great joy to our family, Papa was failing. He was put on oxygen. The doctors told us that two years would be a long life for him. Khalid agreed that I should spend as much time as possible with my father and it was decided that I would commute, living in Virginia with Papa for six months, then bringing Papa back with me to Jeddah for the other six months. I'm so glad I did this, for I had every possible precious moment with my father before he passed away.

We were in Jeddah when Papa took a turn for the worse. I was in bed when my maid knocked on my bedroom door to tell me he was breathing with great difficulty, sweating and with his eyes rolling back in his head. In a panic, I quickly dressed and had my driver and gardener lift Papa out of bed and take him to the car. We raced to the hospital. Just as we arrived at the hospital, Papa looked at me and mumbled, 'Daughter, I am so sleepy.'

I grabbed him, but then he was gone. I jumped out of the car and began running around in the parking lot screaming: 'Help! Help! Help me!' But the nurses and doctors couldn't revive him. Papa was peaceful in death, but I was wild in life.

Nothing is easy in Saudi Arabia, not even death.

Papa, like all Muslims, had cherished a desire to be buried in Mecca, our holy city. But the Saudi government refused us a permit. I called the American Consul and he said he could get permission, but it would take three days. We didn't have three days, because according to our religion we *must* be buried within twenty-four hours of death. So Khalid arranged for my father to be buried in Jeddah. Like so many places in Saudi Arabia, funerals are reserved for men. Saudis believe that women will become too emotional at funerals of their loved ones and might rip out their hair or tear off their clothes, so they are expected to remain at home to mourn behind closed doors. So I was forbidden to attend my father's funeral. For the first time, I had to admit that my father had been right. Saudi Arabia was no place for a woman.

Papa's death hit me harder than Mother's, perhaps because now I was truly orphaned, after Grandmother Mayana and Mother had passed away.

Visiting a gravesite can give comfort to the bereaved. After a week, I decided I would sneak out to visit my father's grave despite the fact that women are forbidden to visit public cemeteries. I forced our driver to take me to the cemetery, then bribed the cemetery official. Once inside I telephoned Khalid. 'Khalid, what is the location of my father's grave?'

'Why do you ask?'

'Because I am in the cemetery and I want to visit my father.'

Khalid shouted: 'You are WHERE?'

'I am going to visit my father's grave. Either you give me directions or I will just wander around and ask everyone I see.'

Khalid groaned in exasperation. He knew I was determined and, terrified I would end up arrested, he gave me directions to the grave, but ordered me to come straight home and make sure nobody saw me. Although there are no tombstones on Saudi graves, there are identifying marks on the ground. Khalid directed me as best he could.

I laid flowers on Papa's grave, said a few prayers, talked to him and felt better for the experience.

I felt so lonely for Papa that I began a habit of visiting his grave once a week, although I never revealed these visits to Khalid. My driver soon accepted the situation and the cemetery caretaker relished the extra funds. It was a great comfort to me.

I didn't care that I was flouting Saudi Arabia's silly taboo against women visiting graveyards. Such preposterous rules are made to be broken.

Living in Afghanistan, and then in Saudi Arabia, taught me over and over that when women have no control, their lives are always in danger. And so it proved for a dear friend, an Iranian/Saudi woman named Soraya. She and I had met in Egypt before I arrived in Saudi Arabia. We had been fast friends since that time.

Soraya called me one day and told me she was in the hospital. She asked me to come quickly. I ran to her side and was startled to see that she was extremely ill, wheezing for every breath. In between each gasp, Soraya began cursing herself for coming to live in Saudi Arabia.

'Soraya! Save your breath! Please tell me what happened.'

Soraya gasped out her story, that she had become ill in the middle of the night with a raging fever. She had called an emergency number for an ambulance to take her to hospital.

'Where is your mahram?' the man answering the emergency line had said, asking for her male guardian.

'He is my brother, but he is out of the country on business.'

'Then you must wait until he returns,' the man said. 'Your mahram must sign for you to be taken by ambulance to the hospital.'

'I will be dead by the time he returns. I think I have pneumonia,' Soraya said.

The man said unapologetically and matter-of-factly, 'If you are not dead when he returns, then call us back.'

Poor Soraya. I nodded at my friend in sympathy. I

had not been allowed to sign for little Duran to be circumcised. I had not been allowed to accompany Khalid's family to Taif, because Khalid had been out of the city on business and unable to sign for me.

But Soraya was a resourceful woman. She slowly dressed then stumbled out of their villa to the main road, where she hailed a taxi and somehow convinced the driver to take her to the hospital. Once there, she faced more obstacles, being refused treatment because her guardian was not there to sign for her to be admitted. Thankfully, a western physician intervened and Soraya was finally admitted to the emergency ward and given medication.

Tragically, the delay had given the pneumonia time to overwhelm Soraya's system. My dear friend did not survive the day, dying soon after my visit. Another good woman was dead only because of the country's absurd restrictions against women.

Once again, I was not allowed to attend Soraya's funeral. But Khalid was feeling guilty about my bruised feelings, so he offered to take me to the cemetery to visit my father on that day. That's when I bragged to my surprised husband that I had been visiting my father routinely.

Poor Khalid slapped his forehead a couple of times, but then drove me to Eve cemetery.

'Why are we here?' I asked, puzzled.

'I thought you wanted to visit your father's grave.'

I felt a rush of anger that my husband had forgotten where his father-in-law was buried. 'He is at Qasuim cemetery.'

Khalid looked at me in astonishment. 'Is that where you have been going? To the Qasuim cemetery?'

'Yes. To my father's grave at the Qasuim cemetery.'

'Maryam, your father is not buried *there*. He is buried *here*, at Eve cemetery.'

'How can that be?' I stammered. 'That is where Stalleh took me.'

Khalid started laughing. 'Maryam, Stalleh did not attend your father's funeral. I sent him on errands on the day of the funeral. He obviously *thought* your father was buried at Qasuim but he was mistaken.'

My temper flared, thinking of the many times I had bribed the caretaker at Qasuim, the flowers I had placed on what I had thought was my beloved father's grave, the prayers I had made, the long hours I had sat on the ground beside his grave – talking to a *stranger*!

'*You and your stupid country!*' I screamed at my husband. 'If I were living in America, I would know where my father was buried and I could visit his grave openly! Even in Afghanistan I would have been permitted to bury my father and visit his grave.'

Khalid found the incident amusing, while I was burning inside. I faced another disappointment when we discovered that the cemetery caretaker at Eve was not open to bribery. I was wounded to the core when Khalid and Duran were allowed inside the cemetery to visit my father's grave, while his daughter was banned, forced to wait outside in the hot sun.

Never once have I been allowed to visit my father's grave, although ironically for some months I tended carefully some unknown man's plot.

Although I was Muslim and had been raised in a Muslim country, I found I was happier socializing with westerners than with Saudis. There were too many hang-ups about women in Saudi society. I became active in the American Ladies of Jeddah Committee, where we were involved in good works.

My little Duran was now four years old, a happy and well-adjusted child with a kindly father and loving mother. He was very bright and, most importantly for me, extremely sensitive and caring about other people. But loving Duran did not alter my love for my first son, whom I now called Big Duran. I thought about Big Duran so many times each day, so sad that I had missed his childhood. Big Duran was twelve years older than Little Duran, so my lost son was now sixteen years old, a teenager, an image I found it impossible to imagine.

When Little Duran reached an age of understanding, I confided that he had an older brother who would one day be a part of his life. Little Duran became very excited and started putting aside his most special toys, saying, 'I will give this to my brother when he comes for a visit.'

The idea that Big Duran was becoming a man without even knowing that he had a mother who had never stopped looking for him pushed me to try to visit Afghanistan yet again. Although Afghanistan was still ruled by the Taliban, I did not care. But Khalid's knowing that Kaiss had threatened to kill me should I set one foot inside my country caused my husband to forbid me from trying. Still, I redoubled my efforts to locate my son, and the development of new technology was to open up new avenues of research for me.

Chapter 24

Once Khalid and I had internet access in 2000, I paid someone to create a web page in honour of Big Duran. There I posted my life's story, and listed all I knew about my son. I signed off with a plea: 'I have not seen my son in nearly 14 years. He was stolen from me when he was only two years old. He will turn 16 on January 27th. In my dreams I am with my son. Please help me find him.'

Many people responded in sympathy, but one person in particular kept sending me messages, teasing me with: 'I know Duran's family.'

I pleaded for further information and was told: 'If you want to know about your son, you must first become good friends with me.'

'I will be your friend,' I promised, 'but first, I must hear directly from my son.'

I never heard from that person again, although I wondered who my anonymous correspondent might have been.

I wrote to three Taliban ministers. Because they were supposed to be religious men, I invoked their piety to plead my case: 'In the Koran, there is a verse that says that heaven is under the feet of mothers. If you are true Muslims, you will help me to contact my son.'

I didn't hold out much hope of an answer, and was startled when one of the Taliban ministers telephoned me at home in Saudi Arabia. He told me firmly, but not unkindly: 'I am very good friends with Duran's father, Kaiss. Duran is a good boy and is loyal to his father. He is doing very well. But Duran belongs to his father. Leave him alone now. He has a family, and that family is here.' I cursed that man, thinking that all men stick together against women.

I began gathering information from friends who had remained behind in Taliban-ruled Afghanistan. I was not surprised to learn that Kaiss had switched allegiance to the Taliban. He now scorned the communist regime he had once served and was in a powerful position close to the Taliban leadership. I also heard that after my letters to the Taliban ministers, they had alerted Kaiss and ordered a guard to be set up to protect my son from his mother. Other friends told me that my son had been trained in computer English and that the Taliban were using his computer skills for their purposes. Perhaps my son was safer than I thought, although I was not pleased to hear of his close association with men I considered to be criminals. Obviously my teenage son was being used as a pawn by his father to increase his prestige with the Taliban rulers.

Just as I thought things couldn't get worse, they did.

I was in Jeddah on 11 September 2001, and watched the horrific scenes coming from America on TV. I bellowed at the sight of all the death and destruction. I loved America and Americans, the country and people who had welcomed me when my own country was burning, and I couldn't bear to see innocents suffering on such a shocking scale.

Once we heard the news that Osama Bin Laden had been behind the attacks, and that he was being protected by the Taliban in Afghanistan, it was obvious that their days were now numbered. America was bound to take military action in response to the attack on their soil.

When American bombs started falling on my homeland, I came very close to a complete nervous breakdown, because for all I knew my son was living where those bombs were targeted. God had kept him safe during the Russian war and the civil war, but now Afghanistan was at war with America, the most powerful nation in the world! Would Afghanistan ever know peace again?

I held the Koran and prayed. 'Allah, please save

the good people in Afghanistan. Allah, please save my son.' The bombs falling on Afghanistan were so devastating that we heard reports people were simply being evaporated. Would my eyes never see my son again? I went to Mecca and held on to the door of the Ka'bah, asking Allah to please keep those bombs away from my beloved son.

By December, American ground troops were moving in, pushing out the Taliban as the new rulers of my homeland. Friends in Afghanistan reported that Kaiss was still with the Taliban and that my son was with his father. My biggest fear was that the American military would kill my teenage son, believing him to be Taliban.

I wrote endless letters to the American Embassy, telling the officials there all I knew about Kaiss and Duran, pleading with them to look for my son and return him to me. I was devastated to be told that since Duran had turned eighteen in January, he was now considered an adult and out of the jurisdiction of American authority. My son was free to live with whom he pleased in the eyes of American law. The only way my son would return to me was of his own free will.

That's when I heard from my cousin Farid that he was going to Afghanistan, to reclaim and reopen our family businesses.

I was alarmed. Outside of a very few American-controlled pockets, Afghanistan was still a wild and violent place. 'But you have a good job in Paris! Please don't risk your life for this, Farid.'

'But this is a special time, Maryam. Our country needs patriotic citizens.' He added: 'Besides, someone has to go in and find your son!'

My heart skipped a beat. Farid had always been my special protector, even now I was a woman grown and married. Farid was a miracle worker. Perhaps he would bring Duran back to me at last.

But before Farid arrived in Kabul, I had a call from another relative, who revealed the most astonishing news: he had managed to meet with Duran! I was told: 'Maryam, your son is a happy boy. He speaks fluent English and he is a computer whiz. He has started his first year of college.'

'I am coming to Kabul right now!' I shouted down the phone.

'No, Maryam, he does not want to see you. I told him about you, Maryam. He knows now that he has a mother, but he has been brainwashed. He believes you sold him to his father for $5,000.'

I put the phone down in turmoil. Although I was sad to hear that my son wanted nothing to do with his mother, I was jubilant to have confirmation that he was alive and that he knew I existed. Well, it was a start, at least.

That was the day hope returned, and my heart told

me I would finally be reunited with my son. Perhaps not tomorrow, or even within the year, but I would see my long-lost son. But knowing that his father would continue to poison him against me, I wondered if it wouldn't be best to see my son on neutral territory. Perhaps I could somehow get him to America?

My sister Nadia travelled to Kabul in the spring of 2002. While there she tried to see Duran, but she found out he was no longer in Kabul. Nadia called me with the information she had uncovered. 'Maryam, at least you don't have to worry about Duran's safety. Kaiss has switched sides once again. First he was a supporter of the Communists, then he switched to the Taliban, now he has turned and is helping the Americans against the Taliban.'

Nothing surprised me when it came to Kaiss. The man had no real loyalty to anyone. He switched political sides as easily as I turned over in bed.

I decided on the spot that I couldn't wait a minute longer. 'Nadia, I am coming too. I am coming home to find my son.'

Nadia screamed at me down the phone. 'NO! Maryam, you cannot. Your presence here will put everyone's life in danger.'

'How is that?'

Nadia put a male cousin on the line, who patiently explained. 'Kaiss has made careful plans for the day when you would try to see your son. He has spread many lies and turned everyone here against you. When he first came back Kaiss reported that Duran's mother was a non-Muslim American woman who was dead. He never admitted the fact that he had kidnapped Duran. When our family reported the truth to the authorities, they called on Kaiss's tribe. Tribal elders have agreed to question Kaiss. They will ask him again why he left America. If they decide he is lying, he will be forced to wear the chador.'

Forcing a man to wear the chador was a huge insult. But sometimes when men lied or behaved in other shameful ways, the tribal elders would rule that they must wear it. If this happened to Kaiss, I knew he would be ridiculed by everyone. In fact, he would be forced to leave the country to hide his shame.

My cousin continued. 'However, Maryam, if it is determined by the elders that you, and not Kaiss, are at fault for the divorce, then you will be put to death, regardless of whether or not you are an American citizen.'

'Oh? So the punishment is to insult the man but to murder the woman?' My blood was boiling. 'You know what? I am coming to Afghanistan and I am going to take my ex-husband to court. With the Americans there it will be a different story.'

My cousin raised his voice. 'Do you think Afghan tribes follow American law? Kaiss will say and do anything he likes and they will believe him because he is a man. You know that women hold no power. You know that a man's word is taken over a woman's word. Nothing you say will be believed, because you are a woman. If you come to Kabul, you are going to start a war between two tribes, Maryam. Then who will look after our children?'

I was trembling with rage when my cousin told me: 'Your son now knows about you. If he wants to see you, he will contact you. If he does not want to see you, then that is your fate. Now, please leave us alone!'

Nadia got back on the phone and said, 'Now do you understand?'

I was devastated with disappointment, waiting impatiently for Big Duran to contact me, day-dreaming about our first conversation. What would I say to my son? What would he say to me? It seemed easy: I would tell my son how much I loved him, and how much I had missed him.

To my despair, however, I heard nothing from Duran. There was total silence. It was clear Kaiss had hardened my son against me. With a heavy heart I recognized I might never see my Big Duran again.

In the summer of 2003, Little Duran and I visited my cousin Zeby who was living in Düsseldorf, Germany. We were enjoying a lazy morning eating breakfast when the telephone rang. From Zeby's words I could tell it was Khalid. Then she whispered into the phone: 'Oh my dear God, thank you.' She began to weep.

I rushed over to her. I saw her write a telephone number on a pad. The first two numbers were '93', which I recognized as the international country code for Afghanistan.

I completely lost my composure and began throwing myself around the room like a child. *Duran's phone number! He called!*

Zeby tried to calm me down.

I could not contain my excitement and grabbed the phone from her.

'Khalid? Khalid? He called? He called?'

'Love,' he said to me in his soft voice. 'Take a deep breath. It is good news for you. Listen, your sister is in Kabul again. She has located your son. He has called you.' Khalid's voice broke. 'He left his number. Call him. I will hang up now. Let me know what he says.'

I was mindless with joy. Perhaps Nadia had finally recognized her role in the loss of my son. If she was the one who brought us together, I would forgive her for everything.

I kept misdialling Duran's number. The combination of trembling fingers and blinding tears made it impossible.

Finally Zeby's husband took the phone from my hands and dialled the number for me.

My heart was pounding too loudly. All my rehearsed words escaped my mind.

A man's voice answered: 'Hello.'

Surely this man was not my little Duran.

'Hello?' I gasped.

The man spoke a second time. 'Hello?'

'Duran?'

'Yes?'

'This is your mother, Duran. Your Mano.' I burst into noisy sobs. 'Remember when you were little you called me Mano?'

A cold voice said, 'Stop crying, please.'

Who was this man on the phone? Where was my baby?

'Stop crying? Stop crying? How can I stop crying? I've waited for this moment for seventeen years!' All the wrong words rushed out of my mouth. 'Listen, I'll come to you right away. I'll catch a flight and come to Kabul.'

But the man shouted back, 'I forbid you to come to Kabul.'

'Forbid me? But, Duran . . . my son . . . my love, I must see you.'

That cold voice was killing me, but it grew colder still. 'Look here, sister, do not come here. If I see your ugly face appear, I'll kill myself.'

I was sobbing. 'Why? Why do you say that? I am your mother. I have lived only to see you again. I—'

'Look here, sister, there is no divorce in Paktia law.'

I could barely think. Why was my son calling me 'sister' in that hateful tone of voice? Why was Duran being intentionally cruel?

When I didn't answer, he shouted at me, 'How dare you divorce my father!'

'Duran, Duran, this is not the time for this. But if you must know, I divorced your father because he beat me.'

'My father said you did not want me after the divorce, that you sold me to him for $5,000. He told me you never loved me.'

My heart pounded painfully. I put my right hand over my chest protectively. 'Duran, listen to me.' My words rushed, one over the other, trying to make him understand. 'That is not true. I can show you papers that prove your father kidnapped you. Duran, your grandfather and I did everything to try and find you. You must believe me.' I paused. 'Duran, won't you call me Mouri?' (*Mouri* means 'Mother' in Pashto).

'Before I call you my mother, there are many questions you must answer,' he said coldly. 'Then I will decide if I will even see you.'

Zeby got on another extension. 'Now calm down, both of you. This is the first conversation. It is a shock for both of you.'

Duran hung up without saying anything more.

I was so shaken I could barely speak. For years I had dreamed of speaking to my son, of telling him of my love, of how I had never stopped looking for him, loving him. Now the dream was a nightmare. My little baby, my adorable Duran, seemed to have no love for his mother. In fact, he gave every indication that he hated me.

Zeby tried in vain to console me. 'Maryam, Duran's father has brainwashed him for seventeen years. The boy doesn't know what to think. He will come round. Give him time.'

Weeping bitter tears I called Khalid and told him what had happened. Khalid was unruffled, as always. 'Don't worry, my love. He will call you back when he is ready. This is going to take some time.'

I was like a wild animal caged, pacing, filled with regrets that I had said all the wrong things. I wanted to shout at my serene husband and take it out on him. Time? Hadn't seventeen years been enough time for me to live without my son?

Duran called again two days later. This time I managed to keep my emotions in check, though it was difficult. I prayed he was calling because of some newly found memory, but that was sadly not the case. He had called me for one reason only. His thoughts were of his father. Duran was worried that I would create problems for his father. 'Your sister told me the story. I will not speak with you again unless you promise to forgive my father. You must not take him to court. You must not make any trouble for him.'

I would have promised my son anything if it meant we could stay in touch. 'My son, I promise you, I will do nothing to hurt your father.'

'You must also forgive my father.'

I paused a long time before uttering those difficult words, although I knew there was little I would not do to be reunited with my son. 'All right, I forgive your father, Duran.'

Instantly his tone changed, and he started sounding friendly, weirdly so, suddenly making plans to leave Afghanistan. 'I think I will go to India to school. I might let you come there to see me. But I never want to go to America. America is where you divorced my father.'

I wanted my son with me in Saudi Arabia, or to meet me in America, but I struggled to be patient. 'Duran, all I want is for you to be happy. I will do whatever you wish.'

He seemed pleased that I was under his control.

A few weeks after I returned to Jeddah, he called me for the third time. Three telephone calls in less than a month! I was over the moon with joy. During that third telephone call he unexpectedly called me 'Mouri'.

'Duran! My son.'

Then, to my astonishment, Duran confessed that he now believed me, that he no longer believed I had sold him to his father for $5,000.

'Listen,' he said, 'I confronted my father. I now know that he has been lying to me. I don't love him any more. I hate him. I am sick of the Islamic life. I have decided I will go to America.'

My son didn't know what he wanted, I thought to myself. First he hated America, and now he wanted to go and live there.

'Why don't you come here, to Saudi Arabia, to be with me and my family?'

'I hate Arabs,' he said, with a troubling certainty. 'Yes, I hate Arabs.'

I said nothing, although his assertion made me feel uneasy. After all, his stepfather was Arab, and his baby brother was half-Arab.

Immediately after our conversation, I made contact with the American Embassy in Kabul and told them my son had finally contacted me. I wanted to arrange the proper paperwork for my son to get an American passport. If Duran wanted to go to America, then his American mother would pull every string to get him there.

A week later Duran called for a fourth time, once more with a disturbing message. 'My father told me that if I see you, he will disown me. He told me I was no longer his son. When I told him I was going to America, he beat me. I had to run away. My father is looking for me everywhere. He is threatening to kill me.'

I gasped in distress. I truly believed Kaiss capable of murdering Duran if that meant he could keep him from me. My mind was racing.

'Where are you now?'

'I have gone into hiding. Fighters of the Northern Alliance are protecting me.'

I didn't like the sound of that at all. Kaiss had been too closely associated with the Taliban, and the Taliban had used my son's skills to further their cause. I knew the Taliban and the Northern Alliance were deadly enemies. Perhaps those soldiers would try to kill my son, too.

To my mind, Afghanistan was full of killers, and all were looking for my son. I would defend Duran with my bare hands if I could get to Afghanistan, but I was in Saudi Arabia, too far away to protect him.

To find my son only to lose him again was too much to bear. That's when I thought of Farid. Thank God Farid was still in Kabul, trying to restart his father's business. I called my cousin, giving him Duran's details, and begging him to find my son and protect him from his father.

'Do not worry, little brother,' he said, laughing. 'I will protect your son with all my heart.'

Indeed, within a few days Farid had managed to locate Duran; how, I do not know. He drove him to the American Embassy in Kabul. There he was interviewed by the consular officials, who said they had no problem issuing Duran with an American passport *if* he was my son, but they would need a DNA test to make certain he was who he said he was.

I decided on the spot to go to my son, to have our DNA tested together, to solve the problem once and for all. It was too difficult to do the tests in Afghanistan, and it was suggested I meet my son in Pakistan. The American authorities would have DNA tests performed there.

The biggest obstacle was the fact that my son did not have a valid passport. It was decided to hire smugglers to take Duran across the border. I didn't know where to start making arrangements but, once again, blessed Farid handled all the details. My cousin found dependable smugglers, men who had been crossing the borders illegally for years.

How could I ever thank Farid? My 'big brother' cousin had shown remarkable devotion to me, time and time again. But a few days before Duran was to leave on the risky journey to Pakistan, Farid called me, his voice filled with concern. 'Maryam, I warn you, do not let Duran use your mobile phone when you meet him in Pakistan. And do not give him money.'

'Why do you say this?'

Farid paused a long moment. 'Maryam, from happiness to disaster is only one small step.'

'What? What are you saying, Farid?'

I sensed my cousin was choosing his words very carefully, too carefully. 'He is your son, Maryam, but I feel I do not know him. Just do as I tell you. Be very careful.'

I knew Farid as well as I knew myself. He was apprehensive. What had happened to make him become suspicious of my son?

I was plagued with worry, but I was too close to a reunion I had dreamed of for nearly eighteen years.

Nothing could keep me from Duran.

The long-lost son on the phone to Maryam
for the first time

Chapter 25

Khalid was very troubled that I was going to Pakistan to meet Duran alone for our first meeting. 'What if you are met by Kaiss? This could be a trick, Maryam.'

I shook my head and held out my hands, pushing Khalid away. 'Wild horses wouldn't keep me from my son.'

Khalid sighed deeply.

'I have not seen my son since 1986, Khalid. This is the chance I have been waiting for.'

Khalid plopped down heavily on the sofa, staring at me.

I tried to make him understand. 'Think how you would feel, Khalid, if someone had Little Duran. No one could stop you. I must go. I am sorry. But promise me, if anything happens to me in Pakistan, please look after Little Duran.'

Khalid choked up. 'I will, my love. I will.'

And I knew he would. My Saudi husband was

nothing like most Saudi men. He had never changed from the considerate suitor he had been when I first met him. I was lucky, and I knew it.

Four days later, on 25 July 2003, Duran departed Kabul for Peshawar in the company of five smugglers. The following day I flew from Jeddah to Islamabad. From Islamabad, I boarded a bus to Peshawar. Some of the windows on the bus were broken and it was hot and crowded, but I didn't care. I was going to see my son.

When I left Islamabad, the sun was rising over the landscape, turning buildings pink and tree shadows indigo. Swirls of dust rose in the air from the vehicles in front. I felt that fine dust in my nose and between my teeth. All the sights and sounds of the world I had grown up in came rushing into my head. Suddenly I was conscious of my age, for I had not been back to the area for over twenty years, since my father and I left Mother in a grave in India and escaped to America. Papa and I had left the area crippled in spirit, for Mother's loss had felt too much to bear. Now I was returning quite alone. If only Papa had lived to see Duran once again.

Duran! I really was going to see my son at last! In my mind, he was still the little fat-faced baby laughing at his Mano. It was nearly impossible to think of my stolen baby as the grown man he must now be.

I daydreamed my way to Peshawar. Neither the

pock-marked face of an overburdened mother sitting beside me nor the singing driver of the bus made much impact on me. All I could see was baby Duran's face. I had memorized the place we were to meet. The Green Hotel in Peshawar, in room 114.

I didn't knock as I rushed into the room. The first thing I saw were five men, all with long beards and dressed in traditional Afghan clothing, the people smugglers who had transported my son across the border. I gave a small cry when I spotted a young unbearded man sitting on the bed. He was dressed casually in western clothes. I ran up to him and stared deep into his face. A profound and unprecedented happiness rolled over me. I grabbed him to me, crying out, 'If this is a dream, Allah, please don't wake me up! My son! My son!'

It felt like the happiest moment of my life.

Duran said nothing in reply.

'You are so handsome, son,' I told him, trying to regain my self-control.

My son held himself aloof, and stared at me coldly. 'Do you think I should have plastic surgery?' he asked unexpectedly. 'I really despise my bony cheeks!'

The five smugglers laughed heartily. One of them shouted through his guffaws: 'The mother cries to see her son. The son is preoccupied with his face!'

My son stared at the men, then at me, and looked

embarrassed. 'I am glad you came for me,' he finally admitted.

My face flushed with pleasure, 'Duran, my son. My son, you will never know how much I have longed for this moment.'

The smugglers exchanged glances, then stood up. 'We will leave you,' the leader said. 'You should talk privately.'

I smiled, urging them to leave quickly. I was eager to be alone with Duran. I longed to close the schism created by time. To accomplish my goal, we must get to know each other, and share the details of our lives in all those lost years.

Duran muttered, 'I saw a photo of you once with my father. You were wearing a white dress. I told my father it looked like a wedding photo to me, and that you looked like a bride.'

'What did your father say to that?'

'Oh, he said he had attended a wedding in America and everyone had wanted their photo taken with him. He said you were a crazy girl who was there. But I never saw that picture again. My father took it away.'

I nodded, feeling that Duran was opening a door for us to talk about his father and the lies that had driven a wedge between us. But I avoided saying anything negative about Kaiss. Perhaps the moment was a test. I thought Duran might be looking for a reason to push me away.

On this day I would concentrate on the positives.

I smiled, staring at my son. I could not get enough of his face and hair and hands. 'Please talk some more,' I said, 'I want to hear your voice.'

He grunted.

I bit my lip, feeling myself dangerously perched above an abyss. One misstep and all would be lost.

'How was your stepmother, Duran? Was she nice to you?'

He shrugged. 'She was OK. She was stupid. She could be kind. She could be mean. When my father beat me, she would sometimes try to protect me.'

'Oh.' I buried my head in my hands. I should have been there to protect my baby. I swallowed with difficulty, then asked, 'Was your father mean to you, Duran?'

'Only if I didn't do what he told me to do. Then he would beat me.'

That was Kaiss. His answer to any loss of control always was to use his fists. I took a deep breath. 'Tell me everything, Duran, everything, the good and the bad.'

And so the dam of silence burst, and my son began to talk.

I heard that when my son was around six years old, he had been looking out of a second-floor window in his father's house when someone pushed him from behind. He tumbled out of the window. He would have been killed but some high bushes broke his fall. He never found out who pushed him, whether it was his father or his stepmother.

I learned that one cold day when Duran had failed to do his homework, his father lost his temper and hit him repeatedly about the head before opening the front door to throw his small son bodily out into the snow. While my son lay there shivering, his father shouted that he should stay out in the snow and sleep there that night. Perhaps that would teach him a lesson.

I learned that my sad little boy had somehow walked all alone for a long distance to his uncle's house, where he was finally taken in to be thawed. I saw my baby struggling through snow drifts dressed only in lightweight pyjamas.

I learned that after Kaiss joined the Russians, my son had watched his father repeatedly get drunk on alcohol.

I learned that Kaiss had purchased a beautiful piano, and that he had made sure my son learned to play.

I learned that after the Soviet withdrawal when the Taliban came to power, the alcohol was barred and the piano was trashed.

I heard that with the Taliban Kaiss had pretended to be a man of religion. Clerics were hired to teach my son to recite the Koran by heart.

I learned that a Taliban leader had come to Kaiss and told him that the Taliban had plenty of people who could recite the Koran, but what they needed was an English-speaking student like my son to learn everything there was to know about computers. And so my son became a computer expert for the Taliban.

I learned that my son grew to hate the Taliban. He had loved the piano and singing and dancing and watching movies, and when the Taliban had come to power, all those pleasures had disappeared or been proscribed.

I learned that my son so hated the Taliban that his hatred had turned him against Islam. I learned that my son was even thinking of becoming a Christian, a thought that caused my Muslim heart to grieve.

As the stories poured out of him, my son began to sweat and look increasingly unwell.

To change the subject that was so troubling, I asked my son to sing to me. I felt my heart swell when he opened up his mouth and I heard his beautiful voice.

That night I slept more peacefully than I had slept since the night before my baby was stolen.

But the following day one of the smugglers took me aside and tried to warn me against my son, whispering to me: 'You know it is possible that his father sent him to you to get an American passport. Perhaps your son is not speaking the truth.'

I looked over at Duran, who was involved in an animated dialogue with two other smugglers. 'That may be the case. But it is a chance I must take.'

I felt compelled to change the topic of discussion, and said to the kindly man, 'I wonder if I would recognize my country now. I wonder if the buildings that were landmarks in my youth are still standing.'

The smuggler lifted one eyebrow. 'Very few. All our treasures are gone. The Taliban destroyed everything that was beautiful.'

I felt so very sad for my country. It had enjoyed a burst of prosperity during my childhood, but those years were long gone, and the worst times in Afghanistan's troubled history had followed. Now all was lost. For the first time in years I wondered what had happened to my family's treasures, like my grandfather Hassen's stamp collection and my own precious coin collection. It seemed a long, long time ago that I had left them carefully hidden in my room. Had some child found them?

The following day we travelled to Islamabad so that Duran and I could have our DNA tests and he could obtain his US passport. Although I knew it was possible that Kaiss had set a trap, and that this young man was one of the many thousands of orphans left behind in the conflict, my heart told me that this young man was indeed my son. But I knew the Americans would never accept a mother's instinct over scientific proof.

The American Embassy had been notified of our mission. They were businesslike in taking samples from us both and informed us that we must wait two to six weeks for the results.

I was aghast. 'Two to six weeks? Where will we stay? We can't stay where we are, a cheap hotel with smugglers.' I looked around. 'Can we remain here?'

The embassy officials didn't care about my predicament. It was not in their interest to become personally involved.

There was nothing to do but to go back to the people smugglers. Those men agreed to guard us and keep us safe for the duration of our enforced stay.

Duran treated me warily, his moods remaining unpredictable. One moment he would share his heart with me, the next he would turn on me with rage and suspicion.

One evening Duran demanded: 'So what if he hit you? That was no reason to get a divorce. He was your husband. And a husband has the right to hit his wife.'

I shuddered. What had Kaiss taught my son? 'No, a good husband does not hit his wife, Duran,' I replied carefully.

'It is written in the Koran that a husband can hit his wife. It is allowed.'

I stammered, 'Well, it is not allowed in the United States.'

His eyes were averted, he would not look at me directly. 'Well, my father says that every woman needs to be beaten. Otherwise they do not know their place.'

'Did your father beat your stepmother?'

Duran slowly nodded. 'Yes. I hated hearing her scream and cry. He would not allow her to see her family. She could not attend female wedding parties. She had to stay at home all the time. I remember one time when he was beating her up, she threatened to kidnap me and disappear, that he would never see me again.'

I made a small noise in my throat. All my worst fears had turned out to be true. Duran had indeed been beaten. He had seen his stepmother beaten. Kaiss was still a sadist, and my son had been trapped in his father's sadistic world.

'After that threat, my stepmother became pregnant. And then my father just kept her pregnant so she couldn't run away. I have seven brothers and sisters, you know.'

'Duran, I am so sorry.'

Duran laughed bitterly. 'It doesn't matter. It made me into a man.'

I felt a chill.

Several times during those weeks, I caught Duran

slipping my cellphone from my purse and making calls to Afghanistan. I remembered Farid's warnings.

I quietly asked him, 'Duran, are you calling your father?'

He replied curtly, 'I don't tell him anything. I just wanted to hear his voice. And he wants to hear my voice.'

'Duran, we risked our lives to meet. If your father discovers our location, it is possible he will come and kill us both.'

Duran laughed harshly. 'He would only kill you, not me.'

I nodded numbly.

I prayed for the DNA test results, assuring myself that all would be well if only I could get Duran out of the region, away from his father's influence and into America.

Three weeks later the DNA test results came back.

They confirmed that Duran was my son.

Things began to move quickly after that. The American Embassy provided him with a passport and we booked flights to take us to Virginia. Duran had decided he wanted to live with Nadia and her daughter Suzie in Virginia and attend school there. I would take my son to my sister, and then I would vacation there every year, as I had when my father was alive. I would see my son at least six months out of every year.

I was in heaven!

Nadia and Suzie were waiting for us at the airport. Everyone was ecstatic ... except Duran. My son seemed strangely unmoved by all the excitement of being reunited with his mother's family. When we arrived at Nadia's home, I showed Duran all the toys and games I had purchased for him over the years. I had saved them all.

Duran was callously uninterested. 'Why don't you give them to your other son?' he said with an indifferent shrug.

Then Duran announced to Nadia: 'I must have a computer and email. There are friends I must contact in Kabul.'

Nadia fidgeted nervously. She had been warned by the state department to be cautious, that after seventeen years of fighting to keep his son away from my family, Kaiss was not likely to give in without a struggle. She spoke to him firmly. 'Yes, Duran, you can have a computer and you can email your friends, but you cannot tell them where you are. You must not give them our telephone number or address. It is dangerous. Just as we will protect you, you must protect us.'

Duran didn't answer but his face flushed red.

He then insisted he must have a post office address of his own.

My son had completed one year at Kabul University where he had maintained an A average. I now enrolled him at NOVA, the Northern Virginia Community College, an institution with many foreign students. We thought Duran would feel at home there and could transfer to a bigger school later. Duran insisted on getting a job on top of his studies. Nadia's office hired him for two days a week and he got a second job at McDonald's. I was relieved that he was working hard at school and at work.

I didn't want to leave my son, but my husband and little boy were waiting for me in Saudi Arabia. As he seemed settled, I felt comfortable leaving Duran for a few months. I returned to Saudi Arabia, telling Duran I would soon be back for a holiday in the States.

Two weeks after I arrived in Jeddah, Khalid and I were shocked to receive a frantic call from Nadia. She told me my son could no longer live with her. 'Maryam, I want your son out of my house right now.'

Khalid and I thought that the crisis would pass so Duran could have the stability of remaining in school. But to be on the safe side, Khalid applied for a visa for Big Duran to come to Jeddah.

As we had hoped, Nadia and Duran made up their quarrel, and he stayed for three more weeks. Then they got into another argument because Duran wanted to go clubbing and Nadia thought he was too young. Duran marched out, and went to stay with Aunt Shagul until his Saudi Arabian visa came through.

One night when Khalid and I were out at a dinner party, our telephone rang at home. When my maid answered, she said a man's voice began screaming at her in English, asking where I was. When she told him I was out, the man asked to speak to Little Duran. When my young child answered the phone, the voice screamed at him, 'I am going to kill your mother, Duran. And I going to kill you too!'

My young son was traumatized. We all thought it must have been Kaiss, although we could not imagine how he had obtained our unlisted home telephone number.

Big Duran arrived in Jeddah a few weeks later. Little Duran was so excited, finally getting to meet the big brother he had heard so much about for years.

When I looked upon the sweet sight of my two sons walking side by side, my heart was filled with joy. How could I have suspected that the threatening caller who had terrified my little one was my eldest son?

A happy mother dances with Little Duran (left)
and Big Duran

Chapter 26

I couldn't resist Big Duran, but he could easily resist me, and those I loved. Even on that first evening, a time of the greatest joy for his mother, my elder son was cold and unfriendly. He even ignored his little brother, who was clamouring to enjoy a warm relationship with his long-lost big sibling.

I began to fret almost immediately, but Khalid told me not to worry, that Big Duran was having to cope with such a lot of change. The adjustment would take time, that was all.

During dinner Khalid told my son: 'Welcome to your new family. I hope you will feel at home here.'

'From now on, you can be my father as far as I am concerned. I hate Kaiss, my son-of-a-bitch father.'

Khalid was shocked, for it is a rare Saudi who will criticize their father, regardless of their character. Khalid spoke quietly. 'You should never call your father names. He is still your father. And I don't want you to use language like that in my home in front of

your young brother. You are here now. You are safe.
Let your anger subside.'

'Are there any rules in this house?' Big Duran
asked, taunting Khalid.

He didn't know my husband, who, I often claimed,
had the calmest temperament in all Saudi Arabia.
Khalid just nodded. 'Yes, of course. Every home has
rules.'

Big Duran began to bargain with him. 'How
would it be if for only two weeks there were no rules?
Let me have some freedom without anyone telling me
what to do. After that, I will obey your rules.'

Khalid and I exchanged glances. I followed my
husband's lead when he laughed the moment off. We
both knew there was not much trouble for Big Duran
to find in Jeddah. Saudi Arabia is conspicuously free
of clubs, bars and movie theatres. Social life in Saudi
Arabia is almost exclusively centred around the
family.

For two weeks all was well. I took both my sons to
the beach. We swam. We played volleyball. We went
to the shopping malls. We seemed normal in every
way, at least everyone but Big Duran.

I was bothered when my teenage son looked at me
and said, 'You dress very sexy.' My heart plunged. I
remembered those words were spoken by Kaiss
before he would beat me.

But then I remembered this was a young man who

had been raised by a brute and he couldn't help knowing nothing of social niceties or manners. So rather than reprimand Big Duran, I hugged him and said, 'Thank you, my son.'

Then Big Duran decided Saudi Arabia was not to his liking. He told us, 'We must move to Virginia. I will go to school there. I give you permission to bring your other son.'

I reminded Big Duran: 'But you didn't like Virginia. You wanted to come out here instead.'

'No. I do not like it here. There is nothing to do. We must go back to America.'

'My husband is here. My younger son is here. We will do as we have always done. We shall live in Saudi Arabia for six months, and then in America for the next six months.'

He didn't answer, but his expression soured. From that time Big Duran became increasingly hostile, losing his awesome temper over the smallest things. I was so happy to have my son back that I took many photographs of him. After the rolls were taken to be developed, all the photographs turned out to be white. The camera shop clerk then looked over my camera and announced it defective. I took it in my stride, and purchased another camera. I sighed sadly and told Big Duran about the destroyed prints. We will take more pictures, I assured him.

But my son's reaction was dramatic. He leapt from

the sofa and started screaming at me. 'You idiot! Why didn't you use a decent camera?' Then he ran around the room like a mad person, picking up objects and breaking them against the wall. He glared at me: 'You stupid woman, you are good for nothing!'

I was in shock. My son was acting like a lunatic, and over nothing. For the first time, I realized how much my son could look and act exactly like his father.

Big Duran threw his head back and screamed as loudly as he could. Then he marched off to his room, slamming the door so hard that the walls shook.

Little Duran was inconsolable. Never before had he witnessed such behaviour. He wanted to go to his brother to make certain he was all right, but something warned me. 'Don't go in there,' I told my youngest son. 'Leave your big brother alone.'

The following day we received Big Duran's cellphone bill from Virginia. He had called Kabul so many times that the bill added up to $1,500 for one month. I was upset but didn't want another explosion from my son. I calmly told him: 'You tell me you are afraid of your father, that he might steal you back to Afghanistan. Yet you are calling him yourself time and time again.'

My son looked at me with angry, hateful eyes. 'I don't call him every time.'

'Who are you calling then?'

'I have many, many friends in Kabul.'

I sighed. 'Well, we are not a rich family. We live on a budget. I will pay this bill, but I cannot do it again.'

Duran's twentieth birthday was coming soon, on 27 January 2004, so I planned a big surprise birthday party for him, the first time I had the opportunity to enjoy that pleasure for seventeen years. The party was held at the pool of an American residential compound where friends of mine lived. I went there early to arrange everything perfectly. Khalid brought the boys over at party time.

From the moment he arrived, Big Duran was so unfriendly that guests began to whisper. My son stood at a distance, shooting me nasty looks and responding to my concerns with snarls. All my guests made an effort to be nice, but my son was so intentionally rude that they soon drifted away. My eldest son had been in a good mood when I left the house earlier in the afternoon, so I asked Khalid, 'Did anything happen after I left?'

Khalid gave me a significant look. 'He was on the telephone for two hours after you left. He was speaking in Pashto.'

My heart plunged. I knew then that my son was maintaining close ties with his father. What were they plotting?

The following morning a close cousin living in

Australia called, wanting to welcome Big Duran back into our family. I listened curiously to the conversation and overheard my son saying to her, 'I want to emigrate to Australia.'

She was obviously taken aback, and must have asked him why on earth he would want to move to Australia.

'I want to come there and get my PhD.'

I imagined my cousin telling him he must first get his bachelor degree.

I walked past my son to go to the kitchen for a glass of juice. When I passed him, he took the telephone receiver and without warning hit me on the head with tremendous force. I gasped from the shock and the pain. Duran glared at me and stalked off.

I picked up the phone and asked my cousin what might have happened to create such anger in my son. She repeated their conversation. I could tell from her tone that she was worried about my situation.

I went up to Duran's room and asked, 'Why would you think of moving to Australia? And why would you hit your mother?'

'I don't want to talk about it,' Duran growled.

I should have punished him then, but I was filled with fear and dread that if I disciplined my son, I would lose him once again. I should have known that by ignoring the problem, bigger problems would only emerge.

* * *

One morning I went to a meeting of the American Ladies of Jeddah, leaving both sons at home, as well as my maid Rahma. When I returned, my home was in turmoil. Little Duran was very upset. Big Duran was locked in his room, refusing to speak with anyone. Rahma was in the kitchen, also disturbed.

'What happened here?' I asked, fear gathering in my heart.

Rahma told me. 'When I went to clean in the television room, I saw your two sons. Madam, your older son's hands were wrapped round your younger son's neck! When the big boy saw me, he released the little one, who came running to me, screaming that he was being strangled. Your big son said he was only playing around.'

Rahma shook her head and turned away.

My younger son heard my voice, and came running. 'Mother, Duran tried to strangle me!' he cried plaintively.

Big Duran was apparently listening through his door. He now made an appearance, laughing, saying, 'Oh no I did not.' He rolled his eyes. 'We were just playing a little game. It was nothing.'

Unwilling to believe my eldest son would seriously try to harm his younger brother, I scolded my youngest son. 'Honey, this is a serious charge. Of course your big brother didn't try to choke you.

Now, you must apologize to him for saying that.'

Big Duran looked at his brother, and then at me, and smiled triumphantly.

When I told Khalid about the incident, he was less certain. 'Maryam, he is unstable. He obviously has a problem with his temper.' When he saw my crest-fallen look, he reassured me he was not blaming Big Duran. 'I do not fault the boy. He was abused and beaten by his father. It's no wonder he is unstable. But I do think he needs the care of a doctor. I think you should take him to Virginia. Find a doctor there. Get your son some help.'

When I said nothing, Khalid insisted. 'We can't take risks with our son's life, Maryam.'

'I will take him over to the States in June, as we planned. I'll take both my sons and go for a long visit.' I repeated, 'Just as we planned.'

'No, Maryam. June is five months away. Anything could happen. Besides, I don't want my son there under these circumstances. Maryam, I do not trust Big Duran with our son. We cannot risk it.'

I bit my lip. I did not want to accept that my oldest son suffered psychological problems and that he was dangerous. I did not want to reprimand him. I had spent too many lonely years looking for him to act in a way that might cause him to turn from me.

Khalid was emphatic. 'Listen to me, Maryam. Your son has hit you. He has thrown things. He is volatile. I think he could become extremely violent, just like his father. If something happens to our young son, you will never forgive yourself.'

It was clear that Khalid had had enough. And who could blame him? Although I couldn't face the idea that Big Duran was guilty of strangling his younger brother, clearly Khalid was not of the same opinion.

But I couldn't bear to leave my younger son for such a long period, to leave one son in order to take care of the other. 'Let me think, Khalid. We'll talk about this later.'

While considering my options, I hired a tutor to help Duran begin studying for the College Board examinations.

'No. Not yet,' Duran protested. 'I want to wait until after my vacation is over.'

'Your vacation has long been over, Duran,' I exclaimed. 'It is time for you to start your studies.'

'You are not a mother,' Duran sneered. 'You are too bossy to be a mother. You think you are my father. Well, you are not!'

I really did not know what to say to that, so I said nothing.

Later that day he was on the telephone again. By this time I was not ashamed to listen in on my son's telephone conversations. I slipped quietly to his door so I could hear everything. Duran was speaking Pashto. My heart told me he was speaking to his father, and that they were plotting. Duran's side of the conversation was not reassuring. 'No, not yet,' he argued. 'I do not want to do it now. No. No. She has promised to get me my American birth certificate. Yes. She said she would. Do not worry. After I get my papers, I will do it.'

My blood rushed through my veins. Do what? What was my ex-husband trying to get our son to do?

I now began to be seriously worried. Had Kaiss so brainwashed our son that he could convince him to physically harm me, or my young son?

Duran and I were sitting in the garden the following day when he said, 'I must make a telephone call.'

'Who is it you want to call, son?'

'I have to make a phone call,' he repeated.

He glared at me and stalked away.

I followed him into the house.

He dialled a number and began speaking in Pashto. When he saw me, he turned his back and walked out into the garden with the phone.

I stubbornly followed, telling him: 'If you are speaking with your father, Duran, I want you to hang up.'

My beloved son looked at me with hatred, screaming, 'The day will come when I will put a knife to your throat and watch the blood flow from your lifeless body! That is when this mission will be over!'

I ran away from my child, my Duran, the child I had loved with all my heart. Where had my loving baby gone? Who was this vicious man who called himself my son?

When Duran finished his conversation, he walked into the house as though he didn't have a care in the world, as though he had not just threatened his mother's life.

Still, a mother's love is difficult to destroy. I reached out to him, wanting desperately to help my son, who I knew had grown up in the most wretched way from the day he was torn from his mother's arms. How he must have suffered! My toddler son had lived through brutal beatings, against a background of insecurity, violence and war, and then later was made to believe his mother had sold him for money: all this must have contributed to his violent behaviour.

I must save my son! I must! I tried to reason with him, to show him I had always loved him, that I had not abandoned him. My voice rose in despair. 'Why, my son, why? How can you hate your mother enough to say such words? Remember that it was your father who stole you away from me when you were a tiny toddler. It was your father who beat you. It was your father who lied to you. While all of that was happening, your grandfather and I were spending all our money and time trying to locate you, to bring you home.'

My son refused to reply.

'Now that you are here, Duran, what is it that you want? What will make you happy, son?'

He looked at me with pure hatred, hatred transported from his father in Afghanistan to me in Jeddah. 'I came here to get money,' he sneered. 'I wanted a lot of money.' He shrugged. 'I thought everyone in Saudi Arabia was filthy rich. I was wrong. I have seen that you and your husband have nothing for me. I don't want to stay if you don't have any money.'

'I am your mother. I love you. I will make many sacrifices for you. I want to get you educated. How can you have no feelings for your mother who loves you beyond measure?'

He laughed hatefully. 'No. You are merely my biological mother. I don't even like you. You are too young to be my mother. I hate the sexy way you look and dress. You do not look like a mother. You are a sex object that turns men's heads.' He stalked away, shouting. 'I want a mother who is pious, who is veiled. I want a mother who stays at home and doesn't do tennis or yoga or go to the beach. I . . .' My son was so angry he was stuttering. 'I want to be just like my father.'

I remained calm, keeping my horror within, acknowledging to myself what I had feared, that my son was seriously disturbed. 'Duran, you said you hated your father. You want to be like someone who beat his wife? Who beat his son?'

'Maybe I hate him. But I want to be like him.' He stalked around the room like a caged bear. 'I have decided to leave and go to live in Germany.'

'*Germany?*' I was dumbfounded.

'I am going to live in the home of my father's brother.'

'But we planned on going to Virginia in June. I—'

'I have changed my plans. My father wants me back. I want to go back to my father.'

'But what of your dreams, Duran? You told me your dream was to get an education and to live in Virginia and—'

'My dream?' He laughed menacingly, moving very close. 'My only dream is to kill you.'

I was brokenhearted. 'Duran. Whatever have I ever done to you but to love you?'

He turned away indifferently.

Frantically I cast around in my mind for something I might say to keep him with me so that I could arrange psychological help. If he left now, he was lost for ever, and I knew it.

'Duran?'

'I've got what I wanted, my American passport. You have no money. You have nothing else I want. I am going to Germany. I will marry a cousin while I am there. Then I will go back to Kabul and live with my father. He promises to give me anything I want.'

'Duran, you said you so hated your father that you were going to change your name,' I reminded him.

He smiled his menacing smile. 'Oh yes, I hate him. But he taught me how to be a good player.'

My heart was breaking. But I couldn't stop him. He was a grown man and he had made his choice. When Khalid heard about the threats he had made against my life, he was horrified and told me I must let Duran go.

He quickly booked my son on a flight to Frankfurt, Germany. He was returning to his father. Khalid and I accompanied him to the airport, still pretending that all would be well, after all.

Despite everything, I still loved my poor disturbed son with a mother's bottomless love. As I wept at the gate, and Duran started to walk away to board the plane, he looked back at me with his dead eyes and empty smile. 'You are so naive,' he said pitilessly. 'See how easily we fooled you.'

And with that, my son was finally and forever gone.

Epilogue

Shortly after my son boarded the flight and left Saudi Arabia for ever, my innocent younger son confided that his older brother had tried to convince him to do something really bad. The act was so terrible, he said, that he would not tell us the details, much as we pleaded with him. As happy as Little Duran had been to welcome his big brother into his life, he was now relieved that Big Duran had left. His big brother has turned into the bogeyman. He had tried to strangle him to death. His big brother had plotted dark deeds against his mother. From the day Big Duran left our home, traumatized Little Duran never again mentioned his name.

There was more bad news. Just when Farid was having great success bringing the family's businesses in Afghanistan back to good order, his throat became sore and did not heal. He became so weak that he left Kabul for Paris to seek a doctor's opinion. I was devastated to learn that Farid, a heavy smoker, had been diagnosed with throat cancer. For him, the dream of helping Afghanistan rise from the rubble was over. Instead he spent his days in a Paris hospital enduring chemotherapy. His prognosis was bleak. On the phone, he spoke to me about Big Duran, advising me to forget my son, that it was an impossible dream to transform the monster that Kaiss had created out of my once-sweet and beautiful baby boy back into a loving son.

Farid knew that he was dying and, when I cried, he told me to dry my tears, that he would soon be with his two mothers and that all would be well.

Farid made a farewell tour to see his family and we met for the last time in Virginia in October 2004. Farid was staying at Nadia's house and I could not believe my eyes when I walked in the door and saw my handsome 'big brother', who was puffy from medication and bald from chemotherapy. He looked like a stranger. But his big eyes were the same and I would have recognized Farid anywhere. He told me, 'I am trying to be brave, little brother. I am trying to be brave.'

He returned to Paris, where his cancer spread but he remained upbeat. His sister Zeby told me that during one of his last conversations, he asked about his 'little brother Maryam'. After that he was silent, but his expressive eyes still followed every movement in his hospital room. Farid soon died, breaking all our hearts.

Although I knew I should greet his demise with an exhalation of relief, I could not, for I miss him every single day. Farid remains the most inspiring figure in my life. There was something so noble about his goodness and care for everyone around him. I knew when Farid, my 'big brother', died that I would not see his like again. I pray that Farid is indeed reunited with his mother, and my mother.

I still continued to dream that my elder son Duran would return whole and cleansed to his mother, that he would learn what it is to love, and to be loved. But sadly, soon after he left, he began to wage un-remitting war against me.

The last time he called, he said, 'Hi. This is your enemy number one.'

I responded lightly, treating his words as a joke. 'Hello to you, enemy number one.' Regardless of his attitude, I still loved my son and was happy to hear his voice.

'I wanted to tell you that I only regret one thing.'

My heart lifted in joy as I waited for his next words, hoping that he would apologize and say he wanted to return, to start anew.

'What do you regret, my love?'

'Oh, I regret that I didn't rape you. I masturbate with you in my mind every night.'

I gasped, then screamed, throwing down the phone in disbelief and horror. I dashed into my bedroom, tore off my clothes and leapt into the shower, scrubbing my face, my body, trying to remove the filth that I felt was crusted over me. Had there ever been such an unnatural son! What had Kaiss done to create such a monster? He had taken the most angelic little boy and turned him into a psychopath who not only wanted to rape and murder his mother but also to murder his innocent, sweet, younger brother.

I fell to the floor of the shower and wept bitter tears, wishing myself back to the moment Duran was born, crying out, 'Allah, why couldn't my child have been a girl? A girl, God!' Kaiss had threatened to kill our baby if it was a girl, but I would have escaped and Kaiss would have never bothered to kidnap a girl. All would have been well had I only had a daughter. 'A daughter, Allah! Why didn't you give me a daughter?'

With passing time I often look back on my life, sadly remembering all the daughters and mothers in my family. I am haunted by one question: why weren't we all stronger? Why couldn't we stand up for ourselves against our men? Grandmother. Amina. Mother. Sarah. Me. All of us. We all struggled but we were weak and fell back into resignation. The forces we were struggling against were not like swimming against the tide . . . but more like swimming against a tsunami. We were swimming against an ancient culture which demands that women always submit, that women always stay weak. So I end where I began ... dreaming a dream that can never come true. For wherever I am in the world, in my mind I am still in Afghanistan, and in Afghanistan only the dreams of boys can come true.

Where are they now?

An update on Maryam's close family members and friends.

Maryam, Khalid and Little Duran still live in Saudi Arabia, although there are frequent trips to the USA to visit Nadia, Suzie and other relatives.

Big Duran: Duran has returned to live in Afghanistan. Although Maryam has never seen her son again, he still communicates with his mother through email messages. Many from time to time are abusive and threatening. Maryam still loves her son and worries about the dangers that surround him in that war-torn country.

Uncle Hakim: Hakim, father to Farid, Zarmina and Zeby, died of Alzheimer's disease in March 1994 in Paris.

Cousin Farid: Farid died of throat cancer in Paris on 5 April 2005. Although Farid married several times, he never had any children. He is buried beside his father in a Paris cemetery.

Cousin Zeby: Farid's sister Zeby is married to a famous Afghan singer. Their son is a keyboard player for his father as well as a fashion model in Germany.

Cousin Zarmina: Zeby's older sister lives with her husband and four children in California. She is a happy homemaker.

Sister Nadia: Nadia lives in Virginia and still practises medicine.

Niece Suzie: Suzie lives in Virginia with her mother, Nadia. In May 2009, Suzie graduated from George Washington University and started training as a doctor.

Auntie Shagul: Sister to Maryam's mother, Shagul died of old age in 2007 in Fairfax, Virginia, where she is buried. She was eighty-six.

Cousin Amina: Amina, daughter of Shair, died a few years ago. Maryam could not learn the cause of Amina's premature death, but fears it was linked to her abusive husband.

Timeline

Anglo–Afghan Wars

During a seventy-year span there were three major Anglo–Afghan wars (between the British–Indian territory and Afghan tribes): 1839–42, 1878–80 and 1919. Although the British won control of Afghan foreign affairs, they were never successful at making Afghanistan a colony. The British lost control of Afghan foreign affairs on 19 August 1919.

Afghanistan Modern-day Timeline: 1919–2010

A chronology of key events

1919: Amanullah becomes King.

1919: After the third war with Great Britain, Afghanistan regains full independence.

1926: King Amanullah introduces social reforms.

1929: King Amanullah is forced to flee due to strong opposition from conservative forces.

1929: Nadir is declared King by an assembly of tribal chiefs.

1933: King Nadir is assassinated at a school-prize competition.

1933: Nadir's son, nineteen-year-old Zahir, is declared King.

1953: General Mohammed Daoud, a member of the royal family, is appointed Prime Minister by King Zahir.

1963: Daoud is forced to resign his post after seeking economic and military assistance from the Soviet Union.

1973: Daoud seizes power during a successful coup against King Zahir, who is forced into exile.

1973: President Daoud declares that the time of kings has ended, proclaiming a republic.

1978: The Soviet Union aligns closer to Afghanistan, making increasing demands for a fuller participation in the Afghanistan government.

1978: President Daoud is killed in a coup led by the People's Democratic Party, who are supported by the Soviet regime. Leaders of the party are Hafizullah Amin and Nur Muhammad Taraki.

1979: Amin and Taraki enter into a power struggle, with Amin the victor. Afghan tribes revolt and the Afghan army faces collapse. The Soviet Union sends in troops to remove Amin. Amin is executed.

1980: Babrak Karmal is installed as ruler, backed by the Soviet Union. Various Mujahedin groups fighting the Soviet forces intensify their resistance as the United States, Saudi Arabia, Pakistan, China and Iran supply funds and arms.

1985: War against the Soviet troops and the Soviet-appointed government further intensifies. An estimated 50 per cent of the Afghan population is displaced by war and flees to neighbouring Pakistan or Iran.

1986: The United States supplies Afghan and foreign Mujahedin fighters with stinger missiles, enabling the fighters to destroy Soviet helicopters.

1986: Babrak Karmal is replaced by Mohammed Najibbulah as head of the Afghan Soviet-backed regime.

1988: The Soviet Union begins pulling out its troops after Afghanistan, the United States and Pakistan sign peace accords with the Soviet Union, although

Najibbulah remains in power, ensuring continuing strife between Afghan factions.

1991: The United States and the Soviet Union agree to end their associations with all fighting factions in Afghanistan. This leaves the pro-Soviet President Mohammed Najibbulah exposed to various Afghan factions opposing any association with communism.

1992: President Najibbulah falls from power when Kabul is captured by the Mujahedin fighters. Rival militias fight each other for control.

1993: Burhanuddin Rabbani is proclaimed President after fighting factions agree on formation of a government.

1994: Factional fighting continues with the Pashtun-dominated Taliban emerging as the main challenge to the government of President Rabbani.

1996: The Taliban, led by Mullah Omar, seizes control of Kabul. Soon after gaining power the new government introduces the most conservative version of Islam. They enforce the strongest Islamic punishments, including stoning and amputations. Women are banned from public life, including work. Many widows and children suffer enormous hardship without a man to protect or provide for them.

1997: Saudi Arabia and Pakistan recognize the

Taliban, while the rest of the world recognizes President Rabbani as the head of state.

1998: Much of the western world first learns about Osama Bin Laden and Al-Qaeda when he is accused of organizing the bombings of US embassies in Africa.

1998: President Bill Clinton orders the launching of air strikes on suspected Al-Qaeda bases in Afghanistan.

1999: The UN imposes financial sanctions and air embargoes against the Afghan government and people in an attempt to force Mullah Omar and the Taliban to deliver Osama Bin Laden for trial for the African embassy bombings. Mullah Omar refuses.

2001: The Taliban blow up the famous Buddha statues despite international efforts to save them.

2001: The Taliban tighten restrictions when they order religious minorities to wear tags indentifying themselves as non-Muslims. There is an outcry from humanitarian organizations world-wide, but protests are ignored.

2001: The legendary Afghan fighter Ahmed Massoud, who is the main opposition against the Taliban, is assassinated by men posing as journalists. Many blame Al-Qaeda or the Taliban.

2001: 11 September, four US airliners are hijacked. Two of the planes are flown into the World Trade Center. One is flown into the Pentagon. The fourth crashes in Pennsylvania. In all, 2,986 innocent people are killed in the attacks on civilian life. Al-Qaeda is named as the organizer of the attacks. The United States government requests that Mullah Omar turns over Osama Bin Laden, the Saudi organizer held responsible for the attacks on America. Mullah Omar stubbornly refuses.

2001: Following the terrorist attacks on New York and Washington on 11 September 2001, the United Kingdom stands by America's side, and from that time the UK is involved in Afghanistan alongside Coalition forces.

2001: In October, led by the USA under Operation Enduring Freedom, the United States and Great Britain launch air attacks against Afghanistan. Royal Navy submarines fire Tomahawk missiles and RAF aircraft provide reconnaissance and air-to-air refuelling capabilities.

2001: In November, UK troops are deployed. Royal Marines from 40 Commando help to secure the Bagram airfield while 1,700 Royal Marines from 45 Commando are deployed as Task Force Jacana. Due to the combined efforts of the USA and UK forces, opposition forces march into Kabul and other key Afghan cities scarcely a month after the first airstrikes.

2001: In December, Osama Bin Laden and his Al-Qaeda followers are forced to flee Afghanistan. During this same month, Mullah Omar and the Taliban flee Kandahar; Mullah Omar's whereabouts remain unknown.

2001: On 22 December, Pashtun royalist Hamid Karzai becomes head of a thirty-member interim power-sharing government.

2002: The first contingent of foreign peacekeepers move into Afghanistan.

2003: Allied forces continue their operations to clear Taliban and Al-Qaeda forces from the south-east region of Afghanistan.

2004: Afghanistan's grand assembly adopts a new constitution.

2004: President Karzai wins re-election with 55 per cent of the popular vote.

2005: Parliamentary and provincial elections take place for the first time in thirty years, with a few women elected to office.

2005–6: Suicide bombings thought to be the

work of the Taliban and Al-Qaeda kill nearly 200 people.

2006: NATO assumes control of Afghan security. (NOTE: During these years of international support of Afghan security, many nations have contributed by sending troops. These nations include: the United States, the United Kingdom, Canada, Turkey, Italy, France, Germany, the Netherlands, Belgium, Spain, Poland, as well as other members of the European Union and of NATO, and Australia, New Zealand, Azerbaijan and Singapore.)

2007: With resistance attacks from the Taliban and Al-Qaeda, surging NATO and Afghan forces jointly launch Operation Achilles, a huge offensive against the Taliban in the south.

2008: The Taliban rejects an offer of peace talks from President Karzai.

2008: Afghanistan and Pakistan governments agree jointly to fight militants in their border regions.

2009: Newly elected US President Barack Obama announces that the United States will increase its presence in Afghanistan by sending in an additional 17,000 troops. Twenty NATO countries pledge to increase their military commitments to Afghanistan.

2009: President Barack Obama announces a new US

strategy for US personnel to train the Afghan army and police.

2009: The United States military launches a new offensive against the Taliban in Helmand province.

2009: Afghan presidential and provincial elections are held amid accusations of voter fraud.

2009: Hamid Karzai is declared the winner of the presidential election against opponent Abdullah Abdullah. Due to accusations of voter fraud, a run-off is called, but Abdullah Abdullah pulls out of the race before the election can be held.

2009: President Hamid Karzai is sworn in for a second term.

2009: UK Prime Minister Gordon Brown announces that the number of British troops deployed to Afghanistan will stand at 9,000 but could increase to 9,500 subject to certain conditions, including that the Afghan national army and Afghan government provide sufficient troops in Helmand to operate alongside British forces there.

2009: US President Barack Obama boosts US troop numbers by another 30,000, bringing the total to 100,000, although the President announces at the same time that the United States will begin to withdraw their troops during the year 2011.

2009: Seven CIA agents are killed on a US military base in Khost when an Al-Qaeda double agent succeeds in a suicide bombing.

As I write, in January 2010, soldiers and civilians continue to die in the region. Additional information regarding UK forces can be found in the Ministry of Defence online factsheets.

Index